Renewing the Earth

Renewing the Earth

The Promise of Social Ecology

A Celebration of the Work
of Murray Bookchin

Edited by
John Clark

**GREEN
PRINT**

First published 1990 by Green Print
an imprint of Merlin Press
10 Malden Road, London NW5 3HR

Copyright © 1990 The Contributors

ISBN 1 85425 001 9

Printed on recycled paper.
Phototypeset by Input Typesetting Ltd., London
Printed in Great Britain by
Biddles Ltd., Guildford and King's Lynn

This collection is dedicated to
MURRAY BOOKCHIN
Director Emeritus, Institute for Social Ecology

by his students, friends, and colleagues, in recognition of his pioneering efforts in the field of Social Ecology, and of his continuing inspiration to us all

Contents

THREE: **A NEW VISION OF THE SELF**

Notes on the Contributors

John Clark teaches philosophy at Loyola University in New Orleans, and works with the New Orleans Greens, the Co-operative Development Center, and the Institute for Social Ecology. He is the author of *Max Stirner's Egoism*, *The Philosophical Anarchism of William Godwin*, *The Anarchist Moment*, and *Bakunin and the End of the Revolution* (forthcoming).

Morris Berman formerly taught at the University of Victoria and is one of the foremost contemporary critics of post-Enlightenment culture. He is the author of *Social Change and Scientific organization* and *The Reenchantment of the World*. His forthcoming work *The Body of History* studies the relation between physical experience and human culture as a whole.

Richard Merrill directs the Horticulture Department and teaches biology and solar energy technology at Cabrillo College, and is Visiting Lecturer in Agroecology at the University of California, Santa Cruz. A major figure in the alternative technology movement, his books include *Radical Agriculture*, *Energy Primer*, and *Bioregional Horticulture* (forthcoming). He was one of the early graduates of the Institute for Social Ecology graduate program.

John Ely has written extensively on ecology, critical theory, feminism, and Green politics. He is the author of *The German Greens*, the most comprehensive critical analysis of that movement to appear in English.

Gary Snyder is one of the world's great poets of nature, culture, and spirit. He has had a profound influence on the development of the bioregional and deep ecology movements. Since his early association with the Beats in the late 1950s, he has been one of the foremost interpreters of Zen to the modern world. Among his many books are *Earth House Hold, The Old Ways, The Back Country, Cold Mountain Poems, Axe Handles*, and *Turtle Island*, for which he won the Pulitzer Prize for poetry.

Daniel Chodorkoff was the co-founder and is now Director of the Institute for Social Ecology. He has worked in the field of community development, and teaches and writes about community and reconstructive anthropology.

Stephen Schecter teaches sociology at L'Université du Québec à Montreal. He has worked with and studied extensively urban participatory politics. He is the author of *The Politics of Urban Liberation* and *T'Es Beau en Ecoeurant*.

John Mohawk is an American Indian teacher, writer, and political activist. He has edited the *Akwasasne Notes*, one of the most highly regarded Native American publications, and he now publishes the Indigenous Press Network's *Weekly Report*. He lectures at the Institute for Social Ecology Summer Program.

Graham Baugh is a political philosopher who writes about anarchist theory. His essays and reviews have appeared in *Telos, Our Generation*, and other journals.

Thomas Simon teaches philosophy at the University of Florida and is active in the anti-apartheid and animal rights movements. He has written extensively on issues of science, technology, and artificial intelligence. He is at work on a book entitled *Democratizing*.

Robert Nicholls has been a community organizer and landscape architect, and continues to write novels, short stories, poetry, and essays. Among his many books are *Slow Newsreel of Man Riding Train, Address to the Smaller Animals, Red Shift*, and the four-volume series of utopian novels, *Daily Lives in Nghsi-Altai*, considered by many to be among the classics of utopian fiction. He lectures at the Institute for Social Ecology Summer Program.

Nancy Jack Todd and **John Todd** are among the best known figures in the alternative and liberatory technology movement. They are co-founders of the *New Alchemy Institute* and *Ocean Arks International*, and publish the quarterly journal *Annals of Earth*. Their latest book is entitled *Bioshelters, Ocean Arks, City Farming: Ecology as the Basis for Design*.

Karl Hess is a writer, speaker, sculptur, and long-time political activist and organizer. He was a major figure in the revival of the libertarian tradition in America. His articles have appeared extensively both in major popular publications and in political journals. He is the author of *Dear America, Neighborhood Power: The New Localism*, and *Community Technology*.

Grace Paley is one of America's foremost writers of fiction, and is well-known for her work in the peace and feminist movements. She is one of the founding members of Woman for Peace on Earth. Her collections of stories include *The Little Disturbances of Man, Enormous Changes at the Last Minute*, and *Later the Same Day*. She was recently named Writer Laureat of the State of New York. She lectures at the Institute for Social Ecology Summer Program.

Joel Kovel is a psychoanalyst, anthropologist, and social theorist. He holds the Alger Hiss chair at Bard College, New York. His books include *White Racism, A Complete Guide to Therapy, The Age of Desire*, and *Against the State of Nuclear Terror*. His most recent work examines the processes of social change in revolutionary Nicaragua.

Chiah Heller is a psychologist, and ecofeminist writer. She is a graduate of the Institute for Social Ecology Graduate Program, and she now teaches courses in ecofeminism at the Institute.

Patricia Mills is Visiting Professor of Philosophy at the University of Toronto. She writes on the topics of feminism, critical theory, and ecology, and is the author of *Woman, Nature and Psyche*.

Stephen Duplantier is an activist in the bioregional movement. He has worked in the field of environmental education, and done extensive research on the ecology of south Louisiana. He is a specialist in the newly emerging field of the ecology of communications.

Jonathan Stevens is a poet and songwriter who lives and works in Western Massachusetts. His poems and music explore the depth of human feelings, the beauty of nature, and the history of popular struggles for freedom. He lectures on art and politics at the Institute for Social Ecology. A selection of his work is presented in his recent record *Creationland*.

Murray Bookchin's work in ecology, philosophy, social and political theory, urbanism, theory of technology, and other fields has been the major inspiration for the development of the Social Ecology movement. His extensive writings, including works like *Post-Scarcity Anarchism, Toward an Ecological Society*, and *The Ecology of Freedom* laid the theoretical foundations for the movement. He founded and has served as Director of the Institute for Social Ecology, where he is now Director Emeritus. He is also Professor Emeritus of Environmental Studies at Ramapo College. Prof. Bookchin resides in Burlington, Vermont, where he teaches and continues research on several major forthcoming works, including *The Politics of Cosmology*, a comprehensive critique of the history of nature philosophy.

PREFACE:

A New Philosophy For The Green Movement

If there is one great need on our planet today, it is a need for rebirth, for regeneration, for renewal. It is a commonplace now that we are in an age of ecological crisis; indeed, that we are threatening our own existence, and that of all the diverse life forms with which we share the earth. The questions of how we are to comprehend this crisis, and find a path beyond it remain. That is, how can we think and act creatively on behalf of life on earth?

The enormous growth of the worldwide Green Movement over the past decade is testimony to the good will and energy of many concerned people who are confronting this problem. It is a movement that is notable not only for the depth of its commitment, but for the breadth of its vision. Of course, the Greens are known for their place in the forefront of battles against air and water pollution, chemicals in foods, hazardous waste production, nuclear energy, and other 'environmental problems'. But, from the beginning, the movement has had more comprehensive concerns.

It has been in several senses a 'global movement'. The Greens have played a major role in the disarmament movement, pointing out that nuclear weapons are the most immediate threat to the biosphere, and that an ecological society must be a peaceful society. They have not hesitated to question the entire system of industrialism and high technology that has degraded the biosphere and produced ecocidal trends like the Greenhouse Effect. They have affirmed that an ecological politics demands a struggle against destructive ideologies like patriarchy, racism, and nationalism. And they have shown that the traditional politics of both Right and Left, far from offering solutions, have succeeded only in aggravating the crisis. In place of these bankrupt traditions, the Greens have introduced a new cultural politics that encompasses bold experiments in democracy, community, and cooperation. On the most profound level, what is emerging is a search for new ways of living together — as members of the human community and the community of nature.

If the Green Movement is to fulfil its promise of reversing the destructive drive of civilization (what Rudolf Bahro has called 'exterminism'), it must develop self-understanding. It must become critically conscious of the roots of the problems we face, the means by which change can take place, and the possibilities open to us in the future. In short, the movement must have a comprehensive philosophy to guide its practice.

Most of the options available in the past have, at best, made a limited contribution to this end. Indeed, some forms of 'environmentalism' have turned out to be strikingly anti-ecological. Thus, approaches like Garrett Hardin's 'spaceship earth' model are not only anthropocentric, but mechanistic, reductionist, and authoritarian. 'New Age' outlooks based on philosophies like that of Teilhard de Chardin are found to be a strange blend of mechanism and mysticism, with a strong dose of technocracy thrown in.

More promising is the growing tradition of 'Deep Ecology'. Its starting-point is Arne Naess' useful distinction between superficial views that merely seek piecemeal solutions to environmental problems, and a truly ecological outlook, which is holistic in its conception of nature, and is based on a respect for the richness and diversity of life. Yet 'Deep Ecology' is less a single philosophy than an eclectic category that includes viewpoints ranging from the most subtle and refined to the most naïve and confused (however 'ecological' the confusion may be!).

Ecological thinking has certainly been advanced through the growth of tendencies like bioregionalism (as developed by Peter Berg and the Planet Drum Foundation) and reinhabitation (as elaborated so beautifully by Gary Snyder). The former has encouraged us to rethink the relationship between our forms of organization and the ecosystems in which we live, while the latter has reminded us of our need for a sense of place, a rootedness, a connection between culture and nature. Yet these hopeful developments do not of themselves constitute the new ecological philosophy; rather, they are indispensable parts of that philosophy.

There is, at this point, one outlook that expresses in a comprehensive, richly developed, and profound manner the deepest strivings of the Green Movement. This philosophy is Social Ecology. According to Social Ecology, the ecological crisis results from a destruction of the organic fabric of both society and nature. Over the ages, the dominant social, political, and economic systems have succeeded in breaking down the complexity of both organic cultures and natural ecosystems. Guided by ideologies of hierarchy and domination, they replaced this organic diversity with a technically complex but mechanized system. According to Social Ecology, our most fundamental problem is therefore one of *regeneration*.

The task of the Green Movement is to initiate at once a double process of 'Renewing the Earth'. On the one hand, we must undertake the regeneration of nature, by reversing the process of destruction of species and ecosystems, and by seeking to cooperate with nature in fostering richness, diversity, and complexity. On the other hand, we must work for the regeneration of society, by pursuing, through mutual aid, cooperation, and respect for individuality, the creation of a non-dominating community in harmony with nature. In this way, both nature and society will manifest the fundamental ecological principle of unity in diversity.

The pre-eminent figure in the development of this conception of Social Ecology has been the philosopher and social theorist, Murray Bookchin. His work in ecological theory over a period of 35 years has laid the foundations for all who have followed in this tradition. In a dozen books, and, most notably, his classic work, *The Ecology of Freedom*, Bookchin has elaborated the theoretical principles of Social Ecology, and applied this perspective to more specific fields like political theory, history, urbanism, and theory of technology. In addition, his courses during the past 15 years at the Institute for Social Ecology in Vermont, have profoundly influenced and inspired numerous students who have applied his ideas in diverse fields, both theoretical and practical. Finally, as an eloquent and indefatigable lecturer, he has vigorously conveyed the message of Social Ecology throughout North America and Western Europe for several decades. It is in view of this magnificent contribution to ecological thought and practice that the contributors to this volume dedicate their work to Murray Bookchin.

Each of the articles in this collection develops in a certain direction the general theme of Social Ecology: the need to replace the society of domination by an ecological society founded on unity in diversity. In fact, the book itself demonstrates the principle, since the articles carry certain central unifying themes in diverse directions.

The first part of the book explores the most general aspects of the 'new vision' offered by Social Ecology. After my overview of Social Ecology as a comprehensive outlook, Morris Berman presents a critique of cybernetic reductionism and the information society, and distinguishes an ecological approach from new forms of mechanism and mysticism. Richard Merrill discusses the connections between the organic viewpoint or 'biological paradigm', our view of science and technology, and holistic concepts like 'Gaia'. John Ely focuses on the relationship between an organicist, vitalistic worldview ('animism'), and the quest for community, freedom, and individuality ('anarchism').

The second, and largest, part of the book considers the most explicitly 'social' aspects of Social Ecology: its vision as applied to questions of community, politics, culture, and technology. Daniel Chodorkoff presents a conception of community development that is holistic, creative, and participatory, and shows how this model has been applied in a New York Puerto Rican community. Stephen Schecter shows how Social Ecology is both a critique of the decay of urban life, and an attempt to recapture the liberatory dimensions of the city and the public realm. John Mohawk explains what traditional, tribal societies can teach us about family, community, nature, and spirituality. Graham Baugh raises important issues about the politics of Social Ecology, and the relation between direct democracy, self-management, community, and freedom. The problem of creating a technics that is at once ecological, participatory, and democratic is addressed by Thomas Simon. Robert Nichols reflects on the nature of a literature of community and of the people. Nancy and John Todd present another practical example of applied Social Ecology in their description of 'Ocean Arks'. And Karl Hess reflects on the implications of notions of political 'rights' as opposed to ecological concepts of reality.

Finally, we turn to Social Ecology's vision of the self, and the personal dimension. Joel Kovel presents a detailed discussion of the nature of the self: the need to go beyond a divided ego based on power; the goal of a richly developed subjectivity rooted in nature and experience; and the relation between selfhood and the realm of 'spirit'. Chiah Heller's discussion of eco-feminism calls for a rejection of both a psychology of adaptation (as in liberal feminism) and one of reductionism (as in certain forms of 'cultural feminism'), and stresses the need to grasp the dialectic between nature, culture, and our aspirations for freedom. Patricia Mills shows how conceptions of nature and 'the natural' affect our ideas of human liberation, especially as concerns women and Black people. And Steven Duplantier explores the social ecology of communication, and the importance in human experience of symbol, ritual, dance, and play.

Social Ecology recognizes the importance of the many dimensions of human experience, as aspects of the rich diversity that is to be balanced and harmonized. It is therefore appropriate that each of the three parts of the book should end with a contribution that reminds us of the connection between our thought and the realms of feeling and imagination. Gary Snyder has given us a new Taoist myth of the immortal Coyote Man, Grace Paley has contributed a poem, and Jonathan Stevens concludes with a song.

We conclude the collection with Murray Bookchin's 'Ecologizing the Dialectic,' which he describes as a good example of his most recent and developed work.

John Clark
New Orleans
1988

PART ONE

A NEW VISION OF THE WORLD

What is Social Ecology?
John Clark

Social Ecology is a comprehensive *holistic* conception of the self, society, and nature. It is, indeed, the first ecological philosophy to present a developed approach to all the central issues of theory and practice. It sets out from the basic ecological principle of organic *unity in diversity*, affirming that the good of the whole can be realized only through the rich individuality and complex interrelationship of the parts. And it applies this fundamental insight to all realms of experience.

In affirming such a holistic approach, Social Ecology rejects the dualism that has plagued Western civilization since its beginnings. A dualism that sets spirit against matter, soul against body, humanity against nature, subjectivity against objectivity, and reason against feelings. A dualism that is intimately related to the social divisions that are so central to the history of civilization: ruler versus ruled, rich versus poor, urban versus rural, 'civilized' versus 'savage', male versus female, in short, the dominant versus the dominated.

In opposition to this dualism, Social Ecology proposes a principle of *ecological wholeness*, which Bookchin defines as 'a dynamic unity of diversity' in which 'balance and harmony are achieved by ever-changing differentiation.' As a result, 'stability is a function not of simplicity and homogeneity but of complexity and variety.'[1] The entire course of evolution is seen as a process aiming at increasing this diversification. Thus, there is an ever increasing richness of diversity, not only in the sense of biological variety and interrelatedness, but also in the sense of richness of *value*.

Accordingly, evolution should be looked upon as a process of planetary development having *directiveness*, and involving the progressive *unfolding of potentiality*. Social Ecology thus forms part of a long teleological tradition extending from the ancient Greeks to the most advanced 20th century process philosophies. Yet Bookchin rejects the term 'teleology' because of its deterministic connotations, and its association with a hierarchical worldview that looks to some transcendent source of order and movement. There is no pre-determined, necessary path of evolution and world history. The unfolding of potentiality is best described as a 'tendency or nisus', rather than 'the "sure win" of classical teleology.'[2]

This directionality of nature is much like the kind of immanent teleology discovered by the early Taoist philosophers. They explained that each being has its own internal Tao, 'way', or striving toward its own particular good. Yet, reality as a whole (or that part of it that was most vividly experienced, living Nature, the biosphere) has a more universal 'way' that can unfold only through the harmonious realization of all individual goods.[3]

It is in this sense that the entire process of development of life and mind is a movement toward the attainment of value. For Bookchin, 'the universe bears witness to an ever striving, developing—not merely moving—substance, whose most dynamic and creative attribute is its increasing capacity for self-organization into increasingly complex forms.'[4] Life and mind are not random, chance occurrences in a dead and unconscious universe. Rather, there is a tendency within substance to produce life, consciousness, and self-consciousness. A tendency to differentiate itself, to issue in diversity and complexity in all realms of being.

In nature, all stages of such development are incorporated in the subsequent stages. As a result, there is an important sense in which a being consists largely of its own history. As Bookchin expresses this idea, 'radical social ecology reads . . . continuity and connectedness in all its gradations, mediations, and moments of development. By absorbing them into the large and contextual whole we call ecology, it treasures the wisdom of the cell and of the body, the natural history of the mind and its structure.'[5] Social Ecology comprehends, in a way that the tradition never has, that mind, like all phenomena, must be understood as rooted in nature and in history.

If natural history is the history of the emergence of life, consciousness, and self-conscious mind, it is correspondingly the history of the development of *freedom*. Social Ecology sees freedom as essentially meaning self-determination. In this sense, it is found to some degree at all levels of being: from the self-organizing and self-stabilizing tendencies of the atom, through the growth and metabolic activities of living organisms, to the complex self-realization processes of persons, societies, ecosystems, and the biosphere itself. For Bookchin, 'freedom in its most nascent form is already present in the directiveness of life as such, specifically in an organism's active effort to *be* itself and *resist* any external forces that vitiate its identity.' It is this 'germinal freedom' that develops along the path of evolution, and finally becomes the 'uninhibited volition and self-consciousness' that is the goal of a fully developed human community.[6]

It is important to see this planetary evolution as a holistic process, rather than merely as a mechanism of adaptation by individual organisms or species. 'Not only do species evolve cojointly and symbiotically with each other: the ecosystem *as a whole* evolves in mutual synchronicity with the species that comprise it and plays a broad role of whole in relation to its parts.'[7] Thus, the progressive unfolding of freedom depends on the existence of *symbiotic cooperation* at all levels—as Kropotkin pointed out almost a century ago. According to Bookchin, recent research shows that this 'mutualistic naturalism not only applies to relationships between species, but also morphologically—within and among complex cellular forms.'[8] We can see therefore a striking degree of continuity in nature, so that the free, mutualistic society at which we aim is rooted in the most basic levels of being.

According to Social Ecology, this holistic, developmental understanding of organic systems and their evolution has enormous importance for ethics and politics. Indeed, only if the place of humanity in nature and natural processes is understood can we adequately judge questions of value. We then see our own experience of valuing and seeking the good as part of the vast process of the emergence and development of value in nature. Value is achieved in the course of each being, according to its particular nature, attaining its good to the greatest degree possible.

Yet, from an ecological point of view, the realization of the planetary good is not merely the sum of all the particular good attained by all beings. For the biosphere is a *whole* of which these beings are parts, and a *community* of which they are members. The common planetary good can therefore be conceptualized only in a non-reductionist, *holistic* manner. The essential place of humanity in the attainment of this good cannot be underestimated. This is true in large part because of the technical capacity of humanity either to aid evolutionary development through judicious and restrained cooperation with nature or to put an end to the process through nuclear annihilation or degradation of the biosphere. But, in a more fundamental sense, humanity's role in nature results from the fact that our species constitutes the most richly developed realm of being to emerge thus far in the earth's evolutionary self-realization.

To say this is not to adopt an *anthropocentrism* that makes humanity the final or even the only end of nature. Neither is it a *biocentrism* that would ignore evolutionary developments for the sake of biological egalitarianism. Rather, it is *ecocentric* in the sense that it requires humanity to situate its good within the larger context of the *planetary good*, and to transform reason into *planetary reason*. As Bookchin states, 'the greatest single role' of an ecological ethics is 'to help us distinguish which of our actions serve the thrust of natural evolution and which of them impede it.'[9]

Human society must therefore transform itself, and renew itself, using ecological wisdom, so that it becomes a social ecological system within a natural ecological system. It must be seen as 'an ecosystem based on unity-in-diversity, spontaneity, and non-hierarchical relationships.'[10] This demands that a new *ecological sensibility* pervade all aspects of our social existence. Such a sensibility perceives 'the balance and integrity of the biosphere as an end in itself.'[11] It also recognizes the intrinsic goodness of the self-realization process (the Tao or 'way') of all the diverse beings that share our planetary ecocommunity.

As the mentality of non-domination replaces the prevailing hierarchical outlook, there emerges 'a new animism that respects the other for its own sake and responds *actively* in the form of a creative, loving, and supportive symbiosis.'[12] The mutualism found throughout nature thereby attains its highest development in a mutualistic system of values and perceptions.[13] This new sensibility will give direction to the process of regeneration that must take place at all levels, from nature, to the community, to the individual person.

The renewal of nature is perhaps the most self-evident task today for an ecological movement. According to Social Ecology, it is necessary to create ecocommunities and eco-technologies that can restore the balance between humanity and nature, and reverse the process of degradation of the biosphere. An ecological community will not attempt to dominate the surrounding environment, but rather will be a carefully integrated part of its ecosystem. Rather than continuing the system of obsessive, uncontrolled production and consumption, the community will practice true *eco-nomy*, the careful attending to and application of 'the rules of the household'. The extent to which humans can have a desirable impact on the ecosystem can be decided only through careful analysis of our abilities to act on behalf of nature, and of the detrimental effects of our disturbances of natural balances.

A pre-condition for the achievement of harmony with nature is the attainment of harmony and balance within society itself. Mechanistic organization based on political and economic power must be replaced by an organic community regulated through common ecological values and a commitment to a common life. The post-scarcity society advocated by Bookchin does not transcend the 'realm of necessity' through vastly increased production and consumption of commodities. Nor by a more 'equitable' distribution of existing material goods to 'the masses'. A society does not fight addiction to harmful substances by even-handedly administering increased doses to each citizen.

Rather, the ecocommunity will achieve abundance through a critical analysis and reshaping of its system of needs. The development of an ecological sensibility will create an awareness of the importance of cultural and spiritual richness: that which comes from close human relationships, from aesthetic enjoyment, from the unfolding of diverse human potentialities, from spontaneity, play, and all activities liberated from the deadening hand of productive and consumptive rationality. The ecocommunity will seek greater simplicity, and reject the mystifying and dehumanizing economic, technical, and political systems that prevail in mass society. It will highly value the complexity of developed personality, of subtle skills, of disciplined intelligence, of liberated imagination. In short, the greatest wealth of an ecocommunity will consist in the flowering of a richy elaborated libertarian and communitarian culture.

The social forms that will emerge from such a culture will themselves embody the ecological ideal of unity-in-diversity. A fundamental unit will be the *commune*, a closely knit, small community based on love, friendship, shared values, and commitment to a common life. It is founded on the most intimate 'kinship', whether or not this kinship is also biological. In addition, cooperative institutions in all areas of social life will be formed: mutualistic associations for child care and education, for production and distribution, for cultural creation, for play and enjoyment, for reflection and spiritual renewal. Organization will be based not on the demands of *power*, but rather on the *self-realization of persons* as free social beings.

Such a transformation requires vast changes in our conception of 'the political'. As Bookchin states it, 'society, conceived of as a diversified and self-developing ecosystem' based on complementarity, poses a very distinct notion of politics' that stresses 'human scale, decentralization, non-hierarchy, communitarianism, and face-to-face interaction between citizens.'[14] The ideal method of decision-making is consensus, which requires an outcome based on a full recognition of the worth and competence of all involved in the process. But to the extent that this is impossible, the most participatory forms of democracy are necessary, if the values of freedom and community are to be synthesized in practice. Ultimate authority must be retained at the level of the local community—the level of lived experience.

For this reason, a political form that is of crucial importance is the town or neighbourhood assembly. This assembly gives the citizenry an arena in which to publicly formulate its needs and aspirations. It creates a sphere in which true citizenship can be developed and exercised in practice. While it is conceivable that ecological sensibility and ecological culture can flourish through a diversity of affinity groups, cooperatives, collectives, and associations, the community assembly creates a forum through which this multiplicity can be unified and coordinated, and allows each citizen to conceive vividly of the good of the whole community.

Martin Buber wrote that 'the whole fate of the human race' depends on the question of whether there will be a 'rebirth of the commune.'[15] He perceived clearly that if the world is ever to emerge from its self-destructive path, it must become a universal community. And such a community, he says, can consist only of a 'community of communities'. If human beings cannot develop a deep sense of community, that is, become *communal beings*, through the actual practice of living in an authentic community of friends and neighbours, then the vast gulfs that separate us from one another can never be bridged.

Such a possibility depends on a renewal at the most personal level: that of the self. As Bookchin has formulated it, Social Ecology sees the self as a harmonious synthesis of reason, passion, and imagination. Hierarchical power has always demanded the repression of many dimensions of the self. As early as the *Odyssey*, we find Odysseus, the paradigmatic model of civilized man, vanquishing, in the forms of Circe, the Sirens, the Lotus-Eaters, Scylla and Charybdys, and so on, the forces of nature, desire, the feminine, the primitive, the unconscious. And in Plato, the first great ideologist of domination, civilized rationality is exalted as the only truly human part of the psyche, while desire is calumniated as the 'many-headed monster' that destroys and devours all.

Social Ecology affirms an ideal of a many-sided self, in which diverse aspects attain a mutually compatible development. The self is seen as an organic whole, yet as a whole in constant process of self-transformation and self-transcendence. The myth of the self as a completed totality, as a hierarchical system with a 'ruling part', is a fiction designed to facilitate adaptation to a system of domination. The self contains, on the one hand, its own individuality: its own internal *telos*, its striving toward a good that flows in large part from its own nature. Yet the nature of that good and the development toward it is incomprehensible apart from one's dialectical interaction with others persons, with the community, and with the rest of nature. The goal is thus the maximum realization of both individual uniqueness and social being.

This conception of self and society does not accept the myth that all tension and conflict can ever miraculously disappear. Indeed, this delusion is more typical of reactionary psychologies of 'adaptation'. Instead, it must be recognized that personal growth takes place only through dialectical interaction within the self, and between the self and others. The interrelationship between reason, passion, and imagination will always be dynamic and tending toward discord. In recognizing the inevitable multiplicity of the self, Social Ecology is in the tradition of the great utopian philosopher Fourier, who exhorted us never to deny or repress the vast diversity of human passions and interests. Instead, all should be recognized, affirmed, and harmonized to the greatest degree possible—so that the self can be as much a complex unity-in-diversity as are the community and nature.

Bookchin has aptly said that the creation of a true ecological community is, above all, *a work of art*. In the same spirit, we might say that the creation of the organic self, this complex unity of multiplicity, is the most exquisite work of art ever undertaken by humanity and nature.

REFERENCES

1. Murray Bookchin, *The Ecology of Freedom: The Emergence and Dissolution of Hierarchy* (Palo Alto, CA: Cheshire Books, 1981), p. 24.
2. Murray Bookchin, 'Radical Social Ecology' *Harbinger* No. 3, p. 35.
3. *See* John Clark, *The Anarchist Moment: Reflections on Culture, Nature, and Power* (Montreal: Black Rose Books, 1984), Ch. 7.
4. Murray Bookchin, 'Toward a Philosophy of Nature.' In: Michael Tobias (ed.) *Deep Ecology* (San Diego, California: Avant Books, 1984), p. 229.
5. Bookchin, 'Radical Social Ecology', *Harbinger* No. 3, p. 30.
6. Murray Bookchin, 'the Radicalization of Nature', in Comment (July 1, 1984), p. 7.
7. Ibid., p. 6.
8. Murray Bookchin, 'Toward a Philosophy of Nature', p. 230.
9. Murray Bookchin, *The Ecology of Freedom*, p. 342.
10. Murray Bookchin, *Toward an Ecological Society* (Montréal: Black Rose Books, 1980), p. 69.
11. Ibid., p. 59.
12. Ibid., p. 268.
13. Murray Bookchin, 'The Radicalization of Nature', p. 15.
14. Murray Bookchin, 'Radical Social Ecology', Harbinger, No. 3, p. 33.
15. Martin Buber, *Paths in Utopia* (Boston: Beacon Press, 1955), p. 136.

The Cybernetic Dream of the 21st Century

Morris Berman

In the future the community of the learned will have to propose this new and humane technology which is natural philosophy and positive magic. . . . However, if the sense of the individual [i.e. of particular entities] is the only good, how will science succeed in recomposing the universal laws through which . . . the good magic will become functional?

> William of Baskerville, fourteenth century, in Umberto Eco, *The Name of the Rose*

The main point is that the world of life is to a great extent created and maintained through the expression of emotional energy. It is this energy through which magic operates. . . . The control and manipulation of emotional energy is the secret of all magic. . . .

> Father Sylvan, in Jacob Needleman, *Lost Christianity*

It was in the mid to late 1960s that an idea with a long but obscure ancestry finally came to fruition, an idea that many of us, myself included, found very difficult to grasp. This idea was that science possessed no epistemological superiority over any other mode of thought, it had no monopoly on the truth, and, in the last analysis, it was a mythology—that is, it functioned as a type of religion for Western industrial societies. On the popular level, this argument was most closely identified with Theodore Roszak, who asserted that science was not some sort of absolute, transcultural truth, but rather a type of cultural construct, i.e. a 'construct in which a given society in a given historical situation has invested its sense of meaningfulness and value.'[1]

Why was this argument so difficult to grasp, let alone accept? Largely, because all of us were brought up within those very philosophical parameters Roszak had chosen to call into question. These parameters have their origins in the Scientific Revolution of the seventeenth century, and are generally summed up by historians of science as the 'mechanical philosophy'. Briefly, this states that spirits of any kind are delusions, that consciousness is epiphenomenal (i.e. arises from a material base), and that matter and motion are the only real entities around. The favorite image of the universe was that of a clock, wound up by the Almighty to tick forever. Nature was thus seen as mechanical, and all explanations of its behavior had to be material ones. And, for the most part, this is still what the dominant culture believes, as can be seen by consulting virtually any modern textbook in the natural or social sciences, or, for that matter, the daily newspaper.

Roszak's idea, as I have already indicated, had a long tradition behind it; a tradition, interestingly enough, that was heavily academic in nature. Edmund Husserl, Martin Heidegger, and Ludwig Wittgenstein had all broached the subject in various forms. The Frankfurt School for Social Research, notably Max Horkheimer and T. W. Adorno, had wrestled with these problems in books such as *Eclipse of Reason* and *Dialectic of Enlightenment*. And the so-called 'externalist' school of the history of science, following up on the general mode of analysis provided by Karl Mannheim, pointed out both the content and the method of modern science were 'situation-bound'. highly localized in time and space. In other words, modern science was put together over a period of roughly 150 years, and principally in four countries—Italy, England, Holland and France. If you studied the social, economic, and religious history of those nations between 1550 and 1700, you began to understand why scientific conceptions of reality would take root at that time and in those places. The logical conclusion was that this whole mode of perception was and is a cultural construct, a mythology, i.e. a complex and elaborate worldview that permeates Western industrial societies and provides them with meaning.[2]

During the 1960s, however, the real critic of the scientific world view was not Theodore Roszak but Herbert Marcuse, whose book, *One-Dimensional Man*, constituted a major attack on the claim of science to be value-free. At a time when it was still fashionable to argue that science and technology could be used for good or evil, Marcuse argued that science possessed no real neutrality, but was from its inception haunted by a particular bias, which he termed the 'logic of domination'. His attack, paradoxically enough, was based on an examination of the one feature that modern science regards as a *guarantee* of its neutrality, viz. its purely formal or abstract character. In a word, the science of Galileo is about relata, not about contents. The law of free-fall, $s = kt^2$, is descriptive rather than normative. Where Aristotle saw a falling body as going 'home', moving toward the center of the earth, and thereby living out its teleological destiny, Galileo saw only an abstract relationship between distance and time. Modern science is thus based on the abolition of the notion of *telos*, or inherent purpose, and it does this by positing a purely formal reality, one that can be bent to any situation. But it is precisely here, said Marcuse, that it reveals its bias, for the ability to be bent to any situation implies a purely instrumentalist character. $s = kt^2$ has a latent but powerful message, for it projects a world of pure form and essentially says that only this is real. In Galileo's time, it was still possible to maintain a notion of two realities. Hence, the father of modern science, as he has been called, supposedly argued before the Inquisition that 'physics tells how the heavens go; it does not tell how to go to heaven'. But it proved to be a feeble dichotomy, and one difficult, as the centuries passed, to maintain. The two realities ultimately collapsed into one; hence the title of Marcuse's book. And having left value behind, this single dimension of reality could then claim to be value-free. But it was precisely this point that Marcuse chose to call into question, arguing that this very neutrality constituted the bias of the whole methodology. There could be nothing neutral about a methodology, said Marcuse, that swallowed up the entire *Lebenswelt;* that created, for literally everyone in the culture, a single mode of seeing and intepreting the world. '[W]hen technics becomes the universal form production', he wrote, 'it circumscribes an entire culture; it projects a historical totality—a "world" '. Amorality, in short, was a species of morality; 'value-free' really meant 'scientific values'.[3]

The combined result of all of this type of thinking, or at least, conspicuously concomitant with it, was the eruption, in Europe and North America, of cults of various sorts on an unprecedented scale. The feeling was, quite simply, that science had gone astray; that if it were a mythology, there were reasons to believe it had outlived its time, and that other realities were equally valid or perhaps even superior to it. By the mid 1970s, interest in the occult was extremely widespread. Astrology, alchemy, sorcery, numerology, witchcraft, Scientology—not since the heyday of the Renaissance had the non-rational enjoyed such a vogue. This was partly explicable in terms of the growing disenchantment with science, but one still has to ask: why magic? What was there about the occult tradition that was so attractive to a large counterculture that was jaded with science? There are undoubtedly many answers to this, but I suspect that one of the most important of these is that magic has strengths in precisely those areas that, according to Marcuse, science is weak. The occult sciences are anything but formal and abstract. They are sensuous and concrete, and magic rituals typically engage all of the senses, including taste and smell. Magic is embodied in a way that science is not; it emerges from the whole person, not just from the intellect. And although magic certainly has a manipulative, or exoteric aspect, its historical context down to the early modern period was a sacred one. That sacred (or ecological) context meant that in overall terms, magic was not value-free or instrumentalist, and there was always a severe injunction against using it in a purely manipulative way. Goethe's *Faust* is, in fact, a modern version of this ancient injunction: the attempt to divorce fact from value has a price, that being nothing less than the loss of the soul. As Marcuse recognized, that divorce is the essential drama of the modern era.[4]

Finally, magic was attractive because it provided an epistemological shock. Many of those who got interested in magical practice, myself included, had a real surprise in store: it works. Reality is flexible enough that perception can influence it; in fact, that is why *science* works, and why it can rightly be called the magic of the modern era. As it turns out, the occult subculture was not the only circle that was interested in alternative realities. Soviet and American intelligence organizations had been investigating ESP, psychometry, psychokinesis, etc., since the 1950s or 1960s, and discovering what magical practitioners have known for centuries: mental attitudes can make a difference for physical effects.[5]

As noted, all of this suggested to many people that Western consciousness may be in the midst of a mythological shift, or that a new scientific revolution might be in progress. This perception, however, was definitely not confined to investigators of occult phenomena. A large 'new paradigm' literature began to develop, arguing for a convergence of modern physics and archaic spiritual tradition, for example, or seeing in ecology or systems theory a new mode of constructing the world.[6] As for myself, I played with magic long enough to satisfy my intellectual curiosity; but I have to confess that I never managed to acquire any great magical powers. Furthermore, my interest was in a post-Cartesian philosophy, not a pre-Cartesian one, and this pretty much put me in the 'new paradigm' camp. And it was at this point that I stumbled across the work of the cultural anthropologist Gregory Bateson, and found what I was looking for: a scientist who talked like an alchemist. Precise, empirical, experimental, Bateson's categories of thought nevertheless had a living, sensuous quality to them. As I began to wade through the opaque prose of his book, *Steps to an Ecology of Mind*, to puzzle over essays like 'The Cybernetics of "Self" ', and 'Form, Substance and Difference', it began to dawn on me that this man had somehow managed to bring fact and value back together in a way that was rationally credible. And although he often used a cybernetic or systems theory terminology, the pages of the book oozed life, because the theory emerged not from abstractions but from concrete situations. Patiently, over the decades of his life, Bateson lived and studied among the Iatmul of New Guinea, the Balinese, alcoholics, schizophrenics, dolphins—it was from such contexts that his most famous concepts, such as schismogenesis, circuitry, and the double-bind, had emerged. Bateson was the living embodiment of his own analysis; the philosophy was incarnated in the practice. This was a 'process' reality, formally identical to the magical tradition, yet radically different in content. There was a clear resonance with Taoism, with quantum mechanics, with the work of Carl Jung and Wilhelm Reich; and it spoke directly to questions of ecology and man's relationship to the environment. The Gregory Bateson of *Steps*, I concluded, could well be the most brilliant, and most desperately needed, thinker of the twentieth century; and that is a view I would still, to a great extent, defend.[7]

Unfortunately, in his later work, Bateson was not able to hold the synthesis of the sensuous and the scientific—what Umberto Eco calls 'natural philosophy and positive magic' —together. The first hint that something was amiss occurred to me in 1979 when Bateson, in the year before his death, published *Mind and Nature: A Necessary Unity*.[8] The holistic epistemology of *Steps* was still there, all right, but despite the subtitle of the book, mind and nature were tending to float away from each other. In Bateson's revision of Darwin, for example, evolution was presented almost entirely as a mental process. Real dinosaurs and butterflies seemed to be absent from the picture. By mid-1980, just before Bateson's death, this tendency was taken to its logical conclusion. His last talk, 'Man are Grass: Metaphor and the World of Mental Process', solves the mind-body problem by doing away with the body altogether. The cybernetic philosophy presented there is, when you come down to it, essentially Neo-Platonic or Augustinian. The flesh withers, the soul is immortal—a convenient philosophy, of course, if you know you are about to die, but a retreat from reality and into a world of pure abstractions nonetheless. By turning into pure form, Batesonian holism succumbed to the very problem that haunted the mechanical philosophy.[9]

Turning to those who seriously reject mechanistic science today, it seems that they largely fall into the two categories I have identified: occult practitioners, and what we might generally call cybernetic or holistic thinkers. I am not going to say anything further about the first category, principally because I do not believe that it has any real future: it is very unlikely that we can turn back the clock and revert to an earlier era and worldview, and I am not convinced it would be a good idea in any event. My attention, therefore, will be focused on the second category; but it is here, quite frankly, that I have begun to have some serious doubts. Whereas Bateson managed, at least for a time, to hold mind and matter together, the holistic or cybernetic thinking of the 1980s is simplifying the problem by dispensing with matter before the game even begins. The result is that, on the philosophical level, we now have an emerging epistemological consensus which, in one form or another, claims to refute and replace the mechanism and materialism of the last 300 years, but which, in most of its forms, falls prey to the same philosophical problems that plague modern science as they were identified by Herbert Marcuse. That is, it is purely abstract and formal, capable of being bent to any reality; and it often has the appearance of being value-free, but in fact projects a *Lebenswelt*, a total vision of reality that circumscribes an entire world. Nor is this occurring just on the philosophical level. The new mythology is now appearing at three levels of society, levels that overlap, interpenetrate, and reinforce each other, and which are often very difficult to distinguish. The first, as noted, is that of abstract philosophy, which includes a rather eclectic *mélange* of writers and scientists, figures as diverse as Ken Wilber, Marilyn Ferguson, David Bohm, Douglas Hofstadter and Rupert Sheldrake.[10] The second level is that of the professional disciplines, including history, biology, education, ecology, and psychology, to name but a few. The third level is the daily life of the ordinary citizen, which is increasingly filled with video games and home computers. Of course, the three levels are not identical; and in sociological terms, there is no way I can prove they are even related. Yet it seems to me that it would be naïve to believe that this new mythology had somehow emerged within our culture at three different points and that these three manifestations were nevertheless not part of the same social process; and I am going to take it as a given that they *are* structurally related, even though I cannot establish any concrete causal connections. And taken as a whole, these three levels serve to propagate the mythology of a new 'process' reality, a type of abstract 'mentation' or consciousness that, despite a fanfare of propaganda about being a new liberatory epistemology, is in fact just as disembodied and 'value-free' as its mechanistic predecessor. These are the problems I see operating on all three of these levels, and which I wish to make the focus of my critique. I shall return to the level of abstract philosophy, or 'new paradigm' literature, toward the end of this article. For now, let me concentrate on the more concrete manifestations of the new cybernetic consciousness.

In many ways, the grass roots level is the most significant, the more so for being the least sophisticated. The Italian historian Carlo Ginzburg has argued that the way to discover what a culture is about is not to study the ideas of its leading intellectuals, but rather to examine what fills the heads of its ordinary citizens.[11] Unfortunately, we are a bit of an impasse here, for it would seem to be a bit too early to discern this.

As far as I am aware, no exact studies have been done of the impact of video games or home computers on the personal or individual level, so I am going to have to rely on general impressions. And the image I have—all of you have seen it—is of a group of teenagers crowded around a Pac-Man machine in a drugstore or games arcade. The thing that interests me most here is the eyes of the players. Have you ever observed the eyes of someone playing Pac-Man? They are glazed. The phrase that recently entered the English language, 'video addict', is quite apropos, because the machine instantly takes the player out of this world. He becomes, in effect, unconscious; his eyes take on an absorbed, drugged quality that reflects the all-encompassing power of the screen. As with any drug, the video screen effectively enables the addict to leave his body and thus the cares of the world; and I recently discovered that an organization called 'Vidanon' has emerged, dedicated to getting people unhooked from this addiction.[12]

In this way, Pac-Man, and frequently the home computer as well, is really the modern fulfillment of the Gnostic vision. For, whether the screen presents a computer program or asteroids to be blown out of the sky, it enables the user to escape, at least momentarily, from boredom, anxiety, and other emotional difficulties, all of which are felt in the body. This is not to say that home computers are identical to video games in terms of intended use, but as things work out in practice, both encourage disembodied activity and both help to diffuse a similar mode of perception throughout the culture. In this way, our culture is starting, without much questioning or critical evaluation, to acquire a kind of 'computer consciousness'. Strictly speaking, home computers fall into the category of professional activity; but it is very doubtful that all or even most of the 27 million units sold between 1978 and 1983 are being used in this way.[13] Exact mode of use, however, is not the point. The real issue here is that both video games and home computers create a similar view of the world for millions of people. Both present the viewer with a screen and a set of images to be operated upon. Both convey the notion that reality is a function of programming, and children as well as adults pick up a certain type of vocabulary from their use. The general result, I suspect, is a vast subculture that lives entirely in its head; that sees reality as essentially neutral, value-free, and, especially, disembodied, a form of pure mental process.

An example of what I am talking about was provided for me by a friend of mine named Susan who teaches high school in northern Florida. Many of her students have home computers. When Susan assigns a paper, her students immediately run home and feed all the key words into their machines, which are hooked up to various data banks and library resources, and proceed to string this information together. The resulting essays tend to look like speeches given by Ronald Ziegler when he was press secretary to Richard Nixon. One of Susan's students, Frank, stayed after class one day to show her his mass of computer printouts on the latest topic she had assigned.

'Frank,' she finally said, 'stop a moment. I think it's great that you've gathered all these facts about the subject, but put them aside just for a second. Look and me and tell me in your own words: what do you *feel* about this issue?'

Frank stared at her for a moment and finally replied, 'I don't know what you mean.'

Susan told me that if she could afford it, she would retire to Key West and spend the rest of her life scuba diving. In fact, she may not have long to wait. Increasingly, the thrust in secondary school education is to do away with teachers entirely. In one survey conducted by the Sperry Univac Corporation, 50% of the high school students polled said they would prefer to be taught by a machine and gave as their reason that they wished to be left alone.[14]

I feel very uneasy with developments of this sort; they reflect a situation in which people get completely caught up in a worldview without any notion that such a thing is happening to them. And I fear we are going to see much more of this in years to come. Recently, the University of Victoria concluded an agreement with IBM Canada whereby the two institutions will work together to develop applications for computer software that will be used by students from the kindergarten level up. Computers are also being designed for the purpose of rocking a baby's cradle and singing it lullabies. 'It is already technically possible', says Seymour Papert, professor of mathematics and education at MIT, 'to make a machine that can interact with a child from the beginning of its life'. Papert's research team discovered that infants can become addicted to computers, and he comments that the interference of parent-infant bonding by such machines is a turning point in the history of child rearing. By cutting these early ties, he says, '[w]e could easily turn up a generation of psychotic children, of psychotic adults'.[15] Susan's student, Frank, may seem like an aberration today, but a decade from now he may be fairly typical. Three decades from now, there may be no problem, in that there may be no one around who does not possess a cybernetic consciousness. The 'psychotic' label is a matter of social definition. In a predominantly psychotic world, psychotic becomes healthy, and healthy, psychotic. It seems to me that we ought to stop and think about developments of this sort before the level of daily life is completely transformed.

Let me turn now to the second level I referred to, that of the professional disciplines. I want to say, as far as this category goes, that I have no opposition to cybernetic technology *qua* technology; its

utilitarian aspect is not the focus of my critique. Computer technology
clearly makes possible a number of desirable things, such as scanning
the retina in eye operations, or arranging airline flights and schedules.
This makes it a valuable tool, and I am personally glad it is available
for such things. What I am worried about, as I presume is obvious by
now, is how it acts on the emotional, social, and perceptual level of
human existence. That is, my concern here is with what the widespread
adoption of all this hardware and software is doing to our modes of
perception, and our relationship to ourselves, to each other, and to the
environment. And at the level of professional research, the impact is
becoming more noticeable every day.

In the field of professional history writing, and indeed in virtually
all of the social sciences, computer studies have become the *sine qua
non* for obtaining a grant, and, in some cases, professional respect.
Robert Fogel and Stanley Engerman's classic work of a decade ago,
Time on the Cross, is a case in point. The computerized data enabled
the two historians to argue that the system of slavery in the American
South was really part of the cash economy and thus, that in material
terms, American slaves were not really an oppressed population. A
number of scholars subsequently challenged the way in which the
authors used and interpreted their statistics, and were able to throw
the argument into serious doubt. Yet the major issue, it seems to me—
and some reviewers did point this out—is that there is something
seriously amiss with the methodology being used, beyond the question
of faulty statistical analysis. What this methodology can never capture
is the experience of slavery as it was actually lived; and this can only
be recaptured, if at all, through testimonial evidence. There will, of
course, always be the problem of how representative any testimony is;
but at least this sort of evidence is not blind to the subjective experience
of daily life. As one black reviewer remarked, 'there are differences
between being slave and being free, even if those distinctions cannot
be analyzed by high-speed computers.'[16] Yet, for the most part, historians and social scientists have tended, in the ensuing decade, to *follow*
the path blazed by Fogel and Engerman, rather than realize that it is
ultimately a dead end. And as they plunge deeper and deeper into this
rarified atmosphere of quantitative analysis, it is the vital subjective
dimension of human life that starts to recede from view. Attitudes,
perceptions, ideologies, emotions, modes of cognition, frequently even
class affiliation—none of these things are very amenable to computer
analysis, and, as a result, they increasingly tend to get dropped from
the research agenda and thus from the historical picture in general. A
good deal of historical research is now being designed with the computer in mind. The tool is thus becoming the master, rather than the
servant, and in doing so it creates a very skewed version of what the

historical record actually contains. Unfortunately, it is in the omitted areas I mentioned that we tend to find the real life of human beings, the locus of meaning, and the value system of a culture. As the Chilean biologist, Francisco Varela, once remarked, the hard sciences deal with the soft questions and the soft sciences with the hard ones.[17] The more the humanities, history, and the social and behavioral sciences succumb to the glamor and professional pull of computer analysis, the more precise they will be and, I suspect, the less they will have to say.

The popular belief with respect to these fields is that we are learning more because we increasingly have more information available. In fact, the range of thought is actually being *narrowed*, because all of the information is of the same kind. In Orwell's *1984*, the goal of the state was to create a system of thought that embraced all the rest. This is what is effectively happening, albeit not through any deliberate conspiracy. The technology itself discourages any kind of thinking that jumps the rails, which is central to truly creative work; and this narrowing tendency is rapidly being incorporated into institutional procedures. Some universities in the US are now considering the feasibility of putting the card catalogues of their libraries on computer tapes, which will do the searching for you. One university library has apparently closed its stacks to students and faculty alike, and all search and request work is done by computer terminals. The outcome of this sort of thing should be obvious. Many scholars will tell you that their best finds have come through pure chance: they went to the stacks to locate some particular item and accidentally stumbled across a book that proved to be a revelation, that altered the entire direction of their work. The new system would make such serendipity completely impossible.

History and the social sciences are not the only disciplines that are being cyberneticized. At least three other fields I can think of—ecology, biology, and clinical psychology —are now being heavily influenced by a systems theory approach. The dominant trend in American ecology since the Second World War has been increasingly reductionist and managerial. The cybernetic approach is to abstract data from the organic context in the form of 'bits' of information. These are then manipulated according to a set of differential equations to generate a 'trajectory' for the ecosystem and plan its 'rational' management. The word 'ecosystem' itself comes from systems theory, having been developed to replace the older, more organic phrase, 'biotic community'. The cybernetic approach to resource management is perhaps exemplified by the Club of Rome, which sees the planet not as a web of life, with regional peculiarities, but as an abstract globe whose resources can and should be moved around according to ecosystem trends formulated by simulated cybernetic models. The result is the destruction of the holistic vision, or organic unity, that lies at the heart of the man-nature relationship, in no less effective a way than the science and technology of the modern era managed to do. This is no less a disenchantment of the world than the one referred to by Max Weber, no less a logic of domination than the one discussed by Herbert Marcuse. Waving a holistic banner here in the name of ecology is truly meaningless.[18]

Cybernetics has also made great headway in biology, and recent textbooks, as well as numerous research papers, are starting to describe living organisms as 'systems of information'. In his book *Algeny*, Jeremy Rifkin notes that 'survival of the fittest' is being replaced by 'survival of the best informed'. Life itself is now described as 'self-programmed activity'. Rifkin warns that if a New Age is indeed dawning, it is the Age of Biotechnology, in which 'cybernetics is the organizing framework . . . the computer is the organizing mechanism, and living tissue is the organizing material'. What is disturbing about this, as in the case of ecology, is that originally, holistic thinking held out the promise of abolishing the fact-value distinction attacked by Marcuse, and of restoring the sense of nature as being alive and sacred. Instead, just the opposite is happening. The one professional field most clearly directed to the study of life is becoming totally disembodied in its theoretical approach—a continuation of the mechanistic paradigm, when you come down to it. 'Life as information flow,' writes Rifkin, 'represents the final desacralization of nature.'[19]

My third and last example of cybernetics come to the professions is that of clinical psychology. On the popular level, a genre of self-help books has appeared, designed to get the reader to induce changes in his life by thinking of himself as a cybernetic system. By and large, these books are translations of Norman Vincent Peale or Dale Carnegie into cybernetic terminology. In *Psycho-Cybernetics*, Maxwell Maltz describes the human unconscious as a 'goal-striving "servo-mechanism" ', and tells his readers that they can achieve their goals by getting this mechanism to oscillate between positive and negative feedback signals. Eugene Nichols, in *The Science of Mental Cybernetics*, provides *his* readers with twenty-three 'mental-action cards', sketches of IBM punch cards with slogans on them. Phrases like 'input', 'feedback', and 'mental data processing' fill literally every page.[20] I should say that although I regard all of this as somewhat amusing, and, to tell the truth, as somewhat sad, it cannot be dismissed as aberrant or even a misapplication of the cybernetic idea. It is only an *application* of the theory, not a *mis*application, for the concept of self-corrective feedback is central to all varieties of cybernetic thinking, and there is no convincing reason, from a theoretical point of view, why it should not get extended to human interaction. And it is not aberrant, because it is precisely through this sort of popular usage that a worldview most effectively spreads. The same thing happened in the early modern period in Europe, when expressions that reflected the clock metaphor began to appear, such as 'running like clockwork' or 'I'm all wound up'.[21] In a similar fashion, we now have a jargon, at least as far as therapy is concerned, that urges the patient to 'erase old tapes' and 'reprogram his consciousness', so that negative events no longer 'push his buttons'. And within the last few years, a whole new therapy, called Neuro-Linguistic Programming (NLP), has arisen, which is based explicitly on a cybernetic model. It would difficult to find a better example of disembodied consciousness, fact-value split, desacralization of nature, and the projection of pure form than NLP. It is truly a New Age gem. The bible of the movement, significantly titled *The Structure of Magic*, by Richard Bandler and John Grinder, was put together by observing three of the great therapists—Virginia Satir, Fritz Perls, and Milton Erickson—at work, and generating a cybernetic model of what they were doing when they treated their patients. All of these three were or are intuitive geniuses, akin to Zen masters, and their talent is legendary. What Bandler and Grinder did was break down all of their therapeutic interactions into 'bits' of information, and then reassemble them into a generalized cybernetic pattern. Hence, the 'structure of magic', which has supposedly been distilled and scientized.[22]

The thesis here, and the authors are clear about this, is that the scientized version of the original therapy is transferable; that anyone with half a brain can copy and apply it successfully. 'Our purpose in this book', they write, 'is to present to you an explicit Meta-model, that is, a Meta-model which is learnable'. They emphasize that the model is purely formal and content-neutral, and claim that this makes it universally available and universally applicable. What the authors fail to grasp, as far as I can see, is that the structure of magic is not the same thing as magic itself. Fritz Perls was able to heal people not because he was following some cybernetic formula, but because of his physical presence, his personal power. Like Erickson and Satir, Perls was a wizard. He had a genius for grasping what his patient's drama was, tricking him or her into a psychological dead-end around the issue, and catalyzing an emotional breakthrough. The crux of his talent was ineffable, and it was hardly a matter of technique.[23] This is what makes the whole approach of NLP so bizarre. What we have here, once again, is really mechanism in updated clothing; we are not better off for having invented a 'process' model of therapy.

So much for the professional and grass roots levels of society. As for the philosophical level, I do not have time to review the work of a number of holistic thinkers in any detail, and shall have to confine myself to one or two examples. It is not an easy task, in any event. The epistemological issues are very complex; and one cannot, as Marilyn Ferguson wishes to do, lump all 'process reality' thinking together. There are varieties of holism, and real differences between them. And yet, with very few exceptions, such as Gregory Bateson's earlier work, all of this theoretical analysis is subject to the same criticisms Marcuse made of mechanistic science. To anticipate some of my conclusions for a moment, classical science and much contemporary holistic thinking, which includes cybernetic thinking, turn out to be not all that different. Both appear to be value-free, at first glance, and yet can be shown to project a *Lebenswelt*, a totality that circumscribes an entire culture; both generate a purely formal, abstract reality that can be bent to any situation; and both are disembodied. Cybernetic thinking, and more generally holistic thinking, does not automatically get you out of the world of Newton and Descartes, as so many holistic theoreticians claim. The cybernetic mechanism may be a more sophisticated model of reality than the clockwork model of the seventeenth century, but it is still, in the last analysis, a mechanism. Two types of holism thus have to be distinguished here: the one, a sensuous, situational, living approach to process, such as is exemplified by the early Bateson; the other, an abstract form, a type of 'process mechanism', which is present in the work of many philosophical spokesmen of the New Age, and which, in a now more psychologically appealing garb, really represents the last phase of classical science, not the beginning of a new paradigm at all. Cybernetics and general systems theory turn out to be the last outpost of the mechanical world view — a continuation of the scientific project of the seventeenth century rather than the birth of a truly new way of thinking.

As noted earlier, many examples of 'holism gone astray' are available. To combat the mechanical philosophy of the last 300 years, we now have 'implicate orders', 'morphogenetic fields', and 'holographic paradigms', among other things. All of these notions are ingenious, and some of them may even be 'true', if the word can be said to mean anything in this context, but, for the most part, they are disembodied, value-free, and content-neutral. David Bohm's concept of the 'implicate order' is purely formal; it deals with boundary relations, in which reality is viewed as a process that Bohm calls 'enfolding' and 'unfolding', or 'holomovement'. Similarly, Rupert Sheldrake's notion of formative causation by means of 'morphogenetic fields' — a brilliant hypothesis if there ever was one — is also purely formal, as the name itself implies. It is not grounded in any concrete or sensuous reality, and it is certainly capable of being bent to any situation. It has been used thus far only in a positive sense, e.g. to explain the growth of the anti-nuclear movement in politics, successful evolutionary adaptation in biology, or the process of learning in general. Yet the very same theory can be used to explain contagion, or the rise of Fascism—La Peste, by Camus, is a perfect description of a morphogenetic field—or the spread of nuclear weapons, or addiction. As with classical mechanism, the theory is not able to discriminate in terms of content. The whole world dissolves in form. Here, as in the case of Bohm's work, and that of so many other 'process' thinkers, human beings somehow disappear from the picture. The whole thing becomes cosmic, a vast mental process divorced from specific physical situations. Alfred Korzybski's famous dictum, 'the map is not the territory', is not without relevance here.[24]

One of the most prominent thinkers in this category—and his work is explicitly cybernetic in nature—is Douglas Hofstadter, whose book Gödel, Escher, Bach appeared in 1979. Hofstadter's work illustrates the general point I am making here extremely well, so I'd like to dwell on it for just a moment. The book is not easy reading, for most of the text deals with the nature of mathematical paradox of the sort formulated by Zeno of Elea in the 5th century BC. Despite its density, the book has been lionized, selling hundreds of thousands of copies and winning Hofstadter the Pulitzer prize and a spot as a regular columnist for Scientific American. As I plowed my way through it, I began to have an uncomfortable feeling: the book had no real content. It was all about puzzles and tautologies, designed to show that everything in our world, including the subjective concept of 'I', was essentially symbolic patterned activity. Reality somehow disappeared from its pages. Everything was programming; the whole world had turned into Artificial Intelligence. I began to sense in Hofstadter a kind of computer jockey who got so fascinated by cybernetic operations that he decided they could and should be extended to the entire world. There is a scene in the film War Games, premiered in 1983, in which the young whiz kid, who has accidentally tripped into the Pentagon terminal and is busy simulating nuclear war on his home computer while the Joint Chiefs of Staff are actually preparing to bomb Russia, asks his machine:

'Is this a game, or is it real?'

His computer replies: 'What's the difference?'

As John Searle pointed out in a review of Hofstadter's second book (co-authored with Daniel Dennett), The Mind's I, this simple point has been lost on Hofstadter. You can, says Searle, get a computer to print out the worlds 'I am thirsty'; but no one in his right mind would attempt to pour a glass of water into the machine as a result. Plainly put, Hofstadter's brand of holism is completely out of touch with reality.[25]

I subsequently had the opportunity to hear Hofstadter speak three years ago at an East Coast university where I was then teaching. Significantly, the turnout was so great that the overflow had to be siphoned off into a room with closed circuit TV. Hofstadter spoke for ninety minutes, and it was vintage stuff: what Achilles said to the tortoise and other Zenonian brain-twisters. Like *Gödel, Escher, Bach*, the talk was rich in form and devoid of content. I was, that year, teaching a course on the historical relations between holistic and mechanistic thought, and so some of the students in that class came up to me after the talk and wanted to know what I thought.

'Well,' I said, 'I'd be curious to know what Dr. Hofstadter thinks dreams are.'

To my surprise, one of my students took off, elbowed his mway through the enormous crowd that surrounded Hofstadter, and came back within ten minutes.

'I asked him,' he said, panting for breath.

'Well? What was the reply?'

'He told me that dreams were confused brain patterns.'

I won't repeat my reaction to this bit of cybernetic wisdom, but I ask you only to contemplate this: more than eighty years after Freud's *The Interpretation of Dreams*, nearly seventy years after Jung's *Psychology of the Unconscious*, and millennia after cultures like the Greeks, the Egyptians, the Essenes, and aboriginal peoples from all over the planet recognized the value of dream symbolism for human life, a leading spokesman of the cybernetic age is telling his audience that dreams are 'confused brain programs'! I wonder if the language of the body is also, for Hofstadter, a type of confused programming, and whether he finds animal and plant life disorganized and in need of cybernetic management. We really have to ponder what it means in the history of a civilization when a thinker of this sort can come to be regarded as a man of penetrating insight, a mind truly to be reckoned with.

Let me conclude, finally, by saying that I am not categorically opposed to holistic thinking. Far from it. I wrote a whole book arguing that mechanism had no philosophical future, and I still believe that. My point is that the real issue, ultimately, is not mechanism versus holism, but whether any philosophical system contains an intrinsic ethic —and not a value-free one—and whether it is a truly embodied approach to the world. On these grounds, mechanism would seem to be disqualified, as Marcuse so effectively argued. But the holistic case is not so simple; there is holism and there is holism. In *The Reenchantment of World*, I argued that what was on the philosophical agenda now was the revival of the magical tradition in a way that was scientifically credible. It is precisely this impulse that underlies the research of people like David Bohm and Rupert Sheldrake, and from that point of view, their work is definitely worthy of our attention and respect. Such thinkers are quite literally the modern equivalents of Descartes and Newton; they recognize that the old paradigm is crumbling and they are out to construct a new one. What I am concerned about is that the magic will somehow get left behind in the process. By 'magic' I do not mean sticking pins in dolls; I mean the affective, concrete, and sensual experience of life. The paradigm I have in mind would be grounded in the real behavior of human beings in the environment. It would incorporate the sort of information that arises from our dream life, our bodies, and our relationship to plants, animals, and natural cycles. And I am absolutely convinced that it would usher in a profoundly creative and liberated period in the history of the West. Unfortunately, most holistic thinking today, and certainly that of the cybernetic variety, is moving in a very different direction. In the name of enlightenment, we are getting reification; we are drifting into a hall of mirrors. What is being lost, on all three of the levels I have discussed, is any sense of unmediated/reality,[26] such as is celebrated in Japanese haiku, for example, or which comes to us through dreams, or through body awareness, or as a result of any extended experience with nature. Instead, what we are now moving toward is a world of pure metaphor, 'programming', 'patterned activity'; what one writer has called 'mysticism without a soul'.[27] 'Mysticism without flesh' might be more accurate.

Yet I do not believe this tendency is inevitable. On the philosophical and professional levels, at least, we might conceivably be able to exercise some epistemological restraint. Cybernetic thinking does not have to be, of necessity, disembodied and formulistic. In his book *The Gift*, Lewis Hyde cites the example of a gift-giving ceremony among the Maori of New Zealand that reveals a cybernetic structure, but Hyde is well aware that the power of this structure is derived from its actual embodiment in a concrete situation: a history, a tradition, a gestalt that is felt to be alive by those who participate in it.[28] Paul Ryan, the American video artist, and the author of a book called *Cybernetics of the Sacred*,[29] once put it to me this way: God is Relationship. By 'relationship' he did not mean a set of abstract relata, but a practice, a praxis, a living and embodied reality. There *are* no 'circuits', there *are* no 'feedback loops'; all that is fantasy. To think such things exist apart from real situations is a Neo-Platonic dream; it is to fall into what Alfred North Whitehead called the 'fallacy of misplaced concreteness'. The French philosopher Maurice Merleau-Ponty recognized this tendency as early as 1960, and wrote the following in his essay, 'Eye and Mind':

Thinking 'operationally' has become a sort of absolute artificialism, such as we see in the ideology of cybernetics, where human creations are derived from a natural information process, itself conceived on the model of human machines. If this kind of thinking were to extend its reign to man and history; if, *pretending to ignore what we know of them through our own situations*, it were to set out to construct man and history on the basis of a few abstract indices . . . then, since man really becomes the *manipulandum* he takes himself to be, we enter into a cultural regimen where there is niether truth nor falsity concerning man and history, into a sleep, or a nightmare, from which there is no awakening. [Italics mine]

Scientific thinking [he continues] . . . must return to . . . the soil of the sensible and opened world such as it is in our life and for our body—not that possible body which we may legitimately think of as an information machine *but that actual body I call mine*, this sentinel standing quietly at the command of my words and of my acts.[30] [Italics mine]

We are at a crossroads now, and it is a crucial one, for this is the heart of the mythological shift I have been discussing. In our eagerness to reject the mechanistic science of the last 300 years, we need to be wary of what we are replacing it with. The thing to ask of any new philosophical statement, any extension of computer hardware into schools, universities, or therapists' offices, and of any new toys such as Pac-Man or Apple II, is only this: does it take me into the things I fear most, and wish to avoid, or does it make it easy for me to hide, to run away from them? Does it enable me to shut out the environment, ignore politics, remain unaware of my dream life, my sexuality, and my relations with other people, or does it shove these into my face, and teach me how to live with them and through them? If the answer is the latter, then I suggest to you that we are on the right track. If the former, then it is my guess, as Merleau-Ponty says, that we are sinking into a sleep from which, in the name of enlightenment itself, there will be no easy awakening.

REFERENCES

1. Theodore Roszak, *The Making of a Counter Culture* (Garden City, N.Y.: Doubleday, 1969), p.215.
2. Edmund Husserl, *The Crisis of European Sciences and Transcendental Phenomenology*, trans. David Carr (Evanston, IL: Northwestern University Press, 1970); Martin Heidegger, *The Question Concerning Technology, and Other Essays*, trans. William Lovitt (New York: Garland, 1977); and Karl Mannheim, *Ideology and Utopia*, trans. Louis Wirth and Edward Shils (New York: Harcourt, Brace and World, reprint of 1936 edition). It should be noted that Heidegger made strict distinctions between the categories of Being, technology, and scientific truth, and it

might be argued that Roszak and others tended to confuse them. It was one of Heidegger's students, however, Herbert Marcuse (see below), who was able to show that although these categories might be philosophically distinguishable, they were not really separable; and that, in actual practice, they easily got scrambled. Thus Marcuse argued, for example, that scientific truth as it developed in the seventeenth century actually had a technological *a priori*, or hidden technological agenda; and that by the twentieth century, this had largely come to define Being in Western industrial societies.

The later notebooks of Wittgenstein reveal his perplexity with the 'grammar of theology' versus the logic of science, and the inability to establish the epistemological superiority of the latter. For a general overview of the Frankfurt School, *see* Martin Jay, *The Dialectical Imagination* (Boston: Little, Brown, 1973). As for the 'externalist' school in the history of science, there is a large literature in this genre, but the classic studies probably remain those of Robert Merton and Edgar Zilsel, done in the 1930s and 1940s. See also the essays in Hugh F.Kearney (ed.), *Origins of the Scientific Revolution* (London: Longmans, Green, 1964).

3. Herbert Marcuse, *One-Dimensional Man* (Boston: Beacon Press, 1966), esp. Chapter 6.

4. For a more extended discussion of this, see Chapter 3 of my *The Reenchantment of the World* (Ithaca, NY: Cornell University Press, 1981). Descriptions of magical practice can be found in various works by the early twentieth-century British occultist, Dion Fortune (Violet Firth). A more recent text is David Conway, *Ritual Magic* (New York: E. P. Dutton, 1972).

5. On Soviet and American research into the paranormal *see* Michael Rossman, *New Age Blues* (New York: E. P. Dutton, 1979), pp. 167–260, and Ronald M. McRae, *Mind Wars: The True Story of Government Research into the Military Potential of Psychic Weapons* (New York: St Martin's Press, 1984).

6. See, for example, Fritjof Capra, *The Tao of Physics* (Berkeley: Shambhala, 1975), Gary Zukav, *The Dancing Wu Li Masters* (New York: William Morrow, 1979), or Itzhak Bentov, *Stalking the Wild Pendulum* (New York: E. P. Dutton, 1977).

7. Gregory Bateson, *Steps to an Ecology of Mind* (New York: Ballantine, 1972).

8. Gregory Bateson, *Mind and Nature: A Necessary Unity* (New York: E. P. Dutton, 1979).

9. Gregory Bateson, 'Men are Grass: Metaphor and the World of Mental Process', 9 June 1980, published by the Lindisfarne Press. I have tended, in this paper, to blur the distinction between the concepts 'value-free' and 'disembodied'. (Marcuse, it seems to me, does this as well.) Strictly speaking, they are not the same thing. Bateson's later work was certainly disembodied, but it was never value-free. His concept of 'circuitry', for example, or of 'Mind' (capital M), both of which he took from cybernetic theory, essentially added up to what in certain Eastern religious traditions is called 'karma', a kind of non-linear law of cause and effect. On this reasoning, the universe is not value-free, but rather is suffused with a pattern that is self-defining or reflexive. Meaning is thus built into the system. In actual practice, however, a disembodied system can easily take

on a purely formal character and fall into the 'value-free' camp, and I
discuss the susceptibility of Bateson's work, and of holistic/cybernetic
thinking in general, to this tendency in Chapter 9 of *The Reenchantment of
the World*. Another way to see this distinction is to examine the difference
between the magical tradition and Aristotelianism. Formally, a *telos* is
definitely present in the Aristotelian worldview, and meaning—e.g. the
concept of natural place and motion —is embedded in the universe.
Natural place and motion are, furthermore, very much a part of the
occult tradition, and fall into the category of 'sympathy', the theory that
'like knows like', a notion which was present in Orphic and Greek
shamanic traditions and in the writings of some of the pre-Socratics.
Aristotle, in fact, may in some way represent the intellectualizing of this
tradition, following the pattern of Plato's 'inversion' of occult sources (on
this see E. R. Dodds, *The Greeks and the Irrational* [Berkeley: University
of California Press, 1951]). The problem is that once the living tradition
gets disembodied, the system is still technically endowed with meaning
or value, but only in an abstract sense. In actual practice, the purely formal
aspect comes to the fore, and Marcuse wrestles with this in *One-
Dimensional Man* (pp. 137–39 and 147), saying that it is a precursor or
anticipation of seventeenth-century science.

This same tension lies at the heart of the problem with Bateson's legacy.
To put it succinctly, the early Bateson was an alchemist, the later Bateson
an Aristotelian. All of his work, as I have noted, was 'value-laden', but
the disembodied character of the later work turned it into a kind of
cybernetic catechism and thus, in actual practice, it would seem to be as
instrumentalist as the mechanism of the seventeenth century.

10. Marilyn Ferguson, *The Aquarian Conspiracy* (Los Angeles: J. P. Tarcher,
    1980); David Bohm, *Wholeness and the Implicate Order* (London: Routledge
    & Kegan Paul, 1980); Douglas Hofstadter, *Gödel, Escher, Bach* (New York:
    Basic Books, 1979); Rupert Sheldrake, *A New Science of Life* (Los Angeles:
    J. P. Tarcher, 1981). Ken Wilber is the author of several works, recently
    published, including *The Spectrum of Consciousness, Up From Eden* and *The
    Atman Project*. Wilber is, however, critical of certain aspects of 'new
    paradigm' thought; *see* Ken Wilber (ed.) *The Holographic Paradigm*,
    (Boulder, CO: Shambhala, 1982), pp. 157–86 and 249–294.

11. Ginzburg develops this theme very effectively in *The Chesse and the Worms*
    (Baltimore: The Johns Hopkins University Press, 1980), and more
    recently, in *The Night Battles* (Baltimore: The Johns Hopkins University
    Press, 1983) (both books translated by John and Anne Tedeschi).

12. 'Addicted to video games? It's Vidanon to the rescue,' *Victoria Times-
    Colonist* (British Columbia), 8 October 1983; from an article in the *Los
    Angeles Times*.

13. This figure was given by Edward Lias of Sperry Univac Corporation at
    a conference called 'Future Mind', held at the University of South Florida,
    Tampa, 14–16 April 1983.

14. *Ibid.*

15. 'Computer Harm to Children', *San Francisco Chronicle*, 26 December 1983.

16. Robert W. Fogel and Stanley L. Engerman, *Time on the Cross* (2 vols;
    Boston: Little, Brown, 1974); review quoted is by N. I. Huggins, writing
    in *Commonweal*, *100* (23 August 1974), p. 459. For an update of the debate,

see 'Historian Calls for "New Moral Indictment" of Slavery' *The Chronicle of Higher Education, 27* (11 January 1984), pp. 7 and 12.

17. At a conference held in Alpbach, Austria, 7–11 September 1983, entitled 'Andere Wirklichkeiten' (Other Realities). For a holistic paradigm which I believe differs from the models being criticized in this essay, see Humberto Maturana and Francisco Varela, *Autopoiesis and Cognition* (Dordrecht, Holland: D. Reidel, 1980). At the Alpbach conference, Varela frequently emphasized the importance of a holism that did not leave human beings out of the picture.

18. 'Cybernetic ecology' is discussed by Carolyn Merchant in *The Death of Nature* (New York: Harper & Row, 1980), pp. 103, 238–239, 252 and 291. For the Club of Rome report, see Donella H. Meadows *et al.* (eds.), *Limits to Growth* (2nd ed; New York: Universe Books, 1974).

19. Jeremy Rifkin, *Algeny* (New York: The Viking Press, 1983), esp. pp. 191, 213, 221 and 228. For a good example of a biology textbook in the cybernetic genre see Lila Gatlin, *Information Theory and the Living System* (New York: Columbia University Press, 1972).

20. Maxwell Maltz, *Psycho-Cybernetics* (New York: Pocket Books, 1969); R. Eugene Nichols, *The Science of Mental Cybernetics* (New York: Warner Books, 1971).

21. For some interesting examples of this see the *Oxford English Dictionary* under the entry for 'clock'. Miners began to describe the direction of veins of ore as 'lying at 9 (or whatever) o'clock'; W. Fenner, in *Christ's Alarm* (1650), says you must wind up your conscience every day 'as a man does his clock'.

22. On this and the following see Richard Bandler and John Grinder, *The Structure of Magic, Part I* (Palo Alto, CA: Science and Behavior Books, 1975), esp. pp. 18–19 and 158. For an example of *body* therapy reduced to cybernetic terms, *see* Yochanon Rywerwant, *The Feldenkrais Method: Teaching by Handling* (New York: Harper & Row, 1983). I am grateful to Mr Brian Lynn for pointing these works out to me and for the helpful discussions we had on current trends in New Age 'therapy'.

23. 'True magic works,' writes Father Sylvan, 'through the phenomenon of resonance. One must know the exact words to say and one must say them in exactly the right place and the right time . . .' (Jacob Needleman, *Lost Christianity* [New York: Bantam Books, 1982], p. 87).

24. On Sheldrake and Bohm, see footnote 10 above and also Renée Weber, 'The Enfolding-Unfolding Universe: A Conversation with David Bohm,' in Ken Wilber (ed.) *The Holographic Paradigm*, pp. 44–104. For an example of morphogenetic fields applied to the political (anti-nuclear) sphere, see Ken Keyes, Jr, *The Hundredth Monkey* (Coos Bay, OR: Vision Books, 1982). Korzybski's statement was first given in *Science and Sanity*, published in 1933, and is repeated in the works of many other writers, including Gregory Bateson.

25. Douglas R. Hofstadter and Daniel C. Dennett, *The Mind's I* (New York: Basic Books, 1981); John R. Searle, 'The Myth of the Computer', *The New York Review of Books, 29*(29 April 1982), pp. 3–6.

26. Strictly speaking, this is not true on the level of Pac-Man. Addictions do provide unmediated experience due to their absorbing intensity. The problem, of course, is that the world in which the addict is absorbed is unreal, and thus the pattern is one that might be termed 'pseudo-holistic'.

Bateson discusses this in his essay, 'The Cybernetics of "Self": A theory of Alcoholism' (reprinted in *Steps*).

27. Father Sylvan, in Jacob Needleman, *Lost Christianity*, p. 140. Cf. Murray Bookchin's comments on the whole issue in 'Sociobiology or Social Ecology, Part II', *Harbinger*, Vol. 1, No. 2 (Fall, 1983), pp. 28–38. Not all criticism of Artificial Intelligence, I am happy to report, comes from traditional 'humanistic' quarters. Joseph Weizenbaum, one of the pioneers of AI, has had some serious reservations about the field and its alienating tendencies, and has discussed this in a review of a book entitled *The Fifth Generation*, by Edward Feigenbaum and Pamela McCorduck, which argues that AI is indispensable to all spheres of life. In this review (*The New York Review of Books, 30*, No. 16 [27 October 1983], pp. 58–62), Professor Weizenbaum writes: 'The knowledge that appears to be least well understood by Edward Feigenbaum and Pamela McCorduck is that of the differences between information, knowledge, and wisdom, between calculating, reasoning, and thinking, and finally of the differences between a society centered on human beings and one centered on machines.'

28. Lewis Hyde, *The Gift* (New York: Vintage Books, 1979), pp. 17–19.

29. Paul Ryan, *Cybernetics of the Sacred* (Garden City, NY: Doubleday Anchor, 1974).

30. Maurice Merleau-Ponty, 'Eye and Mind', trans. Carleton Dallery, in James M. Edie (ed.) *The Primacy of Perception* (Evanston, IL: Northwestern University Press, 1964), pp. 160–161.

A revised version of a paper delivered to the University of Victoria's 'The University into the 21st Century: An International Conference on Social and Technological Change' in May, 1984, and published in W. A. W. Neilson and C. M. Gaffield (eds.), *Tomorrow's Universities: A Mediaeval Institution in the 21st Century* (Montréal: Institute for Research on Public Policy, 1986).

Reflections on Science, Technology and the Biological Paradigm

Richard Merrill

Is There Direction and Purpose? And Where Are We Going?

For more than two centuries now, science and technology have come to dominate human activity; indeed, they have come to replace culture itself. Beguiled by sophisticated machines and chemicals, we seem to hail the new tools that raise us above the animals; our bondage to instinct is loosened, and our limitations to place are transcended.

We believe that technology will help us control nature, and the bigger the technology, the more we can control both nature and human destiny. As a result, science and technology continue to alienate us even further from the natural world we so desperately seek to understand. Are we to believe that space colonies and cosmic explorations will eventually free us once and for all from the polluted confines of our launching pad called Earth? It is as though we were looking for an ultimate freedom from nature itself: to escape from the physical world that seems to exert a sort of tyranny, according to the accepted ideas of human 'progress'.

What has emerged since the Enlightenment is a technocratic world view of material progress in which the triumphs and security of modern technology give it title to rule, not only our lives, but our destiny. We have come to develop a technology as if it were a thing by itself, not from the point of view of what people really require, but of what *CAN* be done. The criteria and priorities for the 'progress' of humanity have become inexorably linked to the goals and achievements of *whatever* is possible in science. Human progress has *become* technological progress.

The degree to which technological progress has molded our view of reality can be seen by the fact that the most highly touted achievements of the last half century (atomic power, pesticides, computer technology, and genetic engineering) also possess an enormous potential for *negative* impacts on human, their culture and environment. The great irony of our times is that the means by which we seek 'security' only deepen the crisis and bring us closer to extinction.

Technology has become too big, too complex, too expensive, and, above all, too violent. It has given us power, growth, and control in a search for security. Perhaps we seek too much security *away from* nature and each other, when we should be seeking security *in* nature and each other.

The insanity of our technological progress points to a most curious aspect of human nature: our inability to say 'no' to the possible. Not only are there no cultural mechanisms for understanding the long-range social and environmental consequences of our technology, but even if there were, we seem unable to deny, destroy, or neglect any 'useful' technology simply because it has possible negative side-effects. This is using technology as an end in itself, creating the milieu for its own proliferation. Our industrial state has immense drive, but little direction, a marvellous capacity for getting there, but no idea of where it is going. To counter this we must re-establish technology as a *means* toward progress, but we must, above all, *redefine* progress, not in another mechanistic direction (bigger machines to the level of the cosmos) but rather within a more comprehensive picture of humanity and nature.

Is Science a Goblin?

Before I describe what a 'more cohesive picture of humanity and nature' might be, we need to take a closer look at the role of 'science' and technology in the picture.

Clearly, it is science that underpins technology and provides the knowledge for technological applications. It is in this sense that science and technology have become synonymous. This is unfortunate and has led to endless debates about the goals of science and the relationship between science and technology. Consider a spectrum of commonly held opinions:

1 The *technocrat* sees science as the fount of technology and the mainspring of human progress. Science allows the state and its industries to function at their most efficient. Science's *raison d'être* is to provide momentum for technical and social progress (which are the same). A technocracy, notes Roszak, is 'a society in which those who govern, justify themselves by appeal to scientific forms

of knowledge. And beyond the authority of science there is no appeal.'

2 The *realist* views science and politics as inseparable. Science can have no meaning outside the existing institutions. Science is as good or bad as society makes it.

3 The *liberal* considers science as subordinate in value to its effect. Efforts should be made to limit research in dangerous areas by changes in institutions or even society itself. Our preoccupation with science leads to never-ending problems which threaten extinction. How far can science stay neutral, and what are the consequencs of technology?

4 A typical *New Left* attitude might view science as a conservative art which gets in the way of the coming revolution (political or spiritual). Science creates the technology which is used by the establishment to preserve its power. The best way to understand the nature of modern technology is to examine the patterns of production, consumption, and activity that maintain the interests of political power. Technology is the tool of the elite and hampers social progress.

5 Those who are *anti-science* see it as inherently evil, and its effects as dehumanizing; science and its technology make meaningless the 'great adventure of living'. Science's alleged objectivity has denatured man's personal experience, taking the mystery and sacredness out of living. Taken to its extreme, this rejection of science slides into an attack on reason itself. Society is seen as irrational in the sense that there is no reasonable relationship between society and the nature of humanity. The old liberal view of a rational and humane society is found to be bankrupt. Reason is rejected because it has failed.

Obviously there are marked differences of opinion about the role of science and technology in society, unlike the 1950s when virtually everybody understood science from the technocrat's viewpoint. We now see a marked divergence of ideas of what science and technology are, and these cannot be reconciled easily. The value of imagination, experience, spontaneity, and community are set against the forces of objective research, authoritative knowledge, division of labour, and specialization; all fragmenting a larger picture of reality. Because there are so many opinions of what science is, we misunderstand the essential meaning of science, and hence misuse it. First, we must assume that reasoning and the human drive for inquiry and understanding are innate characteristics, and are part of the unique experience of being human. We see attempts to organize knowledge and seek principles of order throughout history and across all cultures, in philosophy, religion, art, cultural traditions, and science. What sets science apart from other attempts to organize knowledge is its emphasis on observations coupled with a specific technique of inquiry.

Modern science was born some 200 years ago when a few thinkers decided that appearances were something to be understood and respected, and not just preserved in philosophical images. For the first time, experiments became crucial; theories about reality were supported by close observations. It was the testing of hypotheses that caused a new intellectual excitement to sweep the Western world, a determination to explore, understand and dominate nature, which had hereto dominated humanity. Indeed, such was the faith in 'natural philosophy', as early science called itself, that its practitioners quickly came to believe that all mysteries would eventually yield before it. Science in effect became the new religion.

The Enlightenment of Bacon, Descartes, and Newton came to replace the Greek way of deciding how things ought to be, and gave us our way of observing how in fact things are. They sought to separate the observer from the observed and provide an objective forum for the development of objective knowledge. In their zeal for objectivity, the new scientists of the Enlightenment extended their religious illusions of determinism and duality which confound us to this day. Nevertheless, they laid the foundation for a new way to organize knowledge about how and *where* we are. There was no scientific 'method' then as we know it today. Only simple techniques of observation and measurement (Copernicus destroyed the belief in an earth-centred Universe by simply *observing* the orbital paths of other planets around earth). These were coupled with an emphasis on deciding what kind of questions should be asked. This was a very important aspect of the early *technique* of 'natural philosophy' since it emphasized the need for rejecting valueless problems.

Thinking of science in terms of rote *methods*, rather than a technique for inquiry, came more and more into vogue with the scientific triumphs of the 19th century, and science's great acceleration into the twentieth-century. That tendency reached a peak with Pearsons' 1892 work, *The Grammar of Science* (W. Scott, London), and the formalization of the so-called 'scientific method':

1 A problem is stated;
2 Observations relevant to the problem are collected;
3 A hypothesis consistent with the observations is formulated;
4 Predictions of other observable phenomena are deduced from the hypothesis;
5 Occurrence or nonoccurrence of the predicted phenomena is observed; and

6 The hypothesis is accepted, modified, or rejected in accordance
with the degree of fulfillment of the prediction.

Clearly, such a cut-and-dried method does work in certain cases, call
it 'prediction and control focused science'. But the method of science
does not define it; it says nothing of the goals or nature of inquiry; it
does not tell us how to define the problem (see 1 above). The scientific
method is not a general routine that automatically solves any problem.
It completely ignores the most difficult, most creative, and most important technique of science: the determination of how one decides what
kinds of questions are to be asked. As Karl Popper has noted, 'In
science the question is often more important than the answer.'

The most cogent objection to modern science is that important basic
research has seldom followed the scientific 'technique'. Our stated
problems and applications of knowledge are selective and opportunistic
rather than balanced or holistic. The questions we ask of science are
not based on the larger picture. We fool ourselves, not by the search
for truth or the objectivity of our facts, but by their triviality and lack
of relatedness to the true complexities of human nature-in-nature.

A critique of modern technology, then, should not be a critique of
science or even reason *per se*, but rather of the assumptions behind the
use of scientific knowledge. Clearly, modern science lost its philosophical roots long ago by rejecting ethics and value in the kind of things
that it does, but so have religion, politics, education, etc. The decay
of our environment and institutions is a symptom of our technocratic
culture. We do not live in a wasteland 'caused' by science.

Humanity searches for truth in a variety of ways. Admittedly, science
is only a metaphor for a limited kind of experience. Science does
not have a monopoly on truth. There are equally important paths to
understanding that are non-objective, mystical, and irrational.
Humanity is adrift partly because science, in its obsession with measur-
ing the physical, has neglected those areas of knowledge that all societies have used as steering signals to obtain their essential values, goals,
and sense of meaning. For example, nuclear weapons are not conceivable in a world that considers itself to be a common, living community.
Under these conditions, it *would* be possible to say 'no' to nuclear
weapons.

Science for People and the New Science Paradigm

The growing complexity, danger, and alienation of modern technology, plus the valueless attitude of scientific research, have prompted
many people to search for simpler, safer, and more controllable techno-

logies. Since the early 1970s, there has been a growing movement to re-evaluate technology and make it more useful and less exploitive. The 'soft', 'intermediate', and 'alternative' technology movements of industrialized countries have come to symbolize the search for a technology appropriate to a more sustainable and enriching society. This 'appropriate technology' (AT) stresses community and regionally based economies using ecologically derived technologies plus co-operative modes of action. The cornerstones of AT have been: collection planning, cottage and intermediate industries, recycling of wastes, biologically intensive agriculture, local food economies, use of solar and other renewable energy systems, conservation of non-renewable resources, and bioclimatic architecture. The movement is significant.

For the first time in decades, perhaps ever, an entire new generation of scientists, other professionals, and laypeople are not only seriously criticizing the value system behind science, but doing something about it over a wide spectrum of our society. For these 'new scientists', the nature of the problems facing humanity today are existentially different from the major problems of the past. Human history has shown a preoccupation with responding to the challenges of the natural environment. Now, most future concerns will need to respond to the consequences of our actions for both society and nature. Can scientific activity expand its horizon to include questions of value such as those that follow. What effect does replacing small tractors with large tractors have on soil fertility and stream life? What is the relationship of property tax to *both* the health of a forest and to housing, of clothing fashion to animal populations, of mechanized harvesters to farm laborers, of the goals of our present educational system to future generations? More generally, what is the relevance of technology to poverty, to the physical, spiritual, and mental health of human beings, to the environment all human beings share in common, i.e. planet Earth?

This culture-wide search for scientific value and technological alternatives is especially obvious in agriculture. Formal research, informal research, and in-field experience of growers are being widely shared. Some of the problems being addressed in three major areas of focus are as follows.

1 *The Sustainability of Agroecosystems.* The integration of ecosystem principles to the long-term management of crop production systems; a general substitution of biotechnologies for chemical ones; preservation of ecological buffer areas in surrounding natural vegetation; soil conservation, integrated pest and biological soil management, manipulation of crop diversity for ecological stability, etc. Gradually, these areas of interest are being considered not

just as new disciplines, but as component processes of a larger management unit—the agro-ecosystem.

2 *Appropriate Agrotechnologies*. By its very nature, agriculture has always lent itself to AT. Because of rising energy/labor costs and the fact that growers tend to live on the economic edge, agricultural engineers, the rural counterculture, and ingenious farmers have contributed a great deal to devising conservation techniques and renewable energy hardware for agriculture. On modern farms, the amount of non-renewable (fossil) fuels used for production is far greater than the food energy grown. If agriculture is no longer a net producer, how long can it be sustainable? Is agriculture non-renewable? Should agriculture produce energy?

3 *Rural Socio-economic Concerns*. Not 'How do we get people out of agriculture?' but rather, 'Is there room for a viable rural culture in modern agriculture?' What have been the effects of modern agricultural technology on rural cultures and environments? How does political power control and determine the economic fate of farmers and growers, and the types of technologies they use? What are the consequences to farm labor of agricultural mechanization? How do we support the small farmer with the research, economic incentives, and rural culture so necessary for his/her survival? How do the patterns of land ownership affect the type and scale of technology used in agriculture?

The above list is sketchy, but suggests a rather sweeping re-evaluation of agriculture and its scientific underpinnings. Similar trends can be seen in the areas of architecture, landscaping, medicine, transportation, communication, and biology.

The word 'local' is common in the language of AT. In fact, many aspects of AT are more easily managed on a local or regional scale. 'Bioregions' have been defined as geographic provinces with a marked ecological and often cultural unity, somewhere between a major watershed and a municipality. Bioregions have been studied as units of design and management in an attempt to define a unit of habitat whose resource-use and economy makes sense on a human scale. In many ways, it is also a search for another kind of security; not just to be safe, but to be safe from (have control over) the implications of the technologies around us. At the present, the bioregional model is the closest image we have of a self-sustaining human habitat operating from economic and environmental constraints primarily under its own control.

The broad use of AT within the bounds of a biogregion, or even community, carries with it a certain utopian ring. But such ideas coincide with what many people see as a major juncture in human history at which science and scientists will be forced by circumstances to adopt a completely new value system and frame of reference for their activities—a new paradigm.

Kuhn defines a paradigm (of science) as the 'total pattern of valuing, seeking, and conceptualizing knowledge associated with a particular vision of reality.' Scientific paradigms have occurred throughout history each time someone expanded (or limited) our horizons of reality and place. Copernicus, for example, established a new paradigm of science with his heliocentric universe. Newton did likewise. Darwin and Einstein were important because they expanded our new sense of place by introducing the concept of change through time ('evolution') into the paradigm of science. Stars evolve, life evolves, continents evolve; nothing is static.

It is important to note that the same type of research that led to the atomic bomb also produced the 'paradigm' theories of relativity and quantum mechanics. Together with entropy theory, these theories not only destroy forever the intellectual walls of dualism and determinism (energy=matter, time=space, matter is probability), but they also place absolute limits on what we can do and what we can know. This is a unique aspect of science. It is the only discipline for organizing knowledge that sets limits on what it can 'know'.

The 'vision of reality' implicit in technocracy has led to a paradigm having the characteristics summarized in the left-hand column below. While the form of the emerging paradigm is uncertain at this time, it seems to involve many of the contrasting characteristics and values listed in the right-hand column (in no particular order):

Competition, individualism	Symbiosis, sharing, cooperation
Specialism	Holistic, systemic analysis
Emphasis on prediction and control	Emphasis on guiding human potential and social development
Deterministic models	Biological models
Value as deterrent to objectivity	Value as measure of utility
Exploitive ethic	Ecological ethic
Efficient technology	Appropriate technology
Large, centralized production industry	Small, decentralized economies, bioregions
Non-renewable resources	Conservation and renewable resources
Alienation from nature	Integration with natural processes
Destructive of local and endemic cultures	Local and endemic cultures as vital link in community

Labor and machine intensive	Skill intensive
Energy intensive	Information intensive
Specialized knowledge controlled by a few	Knowledge available to all

Toward a Biological Paradigm

Many of the components of the emerging science paradigm are biological. This is not surprising, since the uniqueness of the human species lies in nature itself, not in any great socio-political triumph. It has a biological basis, and an evolutionary background. No other science has quite the same significance for humanity as biology does, although few people are fully aware of its principles and implications. Biology occupies a unique position among the sciences, being at once marginal and central. Marginal because organic life occupies but a tiny portion of the universe. Central because of all the disciplines it is the one that endeavours to go most directly to the heart of the problems that must be resolved before 'human nature-in-nature' can be framed in other than metaphysical terms.

The foundation of biology rests on the Darwin-Wallace theory of organic evolution. The word 'evolution' means gradual change, and Darwin viewed it as a process of descent with modification. These modifications are selected by the environment which, in turn, may be modified by the organism itself. Life succeeds or fails according to its 'fitness', or its ability to *adapt* to a changing environment, rather than by overpowering it. There is no predetermined plan, no specific direction or goal.

Few ideas have contributed so heavily to the shaping of modern thought, and have so profoundly affected our politics, religion, and science as the theory of evolution. To appreciate the significance of Darwin's scientific paradigm, we need only consider the system it replaced of a permanent, unchanging world. Living things were no longer immutable and, most importantly, all life seemed to have originated from a common ancestor: i.e. all organisms are, to some extent, and, quite literally, related to one another.

This first glimmer of biological interrelatedness was later expanded upon by the discipline of ecology. For a long while, following Darwin, 'ecology' consisted of little more than natural historians describing communities of plants and animals living together in a particular place. Gradually, an understanding of the relationships between organisms began to reveal a definite structure to these natural communities. We now know that a closely knit relationship exists between plant producers, animal consumers, and microbial decomposers. Solar energy, captured and converted to food by plants, is transferred through a series of consumer levels linked together as food chains or, more accurately, food webs. Ecology matured as a discipline when the idea of a loose assemblage of organisms in a community became that of a cohesive ecological system or ecosystem.

During this century, ecologists have described hundreds of ecosystems on earth, together with their patterns of energy flow and nutrient cycles. They have found that the flow of energy through an ecosystem is crucial to its ability to achieve and maintain ecological stability. When the flow of energy is interrupted or exaggerated, food chains become shorter and more simplified, and the general ability of the ecosystem to function is threatened. Ecologically complex ecosystems (in the sense of biological interactions, not numbers of species), such as tropical forests and diversified agriculture, are more resistant to environmental change ('stable') than simple ecosystems, such as pine forests or monocultures. This relationship suggests that ecosystems use energy to create not only structure but also information. Just as a gene may convey information to a cell, a specific plant odor may inform a caterpillar. If an ecosystem uses a great deal of energy to create information, it is considered primitive, unstable, and inefficient. If it uses energy efficiently, it is mature and stable. What can social ecologists conclude from these ecosystems relationships? Possibly three things.

1 Our society is a primitive ecosystem, complicated but not complex. There are not enough viable interdependencies, there are too many large, single-purpose units: large corporations, large bureaucracies, concentrated energy not being used for people. Because ecosystems obviously obey the laws of entropy that affect us all, it is worth asking if ecology can give us models and rationale for the decentralization of society into more interdependent, stable units.

2 The amount of energy we use in society is becoming increasingly less important than what we do with it. It is the quality of the information and structure, the consciousness created with the energy used that counts.

3 Both theoretical and applied ecological research have shown that biological diversity *by itself* does not necessarily lead to ecological stability, but only to certain kinds of diversity. We must be careful not to rationalize diversity as an end in itself, but rather we should argue for the efficient use of energy to *optimize* biological and cultural diversity.

Gaia: Beyond 'Mutual Aid'

Today, ecologists tend to view ecosystems in cybernetic terms, as systems with positive and negative feedback loops and interconnected food webs linked to slow geological and atmospheric cycles. But it is also clear that regardless of where one draws the boundaries, ecosystems are not isolated units of function. Rather they are integrated parts of a collective network in which links of energy join ecosystems across the landscape and over the planet. In fact, all ecosystems, from vast forest stretches to small ponds, are ultimately linked into one ecosystem, the 'biosphere'. The biosphere (realm of life) is the thin veil over the earth in which the properties of light, water, and minerals join to permit organic life. The biosphere includes all land and water masses in a habitable region, about 14 miles deep, from the deepest ocean trenches to the highest mountain top. If the earth were a basketball, the biosphere would be a thin layer of paint. Within these narrow limits, the biosphere is unique and has very special conditions.

Like species and ecosystems, the biosphere has undergone an evolutionary history of its own. This history can be described in terms of the major evolutionary phases leading to the biosphere as we know it today. It is worth describing these phases briefly, as they represent stages of increasing evolutionary rate and ecological diversity.

Phase I: Evolution of Organic Molecules into Organic Life (4.0–3.5 billion BC)

Stage 1: Organic Molecules from Clay.

Recent observations suggest that during accretion, the crystal lattice-work of clay particles can be repeated over and over. This suggests that clay might have served as the original templates for forming free amino acids into protein chains. This would have greatly increased the rate of evolution by avoiding the tedious chance encounter of free amino acids in water.

Stage 2: Macromolecules from Organic Molecules.

It has been suggested that certain amino acids brought together on a clay template formed proteins that had weak catalytic activity. There would have been chemical competition between different types of clay templates for available amino acids and selection for the first organic macromolecules.

Stage 3: Self-Replicating Cells from Macromolecules.

Such a preliminary association of amino acids and nucleic acids would have been the foundation for the first self-replicating cells, and the end of chemical evolution.

Phase II: Biochemical Radiation of Early Life in the Sea (3.5–3.0 billion BC)

The first cells probably resembled chemical-eating bacteria we find today in sediments and other oxygen-poor environments. There was no oxygen on primitive earth. The significant development at this stage was the evolution of complex biochemical pathways in which the waste products of one process became the catalytic agents for the next. This was the most time-consuming period of evolution, but it established the metabolic foundations for all subsequent life and greatly expanded the horizons of evolution.

Phase III: Photosynthesis and the Cosmic Connection (3.0–2.0 billion BC)

Early life soon reached an equilibrium with the chemical and organic nutrients in the sea. Without an outside energy source, the pace of evolution was also at an equilibrium. The development of photosynthesis by cyanobacteria created a cosmic connection to the sun's available energy. By channeling solar energy to the biosphere in an available form (tissue), cyanobacteria greatly accelerated the rate and potential of evolution. With photosynthesis, the flow of energy in the biosphere came to assume its modern form.

Phase IV: Evolution of Oxygen Atmosphere (2.0–1.5 billion BC)

Photosynthesis produces oxygen, which was poisonous to early life. Organisms either developed biochemical pathways to accommodate oxygen, migrated to niches of low oxygen, or became extinct. The gradual accumulation of oxygen in the atmosphere had two profound effects. First, oxygen greatly increases the rate of metabolism and thus accelerates the rate of evolution. Second, free oxygen produces the atmospheric ozone layer, which acts as a chemical shield against dangerous cosmic radiation. Thus protected, ocean life could invade, and radiate across the land.

Phase V: Evolution of Eucaryotic Cells and Sex (1.5–1.0 billion BC)

The endosymbiotic theory of cell evolution suggests that groups of early bacteria with specialized functions evolved as a unit into the common animal and plant cells we see today. These new 'eucaryotic' cells (with a nucleus) were able to concentrate genetic material in a more efficient way, and evolve sex as we know it today. Sexual reproduction greatly increased the genetic information of the biosphere, and accelerated the rate of evolution.

Phase VI: Evolution and Radiation of Multicellular Life in the Sea (1.0–0.5 billion BC)

As eucaryotic cells became larger and more complex, they could not absorb food fast enough to nourish themselves. There was undoubtedly strong pressure to follow the pattern of the past and organize individual eucaryotic cells into larger organisms. A cell was probably selected to forego reproduction whenever it transferred a benefit to the reproducing cells greater than the cost incurred. All efficient interactions were favored, and there rapidly developed a group of cells that did not reproduce but helped to sustain the cells that did. Since the interests of all cells were identical, specialization evolved with little conflict.

Phase VII: Evolution of Land Ecosystems (500 million BC to present day)

The invasion of land by planets, animals, and microbes expanded the biosphere to its present dimensions. Being large, multicellular, and sexual, land creatures could fill the available land niches quickly and evolve vast symbiotic relationships (e.g. insects and flowering plants) which hastened this radiation further.

It has taken over 4 billion years to evolve the biosphere. When seen from the long view, the process seems to have happened in great pulses of increasing evolutionary tempo and levels of biological organization. In fact, if we view the earth in terms of its own time-scale, we see a level of complex activity similar to that found in a living organism. For example, the atmosphere seems to have been created co-operatively by the totality of living systems to carry out certain control functions and to protect the biological systems on earth from cosmic radiation. In addition, the steadiness of the earth's temperature (in spite of the sun getting hotter) and the constancy of the ocean's salt content for the last half billion years strongly suggests the presence of a planetary homeostasis process for maintaining a constant environment for biological evolution.

Lovelock has suggested that the entire range of life, the biosphere, appears to be part of a giant system capable of regulating the earth's temperature and the composition of air, sea, and soil to ensure the survival of life. He termed this the 'Gaia Hypothesis' in honor of the ancient Greek earth mother Gaia. In this context, Gaia signifies the highest level of biological organization, *the* ecosystem of humanity.

It may seem strange to consider the biosphere as being alive, since the metabolism of Gaia takes place on a time-scale completely outside our frame of reference. But many attempted definitions of life have run into difficulty because they failed to decide at which level the term 'life' should apply. Are we 'alive' or simply a collection of specialized cells? Is an ant colony 'alive' . . . or the city of San Francisco . . . or an ecosystem . . . or the entire planet? From our perspective, individuals are convenient units of life, and the larger systems are just loosely associated collections of those individuals. But this perspective may be quite misleading. In fact, the problem of finding the boundary layers of life (along with other problems) essentially disappears if we think of the whole earthly biosphere as a living being.

Science seems to be good or bad depending on how humanity uses or abuses it as technology. One of the positive aspects of science is that since the Middle Ages the history of human consciousness has been strongly linked to the development of scientific paradigms, of theories that expanded understanding of our place in the 'grand scheme of things'. It is tempting to view the concept of Gaia as the foundation of an emerging biological paradigm, a new perspective for science in its search for a more comprehensive and coherent picture of 'human nature-in-nature'. If human beings are early successional animals on a mature ecosystem called Gaia, then perhaps we should measure human progress in terms of the way humanity cooperates in the stewardship of Gaia, by the degree to which we *literally* accept the metabolism of the biosphere as our own. Presently, it is not at all clear what the human role might be in a planetary stewardship. But that is exactly the question that these reflections are meant to pose.

REFERENCES

M. A. Altieri *et al*. Developing Sustainable Agroecosystems. *BioScience* 33: 45–49, 1983.

American Society of Agricultural Engineers, *Agricultural Energy* (3 vols). ASAE National Energy Symposium, (St Joseph, MI: ASAE 1981).

P Berg, and G. Tukel. 1980. Renewable Energy and Bioregions: A New Context for Public Policy. Solar Business Office, Sacramento, CA. or Planet Drum, Box 31251, San Francisco, CA.

M. Bookchin, *The Ecology of Freedom*. (Palo Alto, CA: Cheshire Books, 1982).

F. Capra, *Turning Point: Science, Society and the Rising Culture* (New York: Bantam Books, 1984).

W. Clark, *Dispersed, Decentralized and Renewable Energy Sources: Alternatives to National Vulnerability and War*. (Washington, DC: Energy and Defense Project for Federal Emergency Management Agency, 1980).

L. Dossey, *Space, Time and Medicine* (Boulder, CO: Shambala Publ., 1982).

A. Einstein and L. Infield. 1938 *The Evolution of Physics* (New York: Simon & Schuster, 1966).

G. Feinberg and R. Shapiro, *Life Beyond* (New York: William Morrow & Co., 1980).

G. E. Hutchinson, *The Ecological Theater and the Evolutionary Play* (New Haven, CT: Yale University Press, 1965).

E. Jantsch, *Design for Evolution* (New York: George Braziller, 1975).

H. Jonas, *The Phenomenon of Life: Toward a Philosophical Biology* (New York: Delta Publ., 1966).

R. King, *The Quest for Paradise: A History of the World's Gardens* (New York: Mayflower Books, 1979).

T. S. Kuhn, *The Structure of Scientific Revolution* (Chicago IL: University of Chicago Press, 1962).

E. Laszlo, *Introduction to Systems Philosophy: Toward a New Paradigm of Contemporary Thought* (New York: Harper & Row, 1972).

J. Lawrence et al. *Agricultural Ecosystems* (New York: John Wiley, 1985).

J. Lovelock, *Gaia: A New Look at Life on Earth* (New York: University Press, 1979).

L. Margulis, *Early Life*. (Boston, MA: Science Books Inter., 1982).

L. Margulis, *Symbiosis in Cell Evolution* (San Francisco, CA: W. H. Freeman Co., 1981).

R. May, *Stability and Complexity in Model Ecosystems*. (New York: Princeton University Press, 1973).

R. Merrill, *Radical Agriculture* (New York: Harper & Row, 1976).

J. Monod, *Chance and Necessity: An Essay on the Natural Philosophy of Modern Biology*. (Random House, New York: Vintage Books, 1971).

N. Myers, *Gaia: An Atlas of Planetary Management* (Garden City, NJ: Anchor Books, 1984).

R. Nisbet, *History of the Idea of Progress* (New York: Basic Books, 1980).

K. Polanyi, *Personal Knowledge* (Chicago, IL: University of Chicago Press, 1958).

K. R. Popper, The Logic of Scientific Discovery. (New York: Harper & Row, 1968).

J. Rifkin, *Declaration of a Heretic*. (Boston, MA: Routledge & Kegan Paul, 1985).

T. Roszak, *The Making of a Counter-Culture* (New York: Anchor Books-Doubleday, 1969).

E. Schrödinger, *What is Life? And Mind and Matter*. (New York: Cambridge University Press, 1944).

E. F. Schumacher, *Small is Beautiful: Economics as if People Mattered* (New York: Harper & Row, 1973).

B. A. Stout, *Energy Use and Management in Agriculture*. (No. Scituate, MA: Wadsworth Publ., 1984).

Van der Ryn Calthorpe & Partners, *Sustainable Communities: The Westerbeke Charrette*, (Boulder CO: Solar Energy Research Inst., 1981).

A. Watts, 'The World is Your Body.' In: *The Book on the Taboo Against Knowing Who You Are* (New York: Pantheon Books, 1966).
G. Woodwell and H. Smith. *Diversity and Stability in Ecological Systems.* Upton, NY: Brookhaven National Laboratory, 1969.

Animism and Anarchism

John Ely

Anarchism is a political theory which rejects the necessity of hierarchy and domination as elements in the organization of human life. It stems from the Greek *an-arche*, 'without rule'. From this premise, anarchism opposes all property relations that rely on authority to exploit people's labor. It also rejects any right to extract someone's surplus labor, but recognizes that, in order to exploit labor, the exploited must be subjugated by physical and psychic force, that is, by structures of hierarchical domination which seem natural and irremediable. Hence, anarchist politics advances self-managed forms of human consociation organized by the princples of direct, face-to-face democracy in which production and consumption, creation and enjoyment, are decided by democratic choice, not by the vicissitudes of a market or the forces of authority.

Animism, at first glance, seems to have little in common with this definition of anarchism. Animism refers to a general worldview in which all being, that is everything which exists, is pervaded with life; it comes from the Latin *anima*, and a variety of equivalent roots in Greek, Sanskrit, Gothic, and Germanic, all of which mean 'breath' or 'life'. Animism is thus a broader term than anarchism; it regards not simply political or social organization, but what philosophers call 'ontology', that is, the theory about the conditions of existence or being in general. Animist ontology does not distinguish between the inanimate and the animate, or between human nature and non-human nature.

On the whole, modern anarchism has had little to do with any such idea, though there are signs that this is changing. I want to help facilitate this change by arguing that these two concepts—anarchism and animism—are not unrelated to each other. Nor are they antithetical. Rather, they dovetail: a coherent anarchist social theory can lead one to adopt a animistic worldview, while those who hold an animistic worldview in turn tend toward an anarchist conception of society.

Bourgeois and Marxist conceptions of history were based on a modern view of the cosmos, one oriented towards the instrumental task of scientific and technological progress through the domination of outer or non-human nature. In their basic presuppositions, therefore, they rationlized ontological structures of domination and epistemologies of rule.* In particular, such perspectives were organized in terms of a mechanical, goal-less view of the cosmos which is a perfect analogy in the natural world to the self-regulating market economy: the quantification of matter and the cosmos characteristic of Newtonian science develops in interrelation to the quantification of the world by the market under capitalism, a new world in which everything is apprehended primarily in terms of its price. However, the mechanical cosmos characteristic of capitalist society constitutes only the most virulent and striking example of a general principle developed particularly by German sociologists and romantic anti-capitalist thinking in the early twentieth century. The philosopher Ernst Bloch expresses this relationship succinctly:

> The concept of nature certainly expresses in the first place the society in which it appears; its order or disorder, the changing forms of its dependence. These forms return superstructurally in the concept of nature too: thus the primitive, the magical, the qualitatively ranked and finally the mechanical concepts of nature, are to be understood in large part as ideology. Mechanical natural science was indeed to an especially great degree the ideology of the bourgeois society of its time, ultimately the ideology of the circulation of commodities.[1]

---

*'Ontological structures of domination' and 'epistemologies of rule' are two technical formulations important to the rest of this essay. 'Ontological structures of domination' refers to the way in which the very theory and comprehension of being in general, that is, ontology, is 'structured' by categories and formulation which integrate domination into our most basic conceptual understanding of the world. 'Epistemology of rule' is a term used by Murray Bookchin in *The Ecology of Freedom* (Palo Alto: Cheshire, 1982). Epistemology is the theory of how we know; it concerns the nature and scope of knowledge. Epistemologies of rule, then, are the 'various ways of mentalizing the entire realm of experience along lines of command and obedience'. Hence, as Bookchin observes, 'Just as aggression flexes our bodies for fight or flight, so class societies organize our psychic structures for command and obedience' (p. 89). In an epistemology of rule, thinking about the world, knowing, can be done only as an act which imitates a governing ruler; the knower commands the subjection of the object of knowledge as a type of mastery. Finally, 'rationalized' is also used in a technical sense here; to rationalize something means to justify a potentially unacceptable concept by building it into the 'objective' structure of the world, such that it is at once necessary and 'natural' and therefore seems unobjectionable.

This concept, that cosmology is conceived in definite relation to its respective social system, is central to forming a coherent emancipatory politics. And, I want to argue, the cosmological, or physical, framework from which to articulate anarchist politics (or vice versa) can best be characterized as animist.

Structures of Domination in Nature and Society

I want to support this claim first in a negative manner, by looking at the basic ontological and epistemological structures of coercion characterizing state-organized or 'civilized' societies. Specifically, this means societies organized in cities ('civilization' from the Latin *civitas* for 'city') with a state apparatus formed around a king. Emergent state societies, such as the Sumerian, Andean, Hawaiian, etc., all shared certain basic cosmological and mental structures of domination, those that I want to characterize in terms of the ancient Greek society and its basic framework—what we know today as 'philosophy'.

Lewis Mumford describes the forms of social domination in such 'civilizations':

> Its chief features, constant in varying proportions throughout history, are the centralization of political power, the economic exploitation of the weak, and the universal introduction of slavery and forced labor for both industrial and military purposes.[2]

In such civilizations, religion has constituted the primary form of ideology, that is, the rationalization for such power. The hierarchical dualism between the kingly, spiritual, ruling element and the external nature over which it rules is the central form of cognitive subjection. This is as apparent in the works of Homer as it is in those of the Sumerian author of *The Epic of Gilgamesh* or the Five Books of Moses. Max Horkheimer and Theodor Adorno observe:

> Myth intended report, naming, the narration of the Beginning; but also presentation, confiramtion, explanation: a tendency that grew stronger with the recording and collecting of myths. Narrative became didactic at an early stage. . . . This theoretical element in ritual won independence in the earliest national epics.

Religious doctrine, set in myths of origin, are, say Horkhiemer and Adorno,

> characterized by . . . discipline and power. . . . In place of the local

spirits and demons there appeared heaven and its hierarchy; in place
of the invocations of the magician and the tribe the distinct gradation
of sacrifice and the labor of the unfree mediated through the word
of command. The Olympic deities are no longer directly identical
with elements, but signify them. In Homer, Zeus represents the sky
and the weather, Apollo controls the sun, and Helios and Eos are
already shifting to an allegorical function.[3]

Greek religion, here, is an ontological structure of domination. But,
as they further observe, such distinctions as drawn in authoritarian,
hierarchical terms are carried over into philosophy in the distinction of
the concept from the material components of nature. Greek philosophy,
inaugurating the philosophical enterprise, presents the first systematic
account of domination of concept over material things in its cosmology. What are the basic characteristics of this structure? One basic
characteristic emerges in the way in which the hierarchical metaphysics
of the Greeks makes a distinction between nature and technical artifice;
technical artifice is the locus of human deliberation, and, within a
hierarchical metaphysics, this separation of the kinds of being is used
as the grounds for integrating domination into the cosmos as a whole.

To clarify, let us look at two basic points in the philosophy of
Aristotle. Aristotle distinguishes between those things that exist 'by
nature' and those that exist 'by art'. In this distinction, we find a very
political theme (in the sense of politics as legitimate domination). We
find a formulation of instrumental reason. Here, instrumental reason
justifies the 'use' of things by distinguishing between things that are
capable of being controlled—what we call in modern terminology
'objects'—and the controller, the source of deliberation. For Aristotle,
both the social and the natural realms are the field of means for *techne*,
for 'artifice'. 'In the arts,' says Aristotle, just as with a knife or other
implements to provide us with the 'necessities of life', the 'servant too
is a kind of instrument' (*Politics*, 1253b 21–30). For Aristotle, a thing
'by nature' has a very different logic of action; it has 'within itself a
principle of motion and of stationariness.' However, things 'in so far
as they are products of art,' that is 'a bed or a coat or anything else of
that sort,' says Aristotle, 'have no innate impulse to change.' Here is
the basis of Aristotle's general definition: 'nature is a source or cause
of being moved and being at rest in that to which it belongs primarily
in virtue of itself. . . .' (*Physics*, 192b). Given things by nature and by
art this leaves us, using a modern expression in a rather vulgar but
blunt sense, with a subjective self-acting practice, and one that sees
action in terms of subjects acting on objects.

Addressing the second point in a sketch of the ontology and epistemology of domination in Aristotle, we need to look at the latter form

of being, artifice, the predominant activity of human beings—the process of subjects acting on objects—to see the politics in this distinction
between art and nature. Of those things by art, by technical artifice,
there are many for different purposes. 'As there are many actions, arts
and sciences, their ends are also many; the end of the medical arts is
health, that of shipbuilding a vessel, that of strategy victory, that of
economics wealth. But where such arts fall under a single capacity . . .
the ends of the master arts are to be preferred to all the subordinate
ends. . . .' Hence, we find in Aristotle a hierarchy of priorities and
control of all the activities of human beings in all realms. Within this
hierarchy, however, there is one 'most authoritative art'. 'Politics' says
Aristotle, is 'most truly the master art.' (*Nicomachean Ethics*, 1094a).

The notion of *techne*, as defined by Aristotle, serves as both a description of humanity's relationship to nature, that is, technology in the
modern sense and also as a *prescription* for political control between
human beings. In the ever-present military metaphor of the ship, Aristotle notes the similarities between various sorts of instruments: 'some
are living, some are life-less; in the rudder, the pilot of the ship has a
life-less, in the look-out man, a living instrument.' In both categories,
political and technical management, a dualist and hiearchical relationship structures action—a 'union of those who cannot exist without
each other,[11] particularly the 'natural ruler and subject', and 'male and
female'. For the world of human production, says Aristotle, is better
the more broad the division of labor, as is the case with nature's
fecundity. Nature 'makes each thing for a single use, and every instrument is best made when intended for one use' (*Politics*, 1252b).

Domination, both in the human and natural realms of resources (or
those things accessible to art), is inscribed in Aristotle's definition of
being. The 'art' of political rule, *like all other intentionality*, is conceptualized from within a hierarchical world of control. Aristotle's politics
was the first systematic exposition of the duality between rule and
ruled in conceptual and cosmological terms. These two points in Aristotle thus: (i) distinguish between art and nature; and (ii) establish an
identity in instrumentality *vis-à-vis* humans and other tools—talking
tools, living tools, and silent tools—in hierarchical degrees of what is
today sometimes called 'instrumental action'.

In the Aristotelian framework, art is integrated into a natural teleology of ends, a hierarchy of values. The various 'technical' virtues are
situated within a hierarchical realm of natural virtues in which thinking,
purely transcendent, ruling mind—'god' or *theos*—is supreme. The
technical art of 'using' a slave, directed towards the end of well-
managed household economy, is identical in sense to the technical end
of using a knife, directed towards cutting. *Techne*, in turn, is part of a
hierarchy in which mental knowledge rules supreme. 'Reason,' says

Aristotle, 'is divine'; the rational part of a man is 'the most authoritative and better part of him' (*Nicomachean Ethics* 1178s). And mental knowledge—detached from all natural action and needs—as the height of human virtue, is cast within a cosmos, the structure of the world, capped by pure mind thinking about itself, the *necessity* of the 'prime mover' on which 'depend the heavens and the world of nature' (*Metaphysics*, 1072a, 5–15).

Hence, as the culmination of ancient thought, Aristotle developed what Bookchin calls the first 'epistemology of rule' based on a conception of the rational. Bookchin observes: 'the "conflict" between nature and humanity, woman and man, body and reason . . . permeates Western images of civilization.'[4] Importantly though, not only images of 'civilization', but the 'nature' surrounding it. Causality itself is hierarchical, and the world is, for Aristotle, in its very causality structured hierarchically. The world of nature is ruled by the four causes (*aitia*) just as in the causes of a piece of art, the structure of 'priority' is manifest in a distinction between matter and forms. As Bloch observes: 'Aristotle defined matter as *pure being-in-possibility*, which is, in itself, indeterminate, that which like wax passively receives form and is only in itself that which is imprinted. Form (final cause, final shape, *entelechia*) is, for Aristotle, the only active effector; and the highest form that is totally free of matter, *actus purus*, for Aristotle, is *nous*, the pure thinking god'.[5] Of course, Aristotle and the major strain of scholastic Christian Aristotelianism—the ideologists of ancient and feudal forms of labor extraction—raised mind or *nous* over matter or *hyle*. Mind, or form, constitutes the ruling element. Form rules over matter and constitutes the essence of things within a hierarchical teleology of rule by rule-defining, law-like attributes. Not its potentiality, but its actuality; not its material aspect, but its purely intellectual. 'The form,' says Aristotle, 'indeed is "nature" rather than the matter; for a thing is more properly said to be what it is when it has attained to fulfilment than when it exists potentially' (*Physics*, 193b).

The rule of the universal mind over the multiplicity of material things—the one *over* the many—as a cosmological doctrine of hierarchical rule in Aristotle is manifest; it is not by coincidence that the chapter on the pure formal mind, the ultimate end, in Aristotle's metaphysics, ends with an essentially *political* citation from the *Iliad* which repeats this theme: 'The rule of the many is not good; one ruler let there be.' For Aristotle, as Bloch notes, individual mental activity is constructed by its necessary habitation inside a body—imprisoned, wrapped in bodily experience. It is at worst purely incidental, at best merely matter disposed towards development. Universal mentality, reason in general, the 'impersonal principle of humanness' was for Aristotle detached from material existence. As Bloch observes critically, the notion of

coupling such a formal unviersality with the particulars of material
life was for Aristotle hardly considered. Thus Aristotle, says Bloch,
'regarded the slave only as a kind of tool capable of speech, a being not
touched by matters of the soul or of love.' Indeed, Aristotle regarded all
non-Greek peoples as slaves. Universality was not a generalizable
human attribute but an element of divine spirit above.[6]

It is only in the modern, capitalist world in which really virulent
forms of instrument reason emerge that the relationship between 'truth
and power', as Michel Foucault sees it, becomes encompassing and
pervasive. Teleology, the notion that the cosmos as a whole is directed
towards some ethical, verifiable, and aesthetically beautiful end, is
rejected. Nature *per se* becomes totally mechanical and determined,
metaphorically modeled after a human artifice—the clock. The benefits
of such a 'world picture', in the view of Francis Bacon or René
Descartes, is unlimited ability to master nature for human ends. However, the politics of control are worked inherently and insidiously
into this picture. For the new, modern absolutist state—what Thomas
Hobbes called the 'Leviathan' after the biggest sea-creature then known
to humanity—was ruled by the king in precisely the same utterly
determinate, law-ordered manner in which God created and ordered
the mechanical cosmos, a cosmos so mechanical and so controllable
that Hobbes called it an 'artificial animal'[7] totally reversing the teleological idea in Aristotle that 'art imitates nature' in its quest for the
good. Rather, nature itself was 'artificial', an artifact, as if crafted of
human hands.

Toward a Libertarian Cosmology

Natural philosophy in Aristotle, however, was characterized by a teleological framework in which the ethical world was firmly grounded in
nature, especially in terms of final ends, a final goal or *telos*. It had not
yet lost, as it would later in the early modern age, a rich, non-mechan-
ical (or 'enchanted') view of the cosmos, natural causality, and development. Because of these residual magical elements, in Bloch's view, a
more radical or 'leftist' version of such a natural ethic and teleological
view is possible. Bloch, in this formulation, directs us therefore to a
positive response to the problems raised by the inscribing of domination of cosmos and mind. Bloch, who, as we have already seen,
realized clearly the interplay of social relations and theories of the
'nature of things', uncovered in certain strains of Aristotelianism a
potentiality for opposition to the hegemonic block at the level of
cosmology and natural philosophy. Bloch thus divides later currents
of Aristotelianism into 'left' and 'right' tendencies. The 'left wing'

version of Aristotelianism does not lead to St Thomas Aquinas and scholastic orthodoxy, but to Giordano Bruno and his followers.[8] In the left version, there is no rigid separation between deity or mind (the Greek *nous*) and matter; it gives matter precedence as the source of development in a single united process—as 'continuous movement in itself' and as universally vital. For left Aristotelians, like the Arabic philosophers Avicenna or Averroes, 'a god-nous from outside or from above is no longer necessary.' The Italian Renaissance philosopher Giordano Bruno represents the most radical perspective of this turn away from deistic interpretations towards pantheistic materialism: matter, for Bruno, is a 'fertilized-fertilizing living-whole'. As with the early deity, it is infinite; but there is no hereafter. Left Aristotelianism '*transforms (aufheben) any god-dispensed potency into the active potentiality of matter*' (ibid., pp. 32–3).

This constitutes, at the level where Aristotelian cosmology functions as an ontological base of political domination, a radically subversive element. The entire dualistic structure of mind over nature and of technical ruler wielding power instrumentally over the technically ruled is overturned. The source of activity is matter, the plurality of things as 'being-in-possibility': the notion of a complete, totally determined, infinite, and all-knowing heavenly realm is rejected. For a left-Aristotelian, some notion of hope or utopian imagination replaces it. Teleology thus becomes open-ended, and its basis becomes the notion of a co-relationship in the kinds and levels of animated material being. Indeed, in the Aristotelian doctrine of nature and matter, an intrinsically libertarian option is left open.[9] If form is not regarded as a ruling element, but rather as part of the world's utopian character, the various ways in which rule is metaphorically and semantically constructed in Aristotle cancel themselves out. The final cause is not a perfect, timeless, mental activity or an ultimate god, but rather idealism in the sense of utopianism, what Bloch calls the 'real anticipation' without which 'matter's horizon is not comprehensible'. The ruling element no longer directs its matter, as the 'mind' directs eyes and hands, as the military ship captain his rudder, look-out and crew. The determination of form, actualization, the realization of utopian goals thus occurs as a result of self-organizing material beings. Nature is that which for Aristotle 'has its source of activity within itself.' In a non-hierarchical perspective in which form no longer determines matter, this is an essentially democratic idea: self-management. Matter, through its own striving, through its urge and its self-organizing activity, produces its own horizon of possibilities for development. It 'decides for itself' without some external ruling 'idea'. The cosmos, so to speak, loses its government in so far as its organizing principle is not *purely internal*.

The end result of a left-Aristotelian inversion is a radical *pantheism*, like that of Bruno, in which all matter is ensouled and active. There is no transcendent or transcendental ruling element. More radically, this argument leads to animism: the notion that god is in everything and only in everything (pantheism) is replaced by the god-less notion that everything is alive, inspirited, animate. To find an animistic outlook, Bookchin searches into traditions of thought which precede Aristotle and classical Greek philosophy. As he observes, 'nature philosophy in the classical era [divided] nature itself into "two grades of being"—a residing *logos* or *nous* on one level, over a degraded, irrational, and chaotic "matter" on the other.'[10] In the era before Socrates, the living spiritual or mental aspect lived inside and pervaded all things. For Thales, the early Ionian natural philosopher, the world was animate, alive; it was, as R. G. Collingwood observes, 'an animal'.[11] Since all the world is alive, one's relationship to it works more in terms of care, empthy, and interplay, not in terms of authoritarian law constraining nature or as mind constraining body. Hence, as Bookchin observes, 'animism is a spiritual universe of conciliation rather than an aggressive form of conceptualization.'[12]

An animist mode of conceptualization and activity is 'conciliatory' in several senses; here, I want to discuss only a couple of these senses.

1 For an animist, there is no fundamental distinction between the human, 'social' world and the non-human, 'natural' world. In this sense, it opposes the most basic feature of an epistemology of rule: the distinction between spirit and nature, supernature and nature, between a moral human world of 'practical reason' based on human will 'independent of empirical conditions'[13] and an amoral, mechanical, totally determined world of nature. Hence, for an animist, the notion of a purely human ethics based on 'communication', one that then instrumentally 'directs' the natural world, breaks down. Ethical activity pervades the natural order *per se*, and the relationship is not that of 'rational, communicating' human beings collectively directing a mute nature towards its ends. Rather, the relationship between human beings and nature is conceptualized in egalitarian terms: practical intent and powers do not reside purely in the 'human' end of the equation. As Ernst Bloch characterized it, the relationship between humanity and nature is one of 'co-productivity'.[14] Nature too is a 'subject' and the relationship therefore between humans and nature, like that between human beings is *inter*-subjective. Bookchin deepens and radicalizes this Blochian notion of intersubjectivity through his studies of the 'technological' relationship in early animistic societies, those Bookchin calls 'organic societies'. Indeed, says Bookchin, the craftsperson had essentially a spoken as well as a manual relationship to the material being crafted:

Concrete labor . . . confronted concrete substance, and labor merely participated in fashioning a reality that was either present or latent in natural phenomena. Both labor and the materials on which it 'worked' were *coequally* creative, innovative, and most assuredly artistic. The notion that labor 'appropriates' nature in any way whatever — a notion intrinsic to both Locke's and Marx's conceptual framework — would have been utterly alien to the technical imagination of organic society and inconsistent with its compensatory and distributive principles. So crucial was the coequality of substance with labor, in any understanding of this early technical imagination, that work was distinguished by its capacity to discover the 'voice' of substance, not simply to fashion an inert 'natural resource' into desired objects.[15]

2 Not only is humanity's practical or 'material' relationship to nature totally transformed in the animist world view. Its conceptual contact metamorphoses as well, especially in terms of cognitive relationship to the body and to the corporeality of the planet as a whole. We find an extensive breakdown of the body-world dichotomy. Hence, as David Abram argues in his perceptive essay on 'Merleau-Ponty and the Voice of the Earth', the need to 'regain a genuine depth perception' is an important aspect of addressing today's ecological crisis. Suggesting that the ecological crisis may be seen in relation to 'a recent perceptual disorder in our species', a new manner of experience, a 'recognition of our own bodies as interior to the biosphere of a larger planet-body' must be developed in relation to 'planning and working on behalf of the newly conceived ecological world'. Through a kind of radicalized phenomenology, in Merleau-Ponty's work, 'the full and encompassing presence of the Earth, in all its dense, fluid and atmospheric unity, begins to emerge and to speak.' Abram demonstrates the way in which Merleau-Ponty later in his life began to understand the body-world relationship as more diffuse and spread out. Human beings are enmeshed in 'outer nature' to a much greater degree than the singular, autonomous, monadic notion of a body comprehends. Sight, for example, expands out bodily perception far beyond our skin and means that every human being who sees actually fills a much larger and more complexly organized and mentalized space than that which their 'body' fills in a simple sense. By the same token, Merleau-Ponty works with notions of space as more 'filled', more substantive than empty modern space; like the early Greek natural philosophers, whose space was thicker and whose use of concepts like 'air' connoted a much thicker experience, more like the experience of being in a fluid, surrounding medium.[16] Hence, by developing a more 'bodily' notion of outer, experienced nature, Merleau-Ponty further breaks down the world-

body distinction. As Abram observes, Merleau-Ponty worked in both directions:

> [In] discovering the body, or in discovering a new way of thinking the body . . . Merleau-Ponty was providing the entry into a new way of perceiving the earth of which that body is a piece. To assert, as he did throughout the course of his life, that the human intellect is a recapitulation or prolongation of a transcendence that is already underway at the most immediate level of bodily perception; to asser that is, that the 'mind' or the 'soul' has a bodily genesis, is to suggest that by a strange analogy of elements that stretches back to the very beginnings of philosophy that the sky is a part of the Earth, to imply that the sky and the Earth need no longer be seen in opposition; that this sky, this space in which we live and breathe is not opposed to the Earth but is a prolongation, even an organ of this planet. If the soul is not contrary to the body then the human being is no longer suspended between a dense inert Earth and a spiritual sky, no more than he is suspended between Being and Nothingness.[16]

In terms of both the practical and mental interaction of humanity with the world, a new intersubjective paradigm is coincident with animism's more 'reconciliatory' approach to the natural world.

Problems and Possibilities

A newly conceived 'technical' relationship between humanity and nature, and a deepened perceptual field following from an animist phenomenology are just two important ways in which a 'reconciliatory', 're-enchanted' and dehierarchized worldview characterizes animism. A striking feature of such animist arguments, however, is that they are being advanced frequently by scientists arguing from predominantly empirical grounds. As Bookchin observes, a fascinating aspect of today's cosmological politics is that 'nature is writing its own nature philosophy and ethics—not the logicians, positivists, and heirs of Gailiean scientism.'[17] Since the early part of this century, developments in physics at both the macro and micro levels have radically revised and limited the role of purely quantitative and mechanical approaches to nature inherited from Galileo, Descartes, Newton and the 'scientific revolution'. Erwin Schrödinger, in a fascinating essay entitled 'What is Life?', detailed the manner in which changes in physics due to the development of quantum principles and our understanding of crystal formation have changed the way in which directionality and intention can be conceived in the development of living forms.

More recently, there has been almost a flood of new positions taken in biology, regarding the planetary ecosystem as a self-regulating organismic system—as developed by James Lovelock and Lynn Margalis in their 'Gaia hypothesis'—as well as a breakdown of the life/non-life barrier in early cell evolution. Finally, there have been statements about biological systems in general which have suggested that matter, at various degrees of articulation and complexity, has certain 'inherent self-organizing properties, no less valid than the mass and motion attributed to it by Newtonian physics'.[18] Following in Schrödinger's footsteps, a number a physicists, including Fritjof Capra, David Bohm and Rupert Sheldrake, have taken an interest in what one of them calls 'an organicist view' of physical action.[19] Most of these positions understand critically the relation between modern mechanical science and the modern, Western, capitalist and industrial world. At the same time, they realize the degree to which mono-directional cause-effect determinism arguments cannot explain complex physical phenomena. Hence, for example, Sheldrake advances the concept of 'morphgenetic fields'. Stemming from Greek roots, *morphe* meaning form and *genesis* meaning 'coming-into being', this idea is put forward 'to try to explain the growth and development of organisms, the growth of the plant from the seed, or the growth of an organism from embryo. . . . The idea is that if living organisms are shaped or molded by this new kind of field, the fields themselves must have a structure or organisation which, must, in turn, be explained.' Sheldrake hypothesizes that 'the structure of these fields is derived from the actual structure of similar organisms in the past.' Not only does this 'network' approach to natural systems explain motion in terms of development, in terms of the processual *genesis* of complex systems, but it also rejects a rigid causal or mechanical determinism as the basis of 'scientific' reality. Organisms, says Sheldrake, stabilize in living patterns with what he calls 'morphic resonance', hence explaining the orders and patterns of things in the universe in terms of repetition of what has gone before. 'Morphogenetic fields,' he asserts, 'convey habits of the species, or habits of the individual. I think it is possible that the so-called "laws of nature", which are studied in physics, may indeed be of this general type as well. Instead of there being fixed universal changeless laws of nature . . . ,the laws of nature may . . . be much more like habits of the universe.'[20]

Certainly, the development of many new, and, in many respects, self-consciously politicized approaches to natural phenomena creates an intriguing situation. Indeed, today, as surveys of developments in biological theory indicate, there are competing mechanical and vitalist positions. The mechanical stance is informed, in Evelyn Fox Keller's view, by an epistemology of 'control and domination', whereas the vitalist position advances the perspective of intersubjectivity, of 'letting the material speak to you.'[21] As Martha Herbert makes clear, the reigning position in biological theories of evolution is reductionist, mathematically and architecturally precise, and monocausal in its logic. Thus, in molecular biology, a 'hierarchy of command' is established, 'where DNA gives orders to RNA, which in turn carries out these orders in the construction of specific proteins.' Herbert calls this 'hierarchy of command' the 'central dogma' of molecular biology. However, competing minority perspectives seek to understand biological development less as a rigid monodirectional coding machine and more as an aggregation of different systems, of interplay between them. Hence, as Herbert observes, selection theories have often picked traits assumed to be the product of a species' optimization and adaptation rather arbitrarily. It does not take into account multiple causations and processes of change and interaction. Opposing views are thus 'an attempt to resuscitate the repressed plurality of factors in evolution.'[22]

The debates between more libertarian and more hierarchical, mechanical versions of evolutionary development demonstrate the degree to which such competing paradigms are in a *political struggle* with each other. This is a very important factor in understanding the complex relationship between cosmology and politics. Social ecology emphasizes, in contrast to Marxism or to the Critical Theory of the Frankfurt School, that 'The notion that man must dominate nature emerges directly from the domination of man by man.'[23] It is true that the creation of a mechanical 'paradigm' and the use of science and technology based on it (the 'domination of nature' according to Bacon) was a necessity for progress, progress which then unfortunately led to the instrumentalization of the very people who sought such technical control.[24] Rather, cosmologies and epistemologies of rule have always resulted from the development of hierarchy and domination in society. As Bookchin observes, 'the goal of dominating nature is not a shared human enterprise; indeed, quite to the contrary, it stems from the institutional, psychic, and ideological domination exercised by emerging gerontocracies, patriarchies, and finally, by economic classes and the State.'[25]

In this respect, social ecology raises difficult problems for ecological politics. Modern capitalism was a broad and thoroughgoing social development, changing the very structure of everyday life in countless respects. It was only in this new social context that the determinate, mechanical worldview of modern science could make sense. Undoubtedly, it 'made sense' in a very insidious fashion, forming the categories in which thinking occurs in the terms of necessity and control, but this kind of worldview could only become hegemonic in a capitalistically ordered society. This being the case, the politics of new worldviews

today, those advancing scientific positions in the context of a processual, reconciliatory and animist framework must recognize that such
new views alone will not be the decisive factor. Certainly, it is
intriguing that such new views of society have become widespread,
not only within oppositional sectors of the scientific community, but
also within popular consciousness. Just as intriguing are related developments, like the rapid and recent re-emergence of druids and neo-
pagans in the Western world; for example, an NBC nightly news
report noted the tenfold increase of witches and druids in England in
the last ten years. Such developments suggest the periodic reemergence
of heretical romantic movements which has occurred throughout
modern history. Indeed, the 'Aristotelian left', by the period of the
early Renaissance, when capitalism was just getting off the ground,
presented a serious oppositional 'paradigm'—to use the word somewhat anachronistically—in the early sixteenth century. Bruno's pantheistic views were far more heretical than those of Galileo; and it is highly
inaccurate to place Bruno side by side with such founders of the
mechanical worldview as Galileo, Descartes, Bacon, and Hobbes.
Rather, Bruno was part of a current of emergent pantheism throughout
the Renaissance, a current which included other 'mystics' and heretics
like the philosopher-scientist Theophrastus Paracelsus, who stirred up
peasant revolts in his spare time, and the vitalist Cornelius Agrippa,
who believed in the equality of the sexes, practiced natural magic and
argued against the mining of the earth on the basis of the living nature
of its internal 'flesh'. Movements such as alchemy, Anabaptism and
the 'true levelers', were highly influential in opposing hierarchical doc-
trines of the church, and frequently combined an animate picture of
the world with a qualitative understanding of the earth as a common
realm not distributable into quantifiable properties or exploitable for
commercial uses. Further, as in the work of the later Merleau-Ponty,
there was not the sharp notion of a separated, autonomous individual
in empty, appropriatable space; rather one finds the human soul and
the world soul.[26]

With the consolidation of the mercantile-based absolutist nation-
state, such views were plowed underground. Deism and various forms
of a mechanical and determined worldview created and set in motion
by God became the hegemonic new outlook. Capitalism had taken a
firm hold as a social system, and determined the most basic concepts of
society, concepts which were carried over into subsequent oppositional
developments, most notably Marxism. Periodically, since these early
heretical Renaissance tendencies, there have been 'romantic' and vitalistic attacks on the reigning mechanical paradigm, though never with
such influence as those today. However, it is frequently forgotten
among many writing about the new 'paradigm shift' from the perspec-

tive of 'deep ecology', that underlying the Newtonian, mechanical worldview is the capitalist world system. Without an appreciation of the corrosive but unchecked hegemony of capitalism as the world's economic system, alternative worldviews of a reconciliatory nature will remain marginalized. Hence, those such as Fritjof Capra who predict that we have come to a 'turning of the tide', a 'paradigm shift' in which industrial civilization is now undergoing gradual but steady disintegration, fail to see the manner in which capitalism and the logic of capital accumulation is very much alive and well. Capra observes that 'The decline of patriarchy, the end of the fossil-fuel age, and the paradigm shift occurring in the twilight of the sensate culture are all contributing the the same global process. The current crisis, therefore, is not just a crisis of individuals, governments, or social institutions; it is a transition of planetary dimensions.'[27]

Certainly there are at work at all levels of our 'social' and 'natural' systems widespread crisis tendencies which all seem to have occurred at a similar time: the rise of the environmentalist movement and the 'Limits to Growth' thesis; the crisis of Keynesian economics and the steady decline of the Western economies since the oil shocks of the early 1970s; the problems of 'ungovernability' that many regimes are witnessing, along with the rise of the 'new social movements'; and the rise of technological capabilities of destruction of untold magnitude, with little hope of being able to contain them. But these developments by no means secure as a 'natural' development a new reconciled and holistic worldview at the basic level of the capitalist social system. Indeed, it is quite apparent, *even within some aspects of contemporary green political theory*, that such new 'views' could easily be incorporated into highly mechanistic 'systems theory' which is being used in the social realm by philosophers such as Niklas Luhmann for purposes not at all incommensurate with a highly managed, administrative theory of society.[28] Hence, unless the coincidences between the *market world-system* and the *mechanical world-system* are fundamentally questioned, the new physics and the new biology could very easily be literally *denatured* of their libertarian components. Indeed, systems theory is quite compatible with a socially managed, post-Keynesian, 'post-industrial' capitalist state. Hence, social ecology here tells us of the other side of the dialectic between cosmos and polis as well. It warns us that without confronting the logic of capital accumulation directly, there is little hope for developing a new, reconciliatory worldview.

But by the same token, social ecology shows us how, if we do not take up the basic issues of the manner in which domination and hierarchy are contained in an epistemology of rule, and 'built into reality' through ontological structures of control, they return to haunt us. In this sense, it shares with people such as Horkheimer and Adorno the understanding that a mechanistic view of the cosmos can lead only to a mechanistic view of those who seek control over the nature they have mechanized, so that humanity is enslaved in its own cycle of domination. The interplay between an anarchism which understands its animistic presuppositions, and rejects the modern mechanical world-view, and a animism that is thoroughly political in nature forms the nexus in which this cycle can be broken.

REFERENCES

1. Ernst Bloch, *Erbschaft dieser Zeit*, (Frankfurt: Suhrkamp, 1977), p. 291.
2. Lewis Mumford, *Technics and Human Development* (New York: Harcourt Brace, 1968), p. 186.
3. Max Horkhiemer and Theodor Adorno, *Dialectic of Enlightenment* (New York: Seabury, 1971), p. 8.
4. Murray Bookchin, *The Ecology of Freedom* (Palo Alto: Cheshire Books, 1982).
5. Ernst Bloch, *Avicenna und die aristotlische Linke* (Frankfurt: Suhrkamp, 1977), p. 32.
6. Ibid., p. 36.
7. Thomas Hobbes, *Leviathan* introduction. On the relationship between mechanical science's view of the cosmos and Hobbes' political philosophy, *see also* Thomas Spragens, *The Politics of Motion* (Lexington, KY: Un. Press of Kentucky, 1973).
8. Ernst Bloch, *Avicenna und die aristotlische Linke*, p. 38. John Clark has noted the many ways in which an anarchistic theory of multiplicity and of generation, of 'coming out of non-being into being' have been recurrent in heretical traditions of 'mystical and organismic thought', citing a number of thinkers who clearly fit into the 'Aristotelian left': Taoism 'immediately brings to mind many similar concepts in both Eastern and Western metaphysics. Notable examples include the distinction in Vedanta between Nirguna and Saguna Brahman, Boehme's discussion of the divine *Ungrund* and *Urgrund*, and Eckhart's references to a *Gottheit* that is more primordial even than *Gott*.' Clarke, *The Anarchist Moment: Reflections on Culture, nature and Power* (Montréal: Black Rose Books, 1984), p. 169.
9. Ernst Bloch, *Avicenna*, pp. 32–3.
10. Murray Bookchin, 'Toward a Philosophy of Nature: The Basis for an Ecological Ethics', in Michael Tobias, *Deep Ecology* (san Diego: Avant Books, 1984) p. 200.
11. R. G. Collingwood, *The Idea of Nature* (Oxford: Oxford University Press, 1960), pp. 3–4.
12. Murray Bookchin, *The Ecology of Freedom*, p. 98.
13. Immanuel Kant, *Critique of Practical Reason*, Section 7, 'Fundamental Law of Pure Practical Reason' (Indianapolis: Bobbs-Merrill, 1981) p. 31.
14. Ernst Bloch, *Das Princip Hoffnung* (Frankfurt: Suhrkamp, 1977), Vol. II, pp. 802–813.
15. Murray Bookchin, *The Ecology of Freedom*, p. 233.

16. David Abram, 'Merleau-Ponty and the Voice of the Earth', presented to the Merleau-Ponty Circle, 1984.

17. Murray Bookchin, op. cit., p. 355.

18. Ibid., p. 357.

19. Rupert Sheldrake, 'Religion and Biology', *Resurgence*, No. 111 (July/August, 1985).

20. Ibid., p. 37.

21. Evelyn Fox Keller, 'Feminism and Science', *Signs*, Vol. 7, No. 7.

22. Martha Herbert, 'Evolutionary Theory in Ferment', *Telos*, No. 57 (Fall, 1983), p. 115.

23. Murray Bookchin, *Post-Scarcity Anarchism* (Berkeley: Ramparts Press, 1971), p. 63.

24. Horkheimer and Adorno, in the *Dialectic of Enlightenment*, observed: 'The subjective spirit which cancels the animation of nature can master a despiritualized nature only by imitating its rigidity and despiritualizing itself in turn' (p. 57).

25. Murray Bookchin, Preface to the German edition of the *Ecology of Freedom*.

26. *See* Wayne Shumaker, *The Occult Sciences in the Renaissance* (Berkeley: Un. of California Press, 1972); Carolyn Merchant, *The Death of Nature*, (New York: Harper and Row, 1978); and Morris Berman, *The Reenchantment of the World* (Ithaca NY: Cornell Un. Press, 1980).

27. Fritjof Capra, *The Turning Point* (New York: Simon and Schuster, 1983), p. 33.

28. Murray Bookchin, in his essay 'Toward a Philosophy of Nature' (*op. cit*), critically analyzes the manner in which facters of the ecological theories of Gregory Bateson are themselves formulated in rather mechanistic 'systems' perspective. A more recent example of the manner in which authoritarian and mechanical formulations are integrated dangerously into an ecological perspective is found in Kirkpatrick Sale's *Dwellers in the Land: The Bioregional Vision* (San Francisco: Sierra Club Books, 1985). In this work, the complex developmental logic of such concepts as symbiosis and the stability and growth of eco-communities is reduced to several 'laws' of bioregionalism. Such formulations have a lineage tracing back through figures like Garret Hardin to the social Darwinism of the nineteenth century and ultimately to the *Essays on the Principle of Population* by Thomas Malthus. They can be used in the future to carry out vicious and authoritarian political programs, such as the forced depopulation of urban areas, or to uphold a hierarchically envisioned 'natural order'.

Coyote Man, Mr President, and The Gunfighters*

Gary Snyder

Mr President was fascinated by gunfighters. Expert gunfighters were invited to his White House, three thousand of them, like guests in the house. Day and night they practiced fast-draw and shootouts in his presence until the dead and wounded men numbered more than a hundred a year.

The Senator from the Great Basin was troubled by this, and summoning his aides, said, 'I'll give a basket of turquoise and a truckload of compost to any man who can reason with Mr President and make him give up these gunfights!'

'Coyote Man is the one who can do it!' said his aides.

Pretty soon Coyote Man turned up, but he refused the turquoise. He said, 'If Mr President should get angry, I might go to jail. What could I do with turquoise then? And if I do persuade him, then you'd owe a million wild ducks.'

'The trouble is,' said the Senator, 'Mr President refuses to see anybody but gunfighters.'

'Fine!' said Coyote Man, 'I'm good with revolvers.'

'But the kind of gunfighters Mr President receives,' said the Senator, 'all wear starched uniforms and have shaved cheeks; they glare fiercely,

---

*After the 'Discourse on Swords' in the Third Century BC Chinese *Chuang-tzu* text. Since this book was put together, there has developed an often divisive opposition between some (but by no means, all) Social Ecologists and Deep Ecologists. Gary Snyder's work is widely seen as a major inspiration for the Deep Ecology Movement. It should be understood that his contribution to this book in no way indicates his agreement with Murray Bookchin's position in regard to Deep Ecology, with which he is on some points in very strong opposition. Rather, it is a recognition of the common ground which should unite Social Ecologists and Deep Ecologists, and of Murray Bookchin's important contribution to this shared ecological wisdom. (Editor's note).

and speak in staccato sentences about ballistics and tactical deployment. Men like that he loves! If you go in to see him in your overalls you'd be wrong from the start.'

'I'll get me the uniform of a gunfighter' said Coyote Man.

After a couple of days he had his gunfighter's costume ready and arranged an appointment with Mr President. Mr President's guards had their big Magnum revolvers on Coyote Man as he entered calm and soft.

'Now that you got the Senator to get you an appointment what do you think you can tell me?' said Mr President.

'I heard Mr President likes guns, and so I have come to demonstrate my skill to you.'

'What's special about your skill?' said Mr President.

'My shooting strikes and kills at every shot, and doesn't miss at nine hundred miles,' said Coyote Man.

Mr President was pleased and said 'I'd like to see you shoot it out.' Coyote Man said, 'He who draws the revolver plucks out emptiness, teases on with hopes of dominance. Leaves last, arrives first. Allow me to show my capacity.'

Mr President spent a week checking out his gunfighters. Three dozen were wounded or died in the trials. The survivors were instructed to appear on the lawn and Mr President sent for Coyote Man.

'Today let's see you reach for the revolver with these fine officers. What will you shoot? A long or a short barrel?'

'I'll use any type,' said Coyote Man. 'It happens I have three revolvers. You tell me which to use—but first I'll explain them.'

'Let's hear about your three revolvers,' said Mr President.

'There is the revolver of the cosmos, the revolver of mankind, and the revolver of state.'

'What is the revolver of the cosmos?' asked Mr President.

'The revolver of the cosmos? The Milky Way is its grip, the solar winds, the barrel. Its bullets are stars, it sights by the beams of pulsars. It spits out planets and bathes them, spinning, in heat and light. The ninety-two elements aim it; the secrets of fusion fire it. Wield it, and countless beings leap into life and dance through the void. Conceal it, and whole galaxies rush into nothingness. When this revolver is manifested the whole earth flourishes, the skies clear, the rivers sing, the gardens are full of squash and corn, the high plains rich with Bison. This is the revolver of the cosmos.'

Mr President was at an utter loss. 'So what is the revolver of mankind?'

'The revolver of mankind? The twelve races are the grip; the three thousand languages, the barrel. Forged in the Pliocene, finished in the Pleistocene, decorated with civilization, it aims for knowledge and beauty. The cylinder is the rise and fall of nations, the sights are the philosophies and religions and sciences, the bullets are countless men and women who have pierced through ignorance and old habits, and revealed the shining mirror of true nature. It takes its model from life itself, and trusts in the four seasons. Its secret power is the delight of the mind. Once grasped it brings harmony and peace to the planet; like a thunderbolt it destroys exploiters, and dictators crumble like sand. This is the revolver of mankind.'

Mr President said, 'What is the revolver of the State?'

'The revolver of the State? It is used by men in starched uniforms with shaved chins who glare fiercely and speak in staccato sentences about ballistics and tactical deployment. On top it blows out brains and splinters neckbones; underneath it spits out livers and lungs. Those who use this revolver are no different from fighting cocks—any morning they may be dead or in jail. They are of no use in the councils of mankind. Now you occupy the office of Mr President, and yet you show this fondness for gunfighters. I think it is rather unworthy of you.'

Mr President took Coyote Man to the dining room and the waiter brought lunch. But Mr President just paced around the room.

'Hey!' said Coyote Man, 'Eat your lunch! The affair of the gunfighters is over and finished!'

After that Mr President didn't come out of the Oval Room for three months. All his gunfighters secretly took off their uniforms and sneaked away, back to the businesses and offices in various towns around the land from which they had come.

Originally published in the 'Buddhist Peace Fellowship Newsletter'.

Social Ecology and Community Development

Daniel Chodorkoff

Social ecology, as developed by Murray Bookchin, brilliantly presents a comprehensive theoretical framework for analyzing the crises of modernity. It is perhaps the first such comprehensive approach since Marx, and suggests a reconstructive practice which holds promise of fundamentally transforming people's relation to nature and to other people. The ultimate promise of social ecology is the reharmonization of culture and nature. A vital element in that profound transformation lies in the connection between social ecology and community development.

Community development is an often-abused concept. Perhaps the best way to begin to define it is to state what it is not. As I use the term, community development is not the delivery of services to a needy population by professionals. This is the traditional model put forward for decades by professional development agencies. It is the 'War on Poverty' model that views communities as battlefields on which 'strategic resources' must be brought to bear. It calls for bureaucratic intervention on a massive scale to improve education, health care, housing, nutrition, economic opportunity, and other facets of a community's life. Needless to say, these goals must be incorporated into any meaningful approach to community development. The problem lies with the methodology, the process whereby these noble ends are achieved.

True community development cannot rest on a foundation of outsiders delivering services. Such an approach inevitably fosters dependence on external 'experts' and 'resources'. This dependency hinders the development of indigenous leadership, broad participation and local self-reliance. Ultimately, it often degenerates into a form of social control, strengthening subordination to the dominant culture, furthering the homogenization of communities, and reinforcing centralization of power and policy-making in the hands of outsiders. This approach leads to the disempowerment of communities and citizens, not their development.

Nor can we understand community development in the terms presented by the Reagan administration. Their position is reactionary to the core, and lacks even the good intentions of the 'War on Poverty' approach. They suggest a policy rooted in private-sector investment and a 'trickle down' effect which can lead only to exploitation, domination and community disintegration. Here too, the focus is on absorbing communities into the mainstream of the dominant culture.

The linchpin of this strategy is to offer incentives for private enterprise to 'develop' a community, thus subsidizing its subjugation. Domestic 'enterprise zones' have been proposed which would replicate the domination of Third World nations by corporate investments. The intention is to offer a package of tax deferments, relaxed health and safety standards, and an elimination of both anti-pollution measures and the minimum wage, in order to entice private industry to invest in economically depressed communities.

The definition of community development here is economic. The assumption is that business will provide jobs, jobs equal income, and increased income constitutes community development. Yet, the reality is that although such an approach may possibly increase income for individual community members, it is done at the cost of cultural tradition, community cohesion, a healthy physical environment, and community control of important resources.

A more benign form of private-sector development was attempted in the early 1970s under the rubric of 'Black Capitalism'. Here the effort targeted individual entrepreneurs within a community and aided them in their efforts to establish small businesses. A similar expectation of prosperity 'trickling down' underlay this approach. The reality of Black Capitalism was that the majority of these enterprises failed, unable to compete with their more highly capitalized, better organized corporate competition, and the few that succeeded brought prosperity only to their owners and to a handful of employees. As a result, they increased social stratification in the communities they were supposed to develop.

Another traditional approach to community development, 'urban renewal' through city planning, has had an equally dismal record. The failure of ambitious plans for the rehabilitation of massive areas has been well documented. Yet, planners persist in imposing new spatial relations on neighborhoods with the expectation that their designs can create community. While architecture and planning can help to reinforce particular social relations, community development is not a 'design' problem. Grandiose plans for urban renewal reflect a technocratic mentality which permeates our civilization, a belief in the quick fix of technics. Historically, people have understood that design requires an integration into the social life of a community if it is to enhance the quality of life. There is a tradition which recognizes the holistic nature of community design, but it is largely ignored by the technocrats who populate professional planning.

The tendency of our society to seek technical fixes, technological solutions to what are essentially social problems, is a strong one, and has been carried over into community development efforts. The introduction of 'alternative technologies' into the community development schemes of the 1970s constitutes a case in point. Alternative technology was given a central role in a variety of pilot projects for community development during the Carter administration. But the model of introduction was, in too many cases, one of experts setting up technical systems without significant community participation. As a result, certain ghetto neighborhoods are now littered with rusting solar collectors, non-functional windmills, and graffitti-covered greenhouses. The 'technological solution' to community development means no solution at all.

In addition to the institutionalized approaches that have been described over the past two decades, there have also been a variety of efforts at grassroots community development, some of which have met with more success. These efforts have largely focused on the issues of community participation and control of local institutions like school boards, planning boards, and specific programs in housing and job training. Many of their concerns and approaches to change parallel those of social ecology.

True community development, from the perspective of social ecology, must be a holistic process which intergrates all facets of a community's life. Social, political, economic, artistic, ethical, and spiritual dimensions must all be seen as part of a whole. They must be made to work together and to reinforce one another. For this reason, the development process must proceed from a self-conscious understanding of their interrelationships.

The dominant culture has fragmented and isolated social life into distinct realms of experience. The rediscovery of the organic ties between these realms is the starting point for the development process. Once they are recognized, it is possible to create holistic approaches to development that reintegrate all the elements of a community into a cohesive dynamic of cultural change. Here, social ecology draws an important principle from both nature and 'primitive' society: the integrative character of life in both natural ecosystems and organic communities.

The everyday life of a community needs to be critically analyzed.

Which relationships work, and which are non-functional? Are there traditions of mutualism and cooperation existent which can help a community to realize its goals, or must new forms be created? How can the face-to-face primary ties which characterized pre-bureaucratic societies be recreated in the context of contemporary community?

Is there an existing political sphere which can be expanded and/or transformed to empower the community? Town meetings, block associations, neighborhood planning assemblies, and popular referenda are all vehicles which can be revitalized through the process of community development. How do the existing governmental structures stand in relation to the community development process? The reclamation of politics by the community and the creation of an active citizenry are, from the perspective of social ecology, critical elements in community development.

How can the arts aid in community? Poetry, music, community murals, ritual drama, and literature can all help to foster a unique identity and to reinforce a community's sensibility, if fully integrated into the process.

The spiritual element of a community is important in the developmental matrix as well. From where does a community derive its values, its ethics, and the principles which orient its development? What is its cosmology? How can it gain the inspiration needed to sustain it through the long, difficult process of cultural reconstruction?

The social realm, including family structure, women's roles, social networks like clubs, gangs, and cliques must be examined as well. These relationships underlie many of a community's formal elements, and provide the clearest connection to the primary ties that need to be recreated.

The integration of relational ties, the cultural traditions, myths, folklore, spiritual beliefs, cosmology, ritual forms, political associations, technical skills, and knowledge of a community is crucial. All of these elements must be brought together to provide a base for development. These extra-economic factors are the critical components almost always ignored by the traditional development approaches. But the concern of social ecology is with the development of *community*, not mere economics. Economic development not rooted in a comprehensive understanding of community may well have a disintegrative effect.

However, the economics of a community, and here I use the term in the broadest sense, as its productive relations, are a vitally important aspect of the project. Who owns and controls the productive resources in a community? What can it do to develop its material base, particularly in the crucial areas of food and energy production? How can technology be used in the process? Are there existing functional or vestigial cooperative economic forms or traditions that can be utilized? Food co-ops, producers' co-ops, land trusts, common lands, and credit unions offer possibilities in this area.

In looking for models of ecological social organization, social ecology recognizes that we must consciously look to history to understand our own potential. For example, it proposes that we can separate the liberatory principles of primitive societies from their superstition, xenophobia, and ignorance. Human development and cultural evolution are not linear processes. We still carry the potential for coherent community within us. It is naive to assume that all was good in the primitive world. However, primitivity as a comparative model allows us to understand all that civilization has lost, and that our cooperative potential as a species is much greater than civilization would have us believe.

The form and sensibility of a community are both shaped by and help to shape its environment. This is equally true of tribal communities, the cities of Mesopotamia and Mesoamerica, the Greek *polis*, the cities of Renaissance Europe and the modern metropolis. In the case of the modern metropolis, however, the true substance of the relationship is clouded by the mediating effects of modern technology and the striving for 'mastery' of the natural world. A sense of place, an active relationship with nature, a vision of boundaries, a sense of scale, an organic relationship to a specific environment—have all been central to the authentic sensibility which has informed community life for millenia, a sensibility which has begun to break down only in the very recent past.

This is not to deny the existence of imperial cultures in the past, but to recognize that these existed as a mode of domination, an overlay of oppression which exacted tribute from the local community. These local communities continued to provide a coherent framework for the social life of their residents, a sense of grounding and support that lay hidden beneath the veneer of empire.

It is the breakdown of local community and its total subjugation to the culture of domination which is unique to our own time. Therefore, a primary task in the process of community development is the recreation of local community, and a key component in that task is the identification of humanly-scaled boundaries and the reclamation of a sense of place, be it rural village, small town, or urban neighborhood.

The creation of sensibility of a community—the self-identification of people with place, a sense of commonality, cooperation, and a shared history and destiny—is difficult to achieve, particularly in a social milieu which emphasizes individualism, competition, mobility, and pluralism. The growth of values like individuality rooted in community, cooperation, identification with place, and cultural identity are antithetical to the thrust of the dominant culture. But just as the imperial cultures of the past constituted a mode of domination rather than an authentic form of sociation, the dominant culture of our own time is merely a system of control through exploitation and manipulation. The forms which that exploitation and manipulation take have been effective in destroying community, but they have not replaced it. They have left a vacuum, a hollow place in which resonates the neurotic individualism of Western societies and the collective hopelessness of the East. It is that vacuum, with the often unconcious yearning for reconnection it produces, that the community development process must fill.

Social ecology does not propose an abstract ideal society, but rather an evolving process of change, never to be fully realized. For as soon as we approach the ideal, the ideal changes. Engaging reality with the will to transform it opens up a new realm of possibilities. This is the most profound tradition of utopian thinking, a continuation of that of nineteenth-century Utopian Socialists like Owen and Fourier. Although their plans incorporated fanciful elements, their concern was with a built environment that reinforces community, with an integration of agriculture, industry, social discourse, poetry, spirit, and even, in Fourier's case, emotional diversity. The tradition finds still more explicit expression in the work of the Russian anarchist Peter Kropotkin. To this tradition, social ecology adds a consciously ecological perspective.

The utopian element in the community development process should not be misconstrued. Social ecology understands the limitations of utopia as blueprint, the tendency to retreat from the problems of reality into the cloud cuckoo land of abstract design. It also recognizes the power of utopia as inspiration and as a point of orientation in the day-to-day, incremental process of changing the world. It is the utopian process, holistic, participatory and integrative, that must inform the practice of community development.

This utopian view relies on community empowerment, the ability of a community to consciously plan for its future and to implement those plans. Empowerment can occur only through the creation of real forums for planning and policy-making, forums which are decentralized, participatory, and democratic. Communities must reclaim a public sphere which has become bureaucratized and professionalized. Old forms may be utilizable or new forms may have to be created, but without the initiative of an active citizenry no forum can serve as a vehicle for community empowerment. Empowerment must be rooted in the full participation of the citizenry in the decision-making process, the reintegration of politics into everyday life.

Social ecology also proclaims the ideal of local self-reliance, and dependence on indigenous resources and talents to the greatest extent possible. This does not, however, mean 'self-sufficiency', a condition in which no community has existed since the neolithic. Self-reliance recognizes and encourages interdependence among communities, but emphasizes an ecologially sustainable ethos in the realms of production and consumption, decentralization in the political sphere, and a healthy respect for diversity.

Confederations must be created to help coordinate cooperative activities between self-reliant communities, to administer those interdependent functions which are recognized, and to work to equalize resources between communities. Social ecology suggests that such confederations might form a 'commune of communes', a commonwealth which could extend from the local to the regional to the continental level and beyond, to result in an ultimate unity through diversity. In this goal, social ecology echoes the *telos* of natural evolution itself: a movement towards ever greater complexity and diversity within interrelated webs of life.

The tools and techniques needed to develop communities as unique cultural entities based in the concepts of ecological sustainability and local self-reliance are already available. Decentralized, community-scaled technologies for energy production can help to support the kind of holistic community development envisioned by social ecology. Solar energy, wind power, and small-scale hydroelectric all offer the potential for renewable, non-polluting sources of energy. Food-production techniques like French intensive gardening, hydroponics, bioshelter technology, aquaculture and permaculture can provide a good percentage of a community's food needs on a year-round basis. All of these techniques are proven, and many are commercially available. Given a humanly scaled community, the integration of agriculture and industry relying on alternative technologies and advanced, ecologically sound food-production techniques could provide a viable material base for a self-reliant community.

One measure of a community's sustainability and self-reliance lies in the relationship between town and country. Where the city has become totally alienated from the countryside, as in contemporary urban society, an unhealthly relationship exists. On the one hand, the city dominates the countryside, draining it of resources for its own use; on the other hand, the city is heavily dependent on the countryside, parasitically requiring energy-subsidized forms of agriculture and transportation for its existence.

The ethos of the dominant culture has fostered a specialization of function which has excluded food production from most communities. The industrialization of agriculture has created a dangerous centralized approach to food production, in which population centers are dependent on food producers thousands of miles away for their daily sustenance. This is a situation highly vulnerable to a variety of crises, such as crop infestation, energy shortages, and disruptions in transportation. If any of these disruptions occurred, disaster would ensue. This form of food production also has destructive ecological implications, like destruction of soils, loss of genetic diversity, and vulnerability to infestation by fungi and insects.

Historically, healthy communities have achieved a balance between town and country. The Greek *polis* of Athens, for example, consisted of a central city and an outlying agricultural district. The medieval commune integrated gardens within its walls. Even in our own era, there has been a more balanced relationship. New York City, until the 1950s, got much of its food from Long Island and New Jersey. There were dairy farms on Staten Island, and chicken farms in Brooklyn. Today, the regional agricultural economy has broken down.

The relationship between town and country has other, non-material aspects as well. The predominantly rural values of coherent communities have given way, for the most part, to the *anomie* and alienation characteristic of the city. The breakdown of community grows out of this basic shift in values. The Folk-Urban Continum of Robert Redfield, Max Weber's contrast between *Gemeinschaft* and *Gesellschaft*, the split noted by Marx between town and country are all paradigms which express a social division that is reflected in our own time by the almost total alienation of community from its basis in nature.

The development of healthy communities requires a rebalancing of town and country, a reintroduction of the organic world into the largely synthetic environment of the city. Such an action may initially be rooted in the purely material realm, as in the introduction, through community initiatives, of green spaces, neighborhood gardens, food parks, permacultures, etc. This transformation of the physical environment and the introduction of the skills of nurturance and husbandry needed to transform the physical environment will contribute to the development of a new sense of community, which will reflect these skills as social values.

At this point, a concrete example of community development should help to illustrate the praxis of social ecology. Loisaida is the Puerto Rican section of New York's Lower East Side where residents attempted to actualize elements of this approach in the mid–1970s. There is much to be learned from this experience. Let me describe the way that one of the community's problems was turned into a community resource through the development process.

In Loisaida, there are over one hundred vacant lots. They were rubble-strewn dump heaps, breeding grounds for rats and cockroaches, an eyesore and health hazard. These lots often served as a dangerous 'playground' for neighborhood children, and constituted a blight on the community. Viewed from the perspective of social ecology, however, these lots represented a precious community resource: open space. In an environment of concrete and decaying tenements, these lots, a substantial percentage of the land of the neighborhood, offered valuable sites for recreation, education, economic development, and community cultural acivity.

Local activists recognized this potential and began the development process at the grass roots, organizing residents to clean up the lots and put them to constructive use. Most of the lots belonged to the city of New York, which had done nothing to improve them. The people of Loisaida combined a critical analysis of their problem with direct action. They protested to the city, and they cleaned the lots themselves and began to use them.

They converted some to 'vest-pocket parks', a concept introduced by Robert Nichols, outfitting them with benches and planting green spaces. Others were turned into playgrounds, utilizing recycled materials as playground equipment. Swings were made from discarded lumber and old tires, Jungle Gyms were built from recycled beams. Other lots were turned into community gardens, which became a focal point for intergenerational contact. One large lot was transformed into an outdoor cultural center, La Plaza Cultural, where community poets, theater groups, and local musicians all performed. Several lots were adopted by local schools for use as teaching centers where area youths were introduced to lessons in agriculture and ecology. The transformation of the lots helped to reintroduce the natural world into this ghetto community.

These were simple actions, but their results were profound. The lots were initially transformed by people acting on their felt need to reconstruct their environment. They acted without the official sanction of the city; in fact, in some cases, it was in the face of opposition from the city. This direct action was a first step towards community empowerment.

The initiative came from within the community, from an indigenous leadership which analyzed the problem and sought a utopian (i.e. reconstructive) solution. They did not look to the city for a solution; they created their own. They contested with the city for the material base of their community, the land; and, in most cases, they gained either legal leases to the lots for token amounts of money, or outright title. Several community land trusts were created to remove particular lots from the real estate market forever, and to guarantee their continued use as a community resource. A philosophy of 'doing more with less', the motto of Charas, one of the community groups involved, served as an inspiration to the open-space movement in Loisaida.

Owing to a holistic approach, a number of other elements in the community development process grew out of these simple actions. A problem was turned into a resource, and the health of the community benefited as a result. The people involved in the work gained a sense of pride and accomplishment. Several youth gangs were involved in the movement, and their experience in constructive social action helped to bring them in off the street. A cooperative was formed to manufacture playground equipment from recycled items, creating jobs and income for the people involved.

The gardening groups drew on the traditions of the Jivaro, the Puerto Rican peasantry from which many of Loisaida's living cultural tradition. They were able to draw on a cross-section of the community, young and old, which often remains alienated from the development process. The gardens grew fresh, healthy, organic produce, improving nutrition and lowering food costs for community gardeners. They enhanced the community's self-reliance in an important symbolic way, and the training in gardening led to plans for increasing it further, through the construction of commercial rooftop greenhouses.

The establishment of the cultural plaza created an outdoor space for the celebration of Loisaida's New York Puerto Rican culture. This helped to strengthen the identity of people often traumatized by their move to the mean streets of New York. This identity has been central to the development of an effective movement for change in Loisaida.

Perhaps the most significant aspect of the open-space movement was the empowerment of the people involved. The transformation of their vacant lots drew them into a larger vision of what their community might be. The participants in the open-space movement joined together with other community activists working on issues like health care, education, housing, and job development. Quarterly town meetings were held to chart the progress of the movement, to coordinate and integrate their actions, and to develop a comprehensive plan for the future of their community. An alternative grassroots planning group, the Joint Planning Council, emerged to challange the official city plan for The Loisaida community, previously a disenfranchised, demoralized ghetto, became a force to be reckoned with in New York, and emerged as a model for grassroots, ecologically oriented approaches to community development.

The incorporation of the ideas of social ecology into the process of community development provide a clear demonstration of the power of Bookchin's theories to further movements for cultural change. Social ecology represents a vital source of ideas which will increasingly find expression in an effective praxis. We must continue to develop and articulate its theories in a holistic framework, because social ecology, by virtue of its comprehensive vision and its truly radical nature, represents a challenge to the basic assumptions of our civilization. It is only by developing such a challenge that we can hope to move through our current crises toward an ecological, harmonious, and peaceful world.

The Dialectic of Modernity: Again on the Limits of the City

Stephen Schecter

All roads lead to Rome, or so they once did. Today, they also lead to New York or Paris or Tokyo, to Moscow or Peking, even to Brasilia or Lagos. The history of cities is indeed richly ambiguous, and the contradictory truth that lies condensed in the old adage has shed none of its complexity with the emergence of metropolitan modernity. Ancient Rome, it may be presumed, was a magnet to the denizens of its far-flung empire, who flocked there in search of the magnified experiences and resources which the heart of an empire could offer. Little did it matter that the city itself was overpopulated, congested, and unhealthy, its monumental magnificence masking an underbelly of squalor and poverty that eventually sapped its vitality. The bread and circuses were the spectacular counterparts of the power which exuded from its imperial domination, but as long as its imperium held sway so too did the force of its attraction.[1] A recent article on modern-day Houston suggests that some of the same processes are still at work. The capital of the sun-belt, Houston has witnessed a spectacular growth in recent years, but the accumulation of people and resources has also resulted in the accumulation of growth-related problems: inadequate water and sewage services, polluted air, insufficient transport facilities. Traffic jams have even been noted to end in homicide but, as in ancient Rome, as long as the majority of the population find life there viable and attractive the city will continue to grow.[2] Even revolutionary Havana has managed to suck in more than its share of people and resources, and this despite the stated objectives of Cuban planners to redistribute wealth by redirecting urban and regional growth away from the capital.[3] Has nothing changed in two millennia, or is there, beneath an apparently timeless dialectic, something specifically modern about the modern city that bears particular scrutiny?

Benjamin, writing about Baudelaire's Paris, pointed out the importance of the crowd for the emergence of a heroic consciousness which stands in opposition to the levelling and brutalizing tendencies in modern life.[4] The crowd formed the backdrop to the heroic individual. In it, he could lose himself, finding refuge as he strolled along the boulevards, his critical eye on the lookout for stories and for what the architects of modernity held in store. Yet the crowd was as ambiguous as the boulevard with its many cafés, where the bourgeoisie could gather and devour the latest chapter in the novels serialized in the press. The retrospective brilliance of an Impressionist painting cannot hide the fact that behind this great juxtaposing of strangers lay the watchful eye of the secret police and the idleness of a bourgeoisie which intimates something of the gathering pessimism and eventual demise of liberalism. Baudelaire's Paris was a modern city, concentrating private persons long before the State was to take over the tasks of concentration on an undreamt-of scale. Concentration, while opening up vistas and permitting new social exchanges to occur, also requires more elaborate control. Nineteenth-century Paris was no exception: Haussman's boulevards, the concentration of the working class and its surveillance through a variety of urban and medical reforms designed to regulate social life and discipline its marginal and vagabond elements.[5] If Baudelaire, unlike Hugo, no longer conceived of the masses as the heroic citizens of revolutionary France, it was perhaps because he instinctively placed himself on the other side of the watershed of modernity and deduced, with remarkable intuition, that revolt lay with those who valued mobility over control and refused to let themselves be seduced by the marvels of technique and production:

> Real civilization [I quote Baudelaire again] lies not with gas or steam, nor with ouija boards; it consists of the diminution of the traces of original sin. Aside from that, there are only those moments of existence 'when time and extent are deeper, and the feeling of existence is immensely enhanced.' For Baudelaire, as for his brother, Dostoievski, the city is the appropriate supernatural space where deep history unfolds, the site where the increase or reduction of the traces of original sin is measured.[6]

To live in such a city, to inhabit its time and space, requires the integration of a terrible tension within each individual, a tension that serves as a springboard for encounters and adventures open onto the future. That tension marks not only the solitary hero who mobilizes passions on a suicidal trajectory—Nietzsche and Camus each seizing one side of this dimension of modernity—but also the social space in which the hero is both invited and condemned to appear. Up until the

mid-nineteenth century this social space was still fluid. Romantic pro-
tests and utopian projects could meet up with social forces that had
not yet been encapsulated within the institutionalized norms of an
embryonic welfare state. These forces, to a large extent the uprooted
but untamed pre-industrial masses who formed the revolutionary
movement of the century following 1789, met their last hurrah in the
Paris Commune of 1871. Paradoxically, the arrival of an industrial
working class and the formation of its political organizations signified,
if only in retrospect, the constellation of social forces that was to result
in the consolidation of modern urbanism as a sophisticated process of
social control.

Wallerstein may be right to argue that the problem has been that,
until now, we have not had enough *Stadtluft*, that urbanization has
been the consequence of workers' pressing for a greater relative surplus
wage and hence represents, in the long historical perspective, a drive
for greater liberty on the part of the dispossessed.[7] Yet, this argument
contains a cruel irony, for the workers' drive for access to the cities
has converged with the political organization of society along ever-
increasing centralized, statist, and technocratic lines. In the Soviet
Union, for example, urbanization has proceeded apace, outstripping
the designs of the planners and subverting their paths of development.
Although the planners had wished to decentralize urban growth and
halt demographic increase in the established cities, the combined efforts
of workers seeking material improvement and managers seeking access
to spheres of power pushed Leningrad's population to 4.4 million by
1976, even though the General Development Plan of 1962 had forecast
a population of only 3.2 million by 1980.[8]

In both socialist and capitalist countries, *vast numbers* of humanity
are on the move, in the majority of cases from the country to the city.
It has been estimated that in Latin America, for example, by the year
2000 more than 70% of the population will be living in cities, a figure
which means that urban centers will increase by 9 million inhabitants
per year.[9] In more representational terms, this figure means that people
in Mexico City are renting out rooftops, that *favelados* in the shan-
tytowns of Rio themselves speculate in land, shacks, electricity, and
water.[10] The dominant response by governments and international
agencies has been urban planning, but this response has been to a large
extent ineffectual, and highly ideological in each and every of the
worlds into which the planet has been euphemistically divided. To
stick with the example of the Rio *favelas*, the Brazilian government
decided, in the late 1960s, to relocate upwards of 100,000 inhabitants
by bulldozing over 80 of them and rehousing their squatters in new
complexes built by private contractors but financed by the National
Housing Bank. The residents of the shanty towns did not want to

move. Their new homes were located far from the informal labour market and the homes of the middle and upper classes who often employed their services. They were also costly in comparison to their former dwellings. The *favelados* responded by fiddling the system in a variety of ways, including the renting and selling of their new houses to better-off families ineligible for this program. By 1973, the government agency responsible for the resettlement program, CHISAM, was closed down as the working of the system became more and more extreme. As the rate of default on payments reached 93% in 1974, the program went bankrupt, reflecting a worsening housing situation in general. By 1971, the housing deficit had grown by 76% and most people could not afford payments on homes that were financed by the National Housing Bank.[11] In the end, the National Housing Bank became a subsidy for the upper-income levels, a situation not uncommon in many parts of the Third World. Half-way round the world in Malaysia, the government, following the 1969 race riots, decided to evict squatters. By 1972, almost 28,000 people, mainly Chinese, were evicted; yet less than one-third of the households were rehoused. Of the 2230 low-rent public flats made available, only 44% went to former squatters, the rest going to public servants or members of protective services. Mainly members of the educated Malay and middle classes benefited from UDA, the most important public enterprise in urban development and housing. In an area where unconventional housing—squatting, self-built homes, artisanal labour—accounts for between 25 and 77% of the total housing stock, of what use are plans that do not reach their targets or houses whose cost is beyond the reach of a majority of poor urban households?[12] Under such conditions, urban planning becomes both a joke and an ideology, and as global capitalism becomes reinforced, even the heartland cities do not remain immune. In Detroit, General Motors succeeded in having an entire community razed in order to put up its Poletown plant; yet, since 1978, 90,000 jobs have been lost in the Detroit area, while in 1982 over a third of its population collected welfare payments.[13]

The urban processes to which such statistics and examples refer present, in addition to their technical or economic parameters, dimensions of a political and cultural nature. For even in countries where a more balanced urban development has been achieved—China, Hungary, Cuba, Vietnam—the slowed urban growth, if not outright under-urbanization, has been accompanied by a process of political centralization and state management by a techno-bureaucracy whose outlook and interests, as in the West, conveniently converge.[14] Access to an urban dwelling and to the social and cultural goods that this entails is determined by one's place in the production process, and one is subject to surveillance by the party. The rationale for policies that hide both class domination and political monopoly is couched in language that is well-nigh indistinguishable from that of Soviet or bourgeois planners: maximum utility of productive forces, harmonious regional development, and so forth. As Slater remarked apropos of Cuba, it is a discourse where 'politics are noticeable by their absence.'[15] Yet politics are at the core of the social practice as the state reorganizes social space in order to control the population on an unprecedented level. Nhuân's comment on socialist Vietnam captures this process vividly: 'The thick bamboo hedge that formerly protected the village from the encroachment of the Mandarin bureaucracy has been pulled down so that the workers' collective should be transparent to the party-state'[16] Control, however, comes in many forms, and there is many an equivalent of the bamboo hedge that has been torn down under industrial capitalism to make way for the refined functionalism that dominates our lives. Commenting on the recent modernization of Colombo, an observer remarked how it represented 'a kind of "international" architecture found in so many developing countries' that, in replacing the built structure of a city, ignores the 'built history of a town and a people', while expressing 'a new seizure of Colombo by the expanded interests of capital'.[17]

To ignore the built history of a town and a people, to tear down the walls of communal autonomy, is to reveal the hidden spring of the dialectic of modernity as the erasure of memory, the transformation of time into the commodity-form of the spectacle.[18] The functional line of modern architecture, which houses with equal ease state bureaucracies and multinational corporations, which makes differences between a home, a boutique and a real-estate office difficult to discern, stretches endlessly into a distance from which horizons have vanished. Time and space have met up in an eternal present. The city, once a storehouse of mnemonic opals, is now a place where it is difficult to tell a story. The fluidity of the nineteenth century has congealed into Joyce's nighmare of history, Ulysses' quest ending in Finnegan's Wake.[19] The contemporary hero lacks what Baudelaire's counterpart could still count on: the liberal optimism of his age which even Marx documented in his rather telling admiration of the bourgeoisie's vitality, as described in the Communist Manifesto. That vitality found its architectural representation in the bourgeoisie's transformation of the city, perhaps epitomized in the Ringstrasse of late nineteenth-century Vienna,[20] capital of that empire which already contained those forces that were to explode with 1914, mark the reversibility of progress and introduce into modernity a fissure that has remained ever since. Modern functionalism emerged historically between psychoanalysis and the 'nouveau roman', in a society shell-shocked by its own abdication of the liberalism that had inaugurated it. The tension that had characterized an ascendant bourgeoisie as it struggled to emancipate society from its aristocratic fetters, while multiplying the material and aesthetic possibilities that lay ahead, collapsed. The modern hero, as in Musil's *A Man Without Qualities*, now found himself faced with the dilemma of overcoming a world which had made action seem at once tantalizing, hopeless and lethal but no less urgent.[21]

That Musil could nonetheless draw the contours of the problem, maintain the tension between utopia and things as they are, was in some measure due to the tension that still held in the neo-baroque society of Vienna and Budapest, caught between an archaic conservatism and a socializing modernity. As the political forces that shape the contemporary world continue to homogenize social space, even that tension becomes dissipated. Men and women no longer struggle against a past which all conspire to obliterate, but find themselves enmeshed in a web of institutionalized practices that the self-effacing sources of domination construct from a distance. The world-spirit is still on the move, but now international consultants and planners, coming mainly from the industrialized countries, export techniques, funds, and advice designed to restructure the cities of the Third World along the consumptionist lines of capitalist modernization, however financially havoc-wreaking or socially dubious. The subways and autoroutes of Mexico, Santiago, Abidjan, Tunis, Bogota, Lagos, Bangkok, and Hong Kong are concrete testimony to this process. Against it, however, is created 'a parallel city, often illegal; to the building is counterposed the shantytown, to the car the bicycle, to the autoroute the dirt path.'[22] Humanity is still seeking *Stadtluft*, but as millions of rural dwellers move or are pulled into these burgeoning cities they fashion for themselves what governments cannot provide, only to meet up in the long run with a built environment designed over and against them. Their trajectory is still anarchic, but the price paid for still remaining on the periphery of modernity is an unspeakable misery.

At the other end of the spectrum, marginal groups of people seek, in the centers of advanced capitalism, to appropriate for themselves social space. Squatters' movements in Amsterdam and Berlin, occupying and transforming the built structure inherited from previous eras, create alternative forms of community that, however weak and metaphorical, pose a challenge to the dominant order. In Amsterdam, 20,000 squatters live without the organization of a traditional movement. In Berlin, the squatters of Kreuzberg represent ungovernable elements to the SPD, while the CDU would like to recuperate the themes of self-help in its conservative attack on the welfare state.[23] In either case, the squatters represent people on the move, outside the homogenized patterns of social control, the modern-day counterparts of nineteenth-century vagabonds. Their force, no doubt, is hardly stronger than that of the *favelados* of Rio or the squatters of Malaysia. With them they can form but a metaphorical alliance reminiscent of that formed by Bakunin over a century ago, where self-conscious anarchists imbued migrant peasants with a libertarian culture of revolt that ultimately resulted in the Spanish revolution.[24] Such is the terrain at the inner and outer extremities of modernity: no illusion of unity or identity, but no forgetting either of the echoes of liberty.

Bookchin, in his earlier works as in his recent essays, has tried to capture these echoes from the past in order to open up perspectives on the present.[25] The thrust of his writings has been to signal the utopian dimensions in bourgeois revolutions that remain unassimilated in the political landscape, potential foci of opposition to the homogenizing tendencies of Capital and the State. The city occupies a singular position in this drama, embodying the forms of associative and communal activity which marked popular eruptions into modern history: the American and French revolutions, the Paris Commune, the workers' revolts of the twentieth century. True, these forms lie buried in the institutional networks of the modern state, but they testify to the enduring sense of community that has traditionally made human cultural endeavour worthwhile. It is around this concept of *communitas*, advanced also by Kropotkin, Mumford and Goodman, that Bookchin's idea of libertarian municipalism intersects with his theory of social ecology. His vision of a holistic society based on a dialectic of complexity and interdependence is inconceivable without the rich texture of a democratic, participatory civic culture. The question is: to what extent do the idea and practice of community present a mobilizing counterforce to modern urbanism?

The answer is ambiguous. On one level, it is hard to imagine how people could live without it. Its absence today—not so much as conviviality, though that too—as a public space of discourse makes itself felt in the current reduction of the political realm. Hence, Bookchin's reminder of the traditions where the civic arena was coeval with a vigorous public life, however limited: the Greek *polis*, the Roman *civitas*, the medieval guilds and communes, the city-republics of the Italian Renaissance. Yet, the very examples alluded to were only partial achievements of the ecology of freedom. At other times, and in other places, cities played a quite different role: here, bastions of feudal society, there, allies of a nation state opposed to communal autonomies.[26] Moreover, it was the Roman empire, and not the city-state, that first conferred on all its non-slave male subjects juridical status of citizenship, thereby, in Bookchin's own words, 'vastly enlarging the horizons of the human political community'.[27] The debate over the role of cities in the rise of capitalism suggests that the relationship between city life and liberty is anything but linear, the emerging subjectivity coterminous with modernity being at once dependent on urbanity yet encapsulated within the forces of growing domination. Mumford's sociological archaelogy of the city underscored an even older dialectic.[28] The female-dominated container culture of the neolithic age yielded to a larger city marked by internal stratification and the domination of nature that characterized patriarchal society. Cities, at the same time as they extended horizons, magnified sacred and secular power. Large-scale cooperation and the division of labour opened up new spheres of work and knowledge, but also made possible the surpluses that both protected the community from famine and underpinned royal power. The collective enhancement of life which the urban centers of Antiquity made possible was achieved at the expense of the regimented individuals who inhabited them, and yet the possibility of individual enrichment was itself in turn enhanced by the possibilities which urban congregation unleashed. War and violence became normalized and spread with the rise of cities, but law also assumed a greater role in regulating human intercourse. In short, the history of cities became the recorded history of civilization and its discontents. Significantly, the emergence of formalized religion, first polytheist and later monotheist, played an important part in this transformation. Significantly too, the decline of religion and the death of God accompanied the urban explosion of the nineteenth century, marking a nodal point in the rise of modernity.

Since then, the world has not really recovered from or come to grips with what Nietzsche comprehended perhaps more than any other. The twilight of the idols has forced human beings to confront and to create their own history. The effect has been vertiginous and often disastrous. The city's historic function—its most singular, according to Mumford —has been to store and transmit the symbolic and practical heritage of the human community beyond that which any individual could pass on. Quoting Emerson's remark that the city 'lives by remembering', Mumford went on to write:

> Through its durable buildings and institutional structures and even more durable symbolic forms of literature and art, the city unites times past, times present and times to come. Within the historic precincts of the city time clashes with time: time challenges time.[29]

Paradoxically, this was actual as long as the political community was bounded by transcendental religion. The rise of a secular historic self-consciousness consequent on the death of immortality[30] has made this task more and more difficult. The sociological imagination that flourished in the modern city, though reflective of society independent of its individual members, became more and more the continuous reform

of space and time into the spectacular commodity-form that social life
has today assumed. Bookchin's attempt to seek inspiration from the
more rational and ethical civic cultures of the past is surely an attempt
to combat this tendency:

> To reach back into these historic institutions, to enrich their content
> with our libertarian tradition and critical analyses, and to bring them
> to the surface of an ideologically confused world is to bring the past
> to the service of the present in a creative and innovative way.[31]

And yet, the redemptive power of memory embodied in the city comes
up against the stumbling block of spectacular time, when it is not
ambiguities of these earlier experiments. In the century following Baudelaire and Nietzsche, humanity has indeed been stumbling, in search
of a voice outside the age-old register of jeremiad redemption. At best,
some have managed to stake out the terms of the combat, as in the
following words which Broch put into the mouth of his central character in *The Guiltless:*

> Man has shattered his limits and has entered into multidimensional-
> ity, into the new dwelling place of his self, and in it he wanders
> about lost, lost in immensity. Weave a We, not because we form a
> community, but because our limits coalesce. . . . Man has been
> deprived of his peep-show view, his power of looking into foreign
> countries from home, into the unlimited from the limited; instead
> he has been given something that can hardly be called a view, since
> it operates in the unlimited; it is almost a return to the realm of
> magic, the magic of the perpetual flux between inside and outside,
> less mysterious than the image of former days, but no less
> frightening. . . . Oh, what shattering of limits can be so great as to
> change the unchangeable?[32]

In a global village, where the village that has traditionally replenished
'the miscarriages of life in the city'[33] is being sucked into the vortex of
time and space with which bourgeois society continues to exert its
fascination, the formation of a new sense of community 'because our
limits coalesce,' is, indeed, one way of phrasing the modern equivalent
of Kant's categorical imperative. This equivalent, however, is grounded
in doubt, and also in laughter, the faint, mocking echo of a spirit
willing to take on its World-counterpart on the very terrain of modernity. Bookchin sees signs of its ferment in those new social movements — pacifist, feminist, ecological — that may inject that democratic
body 'the people' with a 'general interest . . . which is larger in its
scope, novelty and creativity than the economically oriented particular

interests of the past'.[34] Perhaps; perhaps not. Perhaps we are still on the threshold of an age of transition that could lead in many directions: space, nuclear war, a continuous restructuring of domination, the reversibility or transformation of progress. The least we can do is be lucid, lest, as Bookchin himself wrote:

> The power of authority to command the individual physically . . . will have laid its hand on the human spirit itself—its freedom to think creatively and resist with ideas, even if its capacity to act is blocked for a time by events.[35]

REFERENCES

1. L. Mumford, *The City in History*, (London: Penguin, 1961), Ch. 8.
2. J. Feagin, 'The social costs of Houston's growth', *International Journal of Urban and Regional Research* (*IJURR*), Vol. 9, No. 2.
3. D. Slater, 'State and territory in postrevolutionary Cuba', *IJURR*, Vol. 6, No. 1.
4. W. Benjamin, *Charles Baudelaire: A Lyric Poet of the Era of High Capitalism* (London: New Left Books, 1973).
5. M. Foucault, *La volonté de savoir* (Paris: Gallimard, 1976); J. Donzelot, *La police des familles* (Paris: Minuit, 1977); J. C. Beaune, *Le vagabond et la machine* (Paris: Champ Vallon, 1983).
6. K. Papaioannou, *La consécration de l'histoire* (Paris: Champ Libre, 1983), p. 167.
7. I. Wallerstein, 'Cities in socialist theory and capitalist praxis', *IJURR*, Vol. 8, No. 1.
8. G. Andrusz, 'Some key issues in Soviet urban development', *IJURR*, Vol. 3, No. 2.
9. N. Ridler, 'Development through urbanization: a partial evaluation of the Colombian experiment', *IJURR*, Vol. 3, No. 1.
10. L. Valladares, 'Working the system: squatter response to resettlement in Rio de Janeiro', *IJURR*, Vol. 2, No. 1.
11. Ibid., and R. Oliven, 'Culture rules OK: class and culture in Brazilian cities', *IJURR*, Vol. 3, No. 1.
12. M. Johnstone, 'Urban housing and housing policy in Peninsular Malaysia', *IJURR*, Vol. 8, No. 4.
13. K. Trachte and R. Ross, 'The crisis of Detroit and the emergence of global capitalism', *IJURR*, Vol. 9, No. 2.
14. N. Nhuân, 'Do the urban and regional management policies of socialist Vietnam reflect the patterns of the ancient Mandarin bureaucracy?'; P. Murray and I. Szelenyi, 'The city in the transition to socialism'; *IJURR*, Vol. 8, No. 1; D. Slater, *op. cit.*
15. D. Slater, ibid., p. 26.
16. N. Nhuân, op. cit.
17. F. Steinberg, 'Town planning and the neocolonial modernization of Colombo', *IJURR*, Vol. 8, No. 4.

18. G. Debord, *Society of the Spectacle* (Black and Red, Detroit, 1977); originally *La société du spectacle* (Champ Libre, Paris, 1971).
19. M. McCarthy, 'Novel, Tale, Romance', *New York Review of Books*, May 12, 1983.
20. C. Schorske, *Fin-De-Siècle Vienna* (NY: Knopf, 1981), esp. Ch. 2.
21. R. Musil, *A Man Without Qualities* (London: Pan Books, 1979).
22. H. Coing, 'La dimension internationale des politiques urbaines dans le Tiers Monde', *IJURR*, Vol. 1, No. 2.
23. S. Katz and M. Mayer, 'Gimme shelter', *IJURR*, Vol. 9, No. 1.
24. S. Schecter, *The Politics of Urban Liberation* (Montreal: Black Rose Books, 1978;) M. Bookchin, *The Spanish Anarchists* (NY, 1977).
25. M. Bookchin, *The Ecology of Freedom* (Palo Alto: Cheshire Books, 1982); *Post-Scarcity Anarchism; Towards an ecological society* and *The limits of the City* (both Montréal: Black Rose Books, 1985), and most recently, 'Theses on Libertarian Municipalism', *Our Generation*, Vol. 16, Nos 3–4.
26. L Holton, 'Cities and the transitions to capitalism and socialism', I. Rév., 'Local autonomy or centralism —when was the original sin committed?', *IJURR*, Vol. 8, No. 1.
27. M. Bookchin, *The Ecology of Freedom*, op. cit., p. 152.
28. L. Mumford, *op. cit.*, esp. Chs. 1–5.
29. Ibid., p. 118.
30. C. Lefort, 'Mort de l'immortalité?', *Le temps de la réflexion*. (Paris: Gallimard, 1982).
31. M. Bookchin, 'Theses on Libertarian Municipalism', op. cit., p. 20.
32. H. Broch, *The Guiltless*, trans. R. Manheim (Boston and Toronto, 1974), pp. 259–60.
33. L. Mumford, *op. cit.*, p. 69.
34. M. Bookchin, 'Theses on Libertarian Municipalism', *op. cit.*, p. 18.
35. Ibid., p. 22.

Distinguished Traditions
John C. Mohawk

A number of years ago I was attending a university function which stressed awareness of Indian culture and which featured speakers from the Indian world who had been asked to talk about Indian values. The speeches were powerful, focusing on the need to maintain relationships between the community, the family, the universe (nature) and a strong self-identity. People were pleased with the presentations and afterwards there was a discussion.

Tom Porter, a Mohawk chief, was one of the featured speakers. He spoke eloquently, emotionally, about his family, his wife and children, his grandmother. The audience was fascinated. He spoke about the oppression which marked his childhood, the feelings he experienced in school systems which let non-Anglo children know that imperfect English is a sign of inadequacy. He talked about the general atmosphere in America and Canada in which family life appears very difficult and therefore community life is threatened. He spoke from his own culture, the culture of the Haudenosaunee or Six Nations Iroquois, and the mostly Anglo audience was sympathetic, sometimes even empathetic, and many were visibly moved.

A few days later, I found myself sitting at my desk where I was then editor of *Akwesasne Notes*, the national publication of the Mohawk Nation. The document with which I struggled was a questionnaire sent to publications. The questions were designed to allow this directory of publications to classify each magazine into their own definitions of political and cultural niches. As I read the questions, I became increasingly uneasy about how alienated Indians really are from all aspects of the mainstream. Is your magazine supportive of family issues? Do you support religious practices? Does your magazine support the idea that the State has an obligation to provide child-care services for working parents? And so forth.

In the end, I declined to answer the questionnaire. Maybe someone else at *Akwesasne Notes* will answer questionnaires like that eventually, but I felt I could not. To give a yes or no answer to these questions would find our publication listed in the same category as conservative magazines which advocate a worldview light years removed in spirit from our own.

Chief Tom Porter speaks to the values of a Traditional society. Traditional societies are varied and have many personalities, but I think it is safe to state that generally speaking Traditional societies are under extreme stress. I could go further and state that Traditional societies are locked in a struggle with what for lack of a better term I will call 'modernism'. Human societies function through institutions. Traditional societies are those in which individuals look to local human institutions to meet their needs—family, community, extended kinship relations. Those societies, I say, are in conflict with and under pressure from societies of the modern age which are characterized by the rise of the centralized Nation-State and under which people look to the institutions of the Nation-State for fulfilling their needs.

I suppose that's an overly simplified definition, but it is one which works for me. It is true that traditional societies have been co-opted in various degrees for centuries, indeed millennia, as the nation states have developed. Some traditional institutions, most notably the Church, have been relegated largely to cheerleading status for the very State ideology which is destroying the Traditional society. Given the vast complexity of history, the many ways in which traditional societies organize themselves, the abberations of those organizations, the blood feuds and the oppressive hierarchies which have manifested in various forms of family and community life, traditional societies have many faces.

Tom Porter talks about the need to strengthen and rebuild the Traditional Haudenosaunee institutions and his discussions often focus on family life as the center of the way of life of his vision. He speaks from a position, however, in which his definitions of those institutions are very different from the definitions of the majority of his audiences, and the differences stem from the specificity of his culture. He is Haudenosaunee, he thinks in Haudenosaunee terms, and his sense of his own humanity is strikingly articulate even if spoken in sometimes halting English.

He is a strong advocate for religion—more properly spirituality— but his is not an exhortation to abject subjugation to authority, and certainly not mindless subjugation to the authority of the state. The Haudenosaunee traditional religion teaches that Nature and the Universe are benign, that people are responsible for coming to morality as the result of coming to ownership of a shared and common thinking about their experiences. The Haudenosaunee story of Creation, for example, tells of a world created by twin spirits, but it's not exactly a story of good and evil. Both twins participate in the creation of this, the real (physical) world that humans experience. In their own way, both contribute to the world we experience. One twin creates the world of ascending life, the green and flowering world of reproduction which delights mankind. The other creates another, perhaps less appealing, aspect of life, which includes creatures like the insects and the vulture. Yet those creations are also necessary for life to continue as we know it.

Haudenosaunee spirituality is an exercise in experiencing and thinking about the world we live in. Each person is responsible for thinking about their role in the universe on every level, including how we relate to the physical world we occupy, as well as the social world we create. Vignettes and parables abound in the oral tradition, each intended to introduce people to a collective mind about reality, but the experience is qualitatively different from what most people experience in Western religions, and for a very good reason. When a parable is told, the Haudenosaunee assembly is reminded that they have a mind, and a responsibility to use their mind to think about that which has been said. A discussion period often follows during which people speak to their feelings and their understanding of the material presented, and in that way people are encouraged to come to ownership of the worldview.

That is quite different, I think, from the Western tradition. Material is presented and analyzed. People are then told what it means and how they are expected to think and behave. They are not required to think. Thinking is the province of 'experts', people appointed for that purpose, and the Common Man's responsibility is to do as instructed. The culture operates with that message in both religion and government because, although the two may be legally separate, they are spiritually rooted in the same thinking.

The foundations of democracy in the Haudenosaunee world spring from that worldview which requires people to be responsible for their own thinking. The moment that people abandon their responsibility to do their own thinking about issues, they have diminished the democratic process. In the Haudenosaunee world, people do not allow other people to do their thinking for them. In its purest sense, that is what pristine Traditional societies are based on.

Societies which follow that principle will find themselves in grave contradiction to modern institutions. It is psychologically healthy for people to view the Universe as a benign force. The alternative is that people find the Universe a place which is disorganized, a 'wilderness', irrational. Such a people will determine that they must bring to that space 'order', a sense of discipline. They will 'tame' the wilderness and adopt a morality of their relationships to the universe which is artificial and, in the end, ecologically irresponsible. Once people accept the idea that Nature is irrational, threatening, and disordered, they cease effectively thinking about Nature and spend their energy thinking about order. Such people are capable of supporting institutions which undertake and allow activities altering the basic relationships of the natural world, including water quality, forest growth, and so forth.

Traditional societies are socialized to existence in a specific place. That is to say, the most Traditional societies are indigenous in the sense that they believe they belong to the space they occupy, be that a desert, a rainforest, or a hardwood forest of the northeast United States. Generation after generation expends energy thinking about what it means to be a people of a forest or desert, and that thinking process develops a conservatism about the ecology which is both healthy and, in the long term, necessary for survival. It is not difficult to contrast that result with a people who spend their time thinking about what it means to be a Nation-State which claims hegemony over deserts and seashore alike, between river systems of vastly different composition and high plains.

Traditional societies create and support institutions which reflect the values of living in a specific environment. All of the Traditional societies with which I am intimately familiar, and I suspect all the indigenous Traditional societies of the world, are founded on institutions which are defined by kinship. This does not necessarily mean blood kinship. Among the Haudenosaunee, kinship is by clan, and people can be adopted into clans and clans extend across national groups. The wolf clan of the Mohawks, easternmost nation of the Haudenosaunee, is considered as one with the wolf clan of the Seneca, the most Western nation. The clan is a political institution which claims an ideology of kinship but which is also based on a historical reality.

The Haudenosaunee follow the same pattern in their governmental institutions. The Great Law of the Haudenosaunee, the governing tradition of the Grand Council, assembles the leaders of the clans to hear issues and to use their very best thinking to solve problems. There is a tradition of consensus decision-making. Given the best possible information, the chiefs will then share their collective thinking on that issue until they 'come to one mind'. Consensus decision-making in this context doesn't mean that everybody necessarily comes to full one-hundred percent agreement, but that all parties do come to ownership of the collective thinking. It is a process that seems to require a certain amount of socialization, a bit of practice.

Religion and government appear to coincide in Haudenosaunee institutions. The same process which characterizes some of the most important traditional teachings (what is now trendily called 'thought facilitation') is also found in the spirit of deliberations of the governing councils and in the community meetings. The principles by which people conduct themselves in such meetings are important. Respect for the other's view, a desire that the outcome not be inconsistent with the profound respect for a benign universe—all of these things require ethics and procedures to which people need to be socialized.

During the process of Haudenosaunee deliberations, for example, each speaker is allowed to speak until he or she has said all they have to say. Conversely, etiquette requires that the speaker be brief and to the point. Everybody is expected to give their full and undivided attention to the speaker. People are to speak to the issues and not the personalities involved. People are expected to speak in a calm and deliberate manner. It is difficult to express exactly how this works, but Haudenosaunee people are socialized to feel uncomfortable in the presence of debilitating harangues and embarrassed for the person who is making such a presentation. The kinds of speeches often heard delivered by American evangelists, for example, would be considered poor manners and somewhat insulting to people who would prefer to deal with specific issues and concrete information and who are required to do their own thinking, rather than allowing other people to do it for them.

Chief Porter speaks to the need for strong family values and spiritual revitalization, for community responsibility and for a reverence for what is nowadays called the ecology. In Iroquois terms, all these ideas are not only consistent but they are homogeneous in a way that most of the West has yet to work out. His discussions about the role of government revolve around the responsibilities of government to the people, not vice versa. His sense of human dignity, of the institutions which actually respond to human needs for nurturance, for psychological safety, for a sense of belonging to community and to a place strike a chord in many of his listeners.

Those ideas need a place in the modern progressive political world. It is not acceptable that the people who advocate family life also advocate military spending. There have to be people who apply rational thinking to the responsibilities of governments and to political agenda which place human development ahead of the interests of centralization of the powers of the State. In my humble opinion, the family can play an important role in these matters, a progressive, positive role as an institution which promotes social goals. It will require that we do a lot of thinking about exactly what such a family looks like, whether it is a pure kinship organization or something else, but the progressive intelligentsia has a responsibility to do exactly that kind of thinking. That the intelligentsia of our time has largely abandoned the institution of the family and embraced the ideology of the State has been one of the great tragedies of our era, and one which has meant that for the most part the American intelligentsia has been in opposition to Traditional society.

It is not acceptable that the entire world of emotional relationships to the Universe, to the forces of creation, to all that is spiritual be owned exclusively by a political/religious faction which favors prayer (i.e. thought control) in the schools. It is necessary that we reinvestigate the role of humanity in the Universe, and that we do some clear thinking about the creation of institutions through which humans can find some rational form of socialization which will enable them to act coherently in their own interest, both ecologically and spiritually.

I would very much like to see these steps taken. The questions on the questionnaire which I declined to answer were unfortunately relevant because they perceived the order of the world in a way which reflected a reality which I find very painful and frightening. I find myself in agreement on many issues with 'radical' politicians for reasons entirely disconnected from their underlying values. I find myself spiritually far from many of them and believe that much of their thinking about the role of institutions needs re-evaluation. That's why I can be in agreement with them on many particular ecological and peace issues, yet at odds with them concerning basic social objectives.

Chief Porter touches all of these people. Whether they are radical politicians, town workers, or college students, his speeches reach them. It is because, I think, he finds a common chord, a piece of humanity which reaches across language and culture and brings them to a place of shared mind. Progressive political thinkers can learn something from that which could potentially spark a truly humanitarian intellectual movement, one which is not as flinty and as alienating as what is currently derided as 'secular humanism'.

The Politics of Social Ecology

Graham Baugh

One of the central insights of social ecology is that the human domination of nature stems from the human domination of other human beings. The idea that society should be reconstituted according to ecological principles of unity in diversity, spontaneity and mutual aid is not based on a simplistic analogy between society and nature but on the idea that relationships between human beings shape and determine their relationships with nature. The elimination of the human domination of nature requires the elimination of domination within human society.

Social ecology demands nothing less than the elimination of all forms of hierarchy and domination. The political question which then arises is whether this requires the complete abolition of politics, or whether it is possible to have politics without hierarchy and domination.

Murray Bookchin has provided the most clearly articulated vision of an ecological society in which hierarchy and domination have been eliminated. In the process, he has begun to distinguish between society, politics and the state in a way that makes it possible to conceive of a political realm distinct from both society and the state, such that one can abolish the state without abolishing all forms of politics. The form

Since this chapter was written, Murray Bookchin has published *The Rise of Urbanization and the Decline of Citizenship* (San Francisco: Sierra Club Books, 1987), an important addition to his earlier writings on politics and society. This work does not deal directly with the political forms appropriate to an ecological society. Rather, it develops a conception of a democratic, municipal politics by which people in contemporary society can begin the movement toward the ecological society that Bookchin still sees as the ultimate ideal. He views the municipality as the basic political unit through which people can recover the political power which has been alienated to the state and thereby assert democratic control over their lives and communities. Insofar as he continues to endorse simple majority rule, the following remarks on self-assumed obligation and minority dissent remain pertinent.

of politics which Bookchin argues is most appropriate to an ecological society can be best described as 'self-managing democracy'. Its most important elements are the self that is to manage the democracy, an authentic public composed of such selves, the affinity groups that will form the basic 'cell tissue' of such a society, and the political practices of direct action and direct democracy.

The underlying purpose of self-managing democracy is to provide each member of society with effective control over her or his life, and its underlying assumption is that everyone is capable of competently exercising such control. To achieve this control, it is necessary to abolish all concentrations of economic and political power, so that decision-making power is evenly distributed throughout society. The resulting form of individual control will not mean control *over* others, but rather control *with* them, in directly democratic popular assemblies. It should not be confused with the instrumental conception of control over something as an object or means for the realization of one's own purposes. The latter concept leads to the objectification and domination of those being used as instruments. For this reason, perhaps it would be better to speak of 'equal participation in the political process' rather than of 'individual control'.

Equal participation, combined with non-hierarchical organization, provides the basis for a self-managing democracy without political specialization which, by its very structure, is meant to prevent the development of political domination and inequalities of power. But self-managing democracy cannot be conceived in purely institutional or structural terms. As with any other form of political organization, it presupposes a particular conception of society. Equal participation itself requires social equality; not equality conceived in terms of equivalence, but a substantive equality conceived in terms of what Bookchin has described as the 'equality of unequals'. To ensure that each person has an equal ability, not merely an equal opportunity, to participate in the management of social affairs requires compensating people for their disabilities, so that they may participate in social life to the same degree as other persons. Instead of treating all people in the same way, people are treated in the way most appropriate to their situation.

However, this does not imply acceptance of inherently unequal relationships of status and power. Relationships of domination based on class, sex, or race are incompatible with a democratic conception of social life. They cannot be compensated for, but must be abolished. To enable each person to participate in social affairs to the same degree requires not only compensating for individual disabilities but also eliminating domination and inequalities of power in interpersonal relationships.

Equal participation, if it is to be more than a mere formality, also requires roughly equal social competence in the management of public life. Self-management, in other words, presupposes a self competent to manage society directly. Such a self is formed not only through participation in the democratic process itself, but through interaction with others in a variety of voluntary, egalitarian social relationships. It is through such interaction that one develops moral character, personal identity, and shared values and beliefs allowing one to engage in rational discourse with others. This shared moral vocabulary of inter-subjective concepts and values provides the basis for and renders mutually intelligible the variety of social practices in everyday life, such as promising. The socially competent self presupposes a richly articulated society in which to develop.

Without this, the self is reduced to an alienated, monadic ego, morality becomes the mere expression of arbitrary preferences, and reason is reduced to the status of an instrument for their achievement. This process is further exacerbated by the introduction of any element of coercion or domination into social life. Instead of acting according to their own reason, people will act on the basis of perceived threats and inducements. Reason will be used to manipulate and dominate others, becoming an instrument of the will to power rather than a means of enlightenment and reciprocal awareness. If democratic decision-making is to be more than an aggregation of arbitrary preferences, and reason more than an instrument of will, the development of a public 'reason' which transcends individual subjectivity, created through interaction with others in a variety of situations and relationships, is absolutely essential.

This requires the transformation of society from the most basic social relationships upward. In contemporary society, perhaps the primary locus of character formation and the development of moral awareness is the nuclear family. Owing to its patriarchal structure, it provides an unsuitable model for an ecological society. It fosters authoritarian character traits, encourages submission to authority, and inhibits the free development of female individuality. It is the male domination of women institutionalized and sanctified by Church and State.

Although putatively voluntary, consent to the marriage relationship, once given, may be withdrawn only with the permission of the State and the Church. Within the marriage relationship itself, in many areas women still may not withdraw consent to sexual relations, because rape by a husband is not recognized at law. The contractual basis of marriage serves to disguise and mystify its true nature. Women, although subordinate to men in status throughout society, are portrayed as free and equal individuals within a voluntary relationship. In exchange for fictitious security and protection (belied by the epidemic of violence against women within familial relationships), women pro-

vide sexual services, child-rearing and unpaid labour. Even by bourgeois standards, it is not a fair exchange.

To ensure equal participation of men and women in social life it
essential to ensure that relationships between them are truly consensual,
egalitarian, and voluntary. Both sexes should be free to develop as
individuals according to their own needs and desires. They require a
new form of intimate consociation within which to develop their individual capacities to act in cooperation with others and to exercise moral
and political judgment. This new form of consociation, which would
form the basic 'cell tissue' of an ecological society, is the affinity group.

The affinity group is a small, non-hierarchical, voluntary association
of like-minded individuals who share not only certain ideals and goals,
but also 'a need to develop new libertarian social relations between
themselves, to mutually educate each other, share each other's problems, and develop new, non-sexist, non-hierarchical ties as well as
activities.'[1] The intimacy of the small group and its voluntary character
foster a genuine solidarity and mutual recognition of each person's
autonomy and self-worth. Involuntary biological ties and the specious
voluntarism of the marriage contract are replaced by voluntary commitment to a non-hierarchical mode of organization in which each person
enjoys equal status and responsibilities. Through interaction in the
affinity group, people develop the non-hierarchical sensibility and social
competence of the liberated self necessary for a self-managed society.

The affinity group does not form an isolated unit in society, but is
rooted in its own authentic locality and united with other groups in
horizontal networks continually evolving in response to changing needs
and circumstances. There is a constant proliferation of social ties as
new combinations of groups arise to fulfil new needs. Each group,
being decentralized, of human scale and based on consensus, remains
comprehensible and responsive to its members. At higher levels of
organization, coordination can be achieved through the use of recallable
delegates with no independent decision-making powers. Bookchin
argues that in a network based on the affinity group structure, 'power
actually diminishes rather than increases at each ascending level of
coordination.'[2]

While the affinity group constitutes the most basic social unit of an
ecological society, direct action constitutes the social practice by which
individuals assert their ability to control their own lives. Direct action
is not just a tactic, but the political expression of individual competence
to directly intervene in social life and manage social affairs without any
mediation or control by bureaucrats or professional politicians. The
individual takes direct action instead of relying on someone else to act
for her or him. This action encompasses a wide range of activities,
from organizing cooperatives to engaging in non-violent resistance to

authority. The affinity group structure often provides an excellent vehicle for direct action, which places moral commitment above positive law. It is not meant to be a last resort when other methods have failed, but the preferred way of doing things. It enables people to develop a new sense of self-confidence and an awareness of their individual and collective power. Founded on the idea that people can develop their social competence and ability for self-rule only through practice, it proposes that all persons directly decide the important issues facing them. In the political sphere, this implies the practice of direct democracy. Instead of relying on elected representatives, people make political decisions themselves in general assemblies.

Bookchin argues that direct democracy requires decentralization and human scale, 'the restoration of city life as a comprehensible form of public life', in which not only the social forms, structures and organizations making up the community are comprehensible to each person, but also 'the very individuals . . . who form the citizen body.'[3] Members of a community, meeting in directly democratic assemblies, can debate issues of common concern and formulate policies for the achievement of collective goals. Participation in the political process has an educative effect, creating an 'enlarged mentality' which transcends particular interests and renders authentic political judgment possible. Public debate and discussion help develop a common conception of the public good in reference to which social life may be ordered and conflict resolved. Social relationships become transparent to all and subject to human control. Through face-to-face communication, people develop both communal and self-awareness. Each person feels part of a physical presence, a body politic, in which she or he is a fully active member. For Bookchin, 'direct participation in social life and the development of selfhood mutually reinforce each other to form the civic virtues and commitments of the citizen.'[4]

Participation in the assembly must be open to all members of the community. This requires more than a formal acknowledgment of individual membership. Each person requires sufficient means to enable her or him to participate in decision-making to the same extent as others. This necessitates an 'irreducible minimum' of material security and free time for all. There is an important public interest in the organization of production and consumption in an ecological society, both to guarantee the 'irreducible minimum', and to ensure that ecologically appropriate technologies and methods are used. For this reason alone, private ownership of the means of production would be inappropriate in an ecological society. The private authority of the boss and the exploitation of wage labour are incompatible with the free and voluntary relationships characteristic of a self-managed society. Although the workplace, by itself, does not constitute an authentic public sphere, it still needs to be organized according to the principles of worker self-management.

Social policy should be decided by all members of the community in general assembly. But when the implementation of policy requires some sort of administrative action, this can be achieved through "strictly administrative bodies subject to rotation, recall, limitations of tenure, wherever possible, selected by sortition."[5] This will prevent the development of political specialization and the emergence of a permanent bureaucracy with its own interests and agenda to uphold. Relations between communities can be based on the anarchist conception of federalism —ever widening associations of freely federated but autonomous communities.

One can provide only a bare sketch of self-managing democracy; its details will need to be worked out in practice by free individuals associated in a variety of voluntary groups organized in a non-hierarchical manner. However, there are some general issues that can be raised regarding Bookchin's proposals for direct democracy, and their relationship with the ecological ideal of a society without hierarchy and domination.

One of Bookchin's most important insights is that it is possible to have politics without the State. Beyond the area of daily social activities and relationships, whether at the workplace or in the intimacy of the affinity group, there is a need for an authentic public sphere where all members of the community can meet to debate and discuss issues, and decide on common courses of action regarding matters of public concern. To argue that government can be replaced by the workshop and simple administration, as Proudhon once did, reveals a misunderstanding of the role of work in society. The workplace is merely one area in which people associate. The interests it represents are too limited and narrow to encompass a more general interest involving all members of the community.

As well, administration is not as simple a thing as nineteenth-century socialists such as Proudhon imagined. Even strictly administrative bodies can develop their own interests and usurp control over certain areas of social life from the community at large. Institutional safeguards, such as limitations of tenure and selection by sortition, are necessary to prevent administrative bodies from constituting a separate source of social power in society. Proudhon himself recognized the limits of his earlier views and came to espouse a form of direct democracy and federalism in his later works.[6]

A faith in mere spontaneity is equally misplaced. One cannot leave it to providence alone to ensure that social life evolves along libertarian lines. In any society, some people will enjoy advantages over others, simply by virtue of personal circumstance, individual talent, and, sometimes, completely fortuitous events. Even in a society based entirely on voluntary association, associations may arise which benefit some segments of society at the expense of others. Where there is no institutional means for dealing with disparities in benefits and power, or for preventing them from arising in the first place, open social conflict and struggle will ensue. Where there is no arena for the public articulation of social values and goals, order may be obtained through unthinking obedience to social customs and traditions which themselves remain unexamined by a critical consciousness.

In a self-managing democracy, the vagaries of fate are replaced by conscious social control by socially competent and aware individuals freely associated with each other. Each member of the community has an equal voice in the management of social affairs. Social relationships are rendered transparent in the light of public discussion and debate. The opacity of custom and tradition is replaced by conscious articulation by the community in assembly of any rules that it may obey. Society is autonomous in the true sense of self-legislating. At the same time as people are bound by the rules they may create, they are superior to them in the sense that they may change them at any time, as new needs and circumstances arise. The assembly provides a forum for the expression of all the many interests of the different members of the community, not just the particular interests of certain groups, such as workers or men. This allows for the development of a truly general interest, and ultimately for the possibility of transcending the very notion of interest as such in favour of more expansive notions of solidarity and community.

Just as self-managing democracy creates a public realm distinct from the merely social, it creates a form of politics distinct from the State. The State is a hierarchical organization exercising centralized power and authority over all those it claims to fall under its jurisdiction. Equal participation in the modern State is simply impossible due to its very size and complexity. The State cannot exist without a permanent bureaucracy and a coercive apparatus to impose order on the disobedient masses excluded from any real power.

Self-managing democracy is decentralized, so that social life is on a comprehensible scale. All members of the community participate equally in social rule. No one is excluded from the assembly, the true seat of collective social power. Both the general assembly and other forms of association, from the affinity group to the workplace, are organized on a non-hierarchical basis. Authority is dispersed among all the members of the community. Bureaucracy is safeguarded against through the use, only where necessary, of strictly administrative bodies subject to recall, limitations of tenure, and selection by sortition. There is no need for any coercive apparatus, because people are subject only to rules which they themselves have created and may change.

The State is above all an involuntary organization. Those who refuse to recognize its authority and obey its rules face imprisonment or exile. To constitute a political form truly distinct from the State, self-managing democracy must be conceived in voluntary terms. Only those who voluntarily agree to participate in the assembly can be bound by its decisions. Its jurisdiction is not based on geography or some notion of sovereignty, but on the notion of self-assumed obligation. By freely associating with others for the purpose of collective decision-making, people create horizontal ties of political obligation between each other, rather than between themselves and some separate entity such as the 'State'.[7]

Some notion of self-assumed obligation is necessary to ensure that self-managing democracy constitutes a form of political organization from which domination has really been excluded. It is based on the idea that democratic voting should be analogous to the social practice of promising. A vote is a public act of commitment by which one binds one's future conduct. Its exercise presupposes the social competence to render political judgment, just as promising presupposes the ability to make moral judgments. Each individual must decide whether she or he ought to commit her or himself to a particular course of future conduct. Thus, both promising and direct democratic voting presuppose, rather than deny, individual autonomy, the ability to reason critically and freely choose one's actions. And just as one can justifiably break one's promises in certain circumstances, without denying their generally binding character, one may justifiably disobey decisions made by a direct democratic vote that are contrary to the basic principles and ideals of the political association. Situations may arise where one's commitment to an ecological, democratic society requires conduct contrary to that decided upon by the general assembly in a particular case.

Through this notion of self-assumed obligation, a better understanding of the nature of the rules to which a general assembly may agree can be obtained. Not only may the assembly change its rules and policies in response to new circumstances, such that the rules are always subordinate to the will of the people in assembly, but those who do not vote in favour of a rule or policy cannot be forced to obey. Enforced obedience would reintroduce domination into the community. Those who do not participate in a particular decision or who vote against it must be free to decide whether, all things considered, they should consent to the will of the majority and agree to abide by it. If all members of the association are deemed equally competent to make political judgments, then minorities cannot be prevented from exercising that judgment when they sincerely disagree with a majority decision. To deny the right to withhold consent and to disobey would be to deny the freedom and equality of those in the minority (or those in the majority who later decide they were mistaken). Direct action will remain as much a part of an ecological society as its institutionalized counterpart of direct democracy.

That each person should be able to decide whether to consent to a majority decision will raise charges of arbitrariness. Such charges are unfounded. In a society of richly articulated and complex social relationships in which the individual is constantly being educated into moral probity, self-awareness and social commitment, such that each person acquires the competence to manage social affairs directly, that social competence will include the ability to make moral and political decisions, including the decision to withhold consent to a policy with which one profoundly disagrees.

From this perspective, a clearer conception of self-managing democracy emerges. If political obligation is conceived in terms of horizontal ties voluntarily created between members of a community, then a more fluid, less institutionalized conception of direct democracy is needed. Instead of one general assembly having jurisdiction over all those in a certain area, as in ancient Athens for example, there will be a multiplicity of political associations freely created for the satisfaction of ever-changing needs and desires, altered in accordance with the wishes of their members in response to new situations and circumstances. Membership in each association will be strictly voluntary, and only those who explicitly agree or consent to a decision within the association will be obligated to abide by it. An authentic public sphere will remain, encompassing those areas of 'social existence in which citizens voluntarily cooperate together and sustain their common life and common undertaking.'[8] By ensuring that social relationships retain their voluntary character in all areas of life, from the personal to the political, the re-emergence of political domination is precluded.

This emphasis on the voluntariness of social relationships is important because direct democracy by itself does not necessarily exclude the prospect of domination. If direct democracy is conceived in purely procedural terms, as merely a different method of decision-making yielding legal rules qualitatively similar to those promulgated by the modern State, then its libertarian potential will be obscured. A libertarian direct democracy must not allow for the coercive imposition of rules on unwilling minorities. The direct democracy of ancient Athens is a case in point. Although it fostered an admirable political 'amateurism' well worth imitating, this was achieved within the context of institutionalized slavery and male domination of women. Within the democratic assembly itself, the 'warrior-citizen' would use his oratorial skills to assert his superiority over others through aggressive verbal duelling. Disobedience and subversion were met by ostracism and capital punishment. Modern anarchists would have felt as unwelcome in ancient Athens as they do in contemporary Greece.

Self-managing democracy, if it is to retain its libertarian character, must reject the notion of legal rules enforced through coercive sanction. In place of coercion, it must rely on the good sense and moral probity of its members. Above all, it must continually strive for the maximum possible degree of voluntariness in social relations, realizing Kropotkin's vision of an organic society which combines 'the most complete development of individuality . . . with the highest development of voluntary association in all its aspects, in all possible degrees, for all imaginable aims,' constantly assuming 'new forms which answer best to the multiple aspirations of all.'[9]

Kropotkin's fellow anarchist, Michael Bakunin, once wrote that whoever says politics says domination. Perhaps it is now possible to have politics without domination: the politics of social ecology.

REFERENCES

1. Murray Bookchin, *Toward An Ecological Society* (Montréal: Black Rose Books, 1980), p. 48. Bookchin's essays in this collection should be read in their entirety. The short summary attempted here cannot do justice to his views.
2. Ibid., p. 49.
3. Ibid., pp. 187–188.
4. Ibid., p. 238.
5. Ibid., p. 216.
6. *See*, for example, Pierre-Joseph Proudhon, *The Principle of Federation*, trans. R. Vernon (Toronto: University of Toronto Press, 1979).
7. The following discussion of self-assumed obligation is drawn from Carole Pateman, *The Problem of Political Obligation* (London: John Wiley & Sons, 1979).
8. Carole Pateman, p. 174.
9. Peter Kropotkin, 'Anarchism: Its Philosophy and Ideal.' In: R. Baldwin (ed.) *Kropotkin's Revolutionary Pamphlets*, (New York: Dover, 1970).

Beyond Technological Things

Thomas W. Simon

Things and Things

Things

We are surrounded by them. At times I think that my very being is being devoured by them. I no longer talk to people even through the mediation of the telephone. Now I swap messages on answering machines—thing to thing 'communication'.

All about me I find things: swivel lamps, cluttered papers, books and more books, Great Crisps, Acction digital watch, Sony 7–band SW Spread Dial Radio. . . . A moth flickers an interruption on the thing-scape. Outside my Croft windows the flora and fauna become rarer with the passing of each day and with the accumulation of each thing.

Some things remain just things ("Hand me that thing over there."). Those difficult to classify become 'thingamabobs' and 'thingamajigs'. Only a few things get classified as technologies. To the modern mind, papers and books do not qualify as technological things; watches and radios do. To the common mind, technologies are those things that do something. Books don't do anything; Radios do. Therefore, Bookchin claims that

> To the modern mind, technics (technology) is simply the ensemble of raw materials, tools, machines, and related devices that are needed to produce a usable object.[1]

My claim is that technology to the modern mind is not even that; it is much simpler. For example, most people do not even recognize that the raw materials used in making computers are themselves dangerous chemicals. Technology is a subset of things; technology is an isolated set of things, whose history and context is almost entirely blurred. The thinghood of modern technology is an essential characteristic.

Of course, this way of viewing technology was not always so. As Bookchin points out, the classical Greek sense of technology (*techne*) had a much broader meaning than the modern one. In the classical sense, *techne* includes an ethical, rational, and social framework. Technology was not an isolated thing. One purpose of this essay is to take technology beyond thinghood, into that broader, contextual, classical framework.

Oddly enough, there is another sense of thing. Etymologically (and theoretically), the first Western democratic republic began in 930 AD when the first Al*thing*, or national assembly, was convened on the gloomy plains of *Thing*vellir in southwest Iceland. This planting of the democratic seed is quite revealing. At Thingvellir, some 400 chieftains, who had parceled out all habitable Icelandic land, would meet in order to 'legislate' the laws. These laws, however, were unwritten, unenforced, and unenforceable except by the practice of 'might makes right'.

> When one searches the Landnambok, a contemporary Icelandic history which lists almost every man and woman of importance who lived in Iceland during the first decades of its occupation by the Norse, it is difficult to find references to more than a handful of men who died natural deaths. The majority seem to have died violently at the hands of their fellows.[2]

I will leave it to the reader to decide whether democracy has radically changed since the days of Eric the Red. In any event, a not too dissimilar gap between the theory and practice of democracy exists with respect to modern-day thinking about technology. One purpose of this discussion is to develop a participatory democratic praxis for technology so that the gap between theory and practice can be bridged. In other words, I will be trying to show how our theory and practice of technology can go beyond the first sense of thing (thing 1) and toward the second theoretical sense of thing (thing 2). First, however, we need to describe the technological landscape before us.

The Highs and Lows of Technology

High-technology may not be too easy to define. The prefix 'high' has always bothered me. Sometimes it is written as 'hi-tech', as if technology is giving some sort of friendly, salutatory greeting. Or does this form of technology assure civilization of some exhalted, 'high' state? These facetious remarks are simply intended to show the futility of trying to define high-technology when the high-ground has already been staked out through using the word 'high' in the first place.

Definitional quandaries aside, high-technology is certainly easy to recognize. The monstrous nuclear power plant just down the road from me at Crystal River easily qualifies as high-technology, as does all the laser star-wars gadgetry my employer, the University of Florida, is so fond of promoting. Concords, Tridents, computerized whatever, genetic engineering—I suppose even videos—make the list of high-technologies.

Low-technology (if we accept the terms of the debate) has, of course, an inferior status. Like high-technology it is difficult to define, but, unlike high-technology, it cannot be easily recognized. Bicycles easily qualify as low-technology while electric cars are debatable.

Low-technology adherents have tried to recast the terms of the debate by promoting variations of the low-technology theme: intermediate, appropriate, alternative, liberatory, feminist, democratic, ecological, convivial, modest, soft, indigenous, radical, etc. The list seems endless. Opposition to high technology appears, at best, to be an incoherent hodge-podge of conflicting opinions. Perhaps low-technology is no more than the negation of high-technology.

Despite these misgivings, there is more coherence to the low-technology movement than might first meet the eye. Of all the low-technology variants, appropriate technology (AT) is certainly the dominant version, and within the AT movement a further dominant strain can be found. Yet, this strain of AT is part of the problem and not part of the solution. Basically, high-technology and the mainstream of AT are cut from the same cloth. Both treat technology as a thing in the first sense, as an isolated object. Secondly, both ignore technology as a thing in the second sense, as critically involving deliberate and democratic participation. As we will see, a way to go beyond AT is to blend together some of these other conceptions of low-technology: liberatory, feminist, democratic, and ecological.

Beyond Things 1

Liberatory and Liberation Technologies

As noted above, what allegedly separates technology from normal, everyday things is that technology does something. Things just lie around, inert. Technology is active—crunching, playing, devouring, generating—in short, producing. Technology works. With a spelling program on hand, a word processor produces magic, correcting most of my errors. Technology is a productive thing, a thing 1.

The General Electric Carousel of Progress vividly displays all of the wonderful things produced by electricity. Marx, of course, emphasized the productive forces of society. Alternative technology is no exception to this emphasis on production. If you review the AT literature on the Third World, you will find manual production almost being worshipped. As an example, take this description of ten beggars in India put to work through the use of AT:

> They are completely rehabilitated now. They are well-dressed; they are happy, and are now completely different people. . . . It just shows that if one has the imagination, almost anything can be done.[3]

Technology is cast into the role of 'rehabilitation', which translates as 'putting people to work'. This is the AT Carousel of Progress. Yet, it is not necessarily progressive. A technology freeing people from arduous tasks can be just as important as one creating jobs. After reading AT literature, it is difficult to avoid the feeling that major labor-saving technologies are reserved for the First and not the Third World.

In the mid–1960s Bookchin developed a novel conception of technology which should have overcome this AT shortsightedness. Liberatory technology is what is needed to free us from want and toil. Too often, technological proposals assume a form of work and then try to invent technologies that will alter but never eliminate that form of work. For Bookchin, however, there are many forms of human production well worth eliminating. For example:

> The abolition of mining as a sphere of human activity would symbolize, in its own way, the triumph of a liberatory technology.[4]

The task of technological innovation, then, is, in part, not to create more work or to make work more efficient, but to eliminate toil and drudgery altogether.

While Bookchin has developed his views on technology far beyond his earlier conception of liberatory technology, it is still worth noting a problem with it. Liberatory technology, like so many other philosophies of technology, clings to the idea of technology as a productive thing. In the liberated society, 'the machine will remove toil from the productive process.'[5] Technology is useful in so far as it relates to the production process. High-technology aims to make that production process more efficient; AT tries to employ more people in the process; liberatory technology would like to eliminate certain production processes.

To see one of many problems with this production emphasis, we only need to see the sexist bias in these conceptions of technology. Reproductive technologies are seldom addressed. Moreover, only the masculine aspects of technological development—innovation, design, construction, supply —merit time and attention. The other aspects of technology (the non-productive, non-thing 1 side)—daily operation, maintenance, use, care, responsibility—are shoved aside. The heroic element gets rewarded while the nurturing side gets ignored.[6]

This sexual division of technology has had devastating consequences, including the failure of many AT projects. In the 1970s windmills were sprouting up all over the northeastern part of the United States, including one atop a rehabbed building in New York City in the Loisaida project. That was the exciting phase. Now few of these wind-mills are turning. One of the reasons is that maintenance on them was neglected. The seemingly dull, nurturing phase was largely bypassed. Likewise 'soft', or what I call liberation, technologies, such as cooking, sanitation, and education, take a back seat to the gadgetry and engineer-ing feats needed to build an appropriate technology.

We need to go beyond thing 1, beyond viewing technology as an isolated productive thing. Technology is part and parcel of a context.

Towards Thing 2

Democratizing Technology

Normally, we think of what technology does for us. From microwave to electric-can opener, life in the kitchen has certainly been made easier. Seldom do we consider how we as individuals end up doing things for the technology. This is what Winner calls reverse adaptation: we end up serving the technology rather than the technology serving us.[7] It turns out that those 'labor-saving' devices in the home did not emanci-pate women. Women still spend 60 or more hours per week on dom-estic tasks. Finally, even rarer are thoughts of how we can reverse reverse adaptation and gain control of technology.

The political situation with technology is not that different from the Althing. We may talk of the emancipatory effects of technology, but the political reality shows little that is democratic about modern tech-nology. The chieftains of modern technology legislate the laws of technology, laws that are largely unwritten, unenforced, and unen-forceable. Nobody asks me what I think of getting a new computer in the office or of having fuel injection put in my car. The rules for introducing technology remain unwritten for the public at large. Some-body must be making these decisions. All I know is that it isn't me and that it probably isn't you. Technology is something we consume, not something upon which we deliberate.

Participation in technology only extends to concerns like user-friendly computers. Attention is given to how people interact with the machines, but not with how people interact with the entire process of technological development. This charge holds true against AT just as much as it holds true against high-technology. Look at the following AT examples. In India, only the rich farmers are able to make use of a methane gas plant. The two people able to afford a solar pump now monopolize the sale of previously free water in a Mauritanian village.[8] Small irrigation machines in Gao, Mali, enable farmers to sell enormous quantities of melons to Parisian tables, while food crops are in short supply for their hungry people.

How can democracy be made more participatory and more democratic? Let me provide just one small way in which that question can be approached. In general, a radical, participatory sense of democracy implies professional suicide. As more and more people take power and control over their lives and surroundings, the power and control of professionals and experts diminishes. The more power people attain over their own health and the health-care system, the less power medical doctors have. The home-birth movement is partially an attempt to democratize technology, to optimize the participation of not only the pregnant woman but also of significant others, including the midwives. In effect, the professional commits professional suicide the more successful she or he becomes. The lawyer's task is to return the area of dispute to the people through community dispute centers, instead of monopolizing the dispute process. The lawyer, like most professionals, needs to become superfluous.

Architects are usually not thought of as technologists, but that is a problem with our limited vision of technology. Architecture is one of the potentially suicidal professions. Architects provide designs and blueprints for buildings and even for communities. Customer and community involvement in architecture depends on numerous factors, but rarely is participation optimized. Participation is partially dependent upon how much the architects succeed in teaching the others to become architects. In other words, it depends on how little the architects are needed.

The extent to which a professional/expert is no longer needed is partially the extent to which a process has become democratized. It is the extent to which we are able to make the professional terrain a deliberative assembly.

From Things to Nature

Eco-Technology

Ecology and technology—a strange juxtaposition. Ecology deals with the animate world; technology with the inanimate. Ecology and technology take their places on opposite sides of the battlefield. Ecologists try to preserve nature against the onslaught of technology. Technologists use nature to serve their own ends.

Bookchin's innovative concept, eco-technology, sounds like an oxymoron, akin to 'military intelligence' or 'bankers' trust'. Nonetheless, eco-technology is a critical concept. Traditional conceptions of technology, of both high and low varieties, have a very anthropocentric bias. In the adoption of a particular technology, the primary interest is in what that technology does for humans. True, proponents of AT (and some of high-technology) do worry about environmental effects, but the impact on the environment is still considered a 'secondary' or 'side' effect.

In contrast, eco-technology is not simply a thing. Rather, the first step in acquiring an ecological identity would be to design technical components

> *as part* of ensembles—as technical *ecosystems* that interpenetrate with the natural ones in which they are located, not merely as agglomerations of 'small', 'soft', 'intermediate', or 'convivial' gadgets. The principal message of an ecological technics is that it is integrated to create a highly interactive, animate and inanimate constellation in which every component forms a supportive part of the whole.[9]

The environment, then, is not merely a secondary consideration placed conveniently in the background. All too often, alternative technologies are engineering feats and not ecological integrations.

Not only is eco-technology not merely a thing, it is not even necessarily a productive thing. It may well be, as Bookchin describes preindustrial technology, *adaptive* rather than innovative.[10] Why do we always demand novel production from technology when creative adaptation will do? And adaptive technology need not be active. The best technics in some circumstances is a technics capable of *doing nothing*. Allowing an ecosystem to run its course may not be classified as technological activity, but we need to stretch the concept of technology in this adaptive direction.

Before concluding that eco-technology is the panacea for taking us out of the many quandaries outlined here, some cautionary notes are in order. The ecology concept itself should remind us that no single adjective when attached to the noun 'technology' will do the trick. Just as ecology implies diversity, so we need a diversity of qualifiers to re-dress technology in a more appropriate apparel. Liberatory, liberator, feminist, democratic, ecological—all converge in a technology web. Bookchin rejects 'democratic technics' because it is 'not necessarily a nonhierarchical or ecological one.'[11] That, of course, depends on the sense of 'democratic'. A representative democracy is by definition hierarchical, whereas a participatory democracy is nonhierarchical and is closely akin to ecology. Conversely, eco-technology is not necess-arily democratic and participatory. All of these nodes are necessary for re-conceptualizing and re-feeling the technology web.

Above all, it is important to realize that a technological choice is not an isolated one. We are not simply choosing a thing, we are choosing a self, a way of relating to nature, a politics, a society, a way of being and becoming.

REFERENCES

1. Murray Bookchin, *The Ecology of Freedom* (Palo Alto, CA: Cheshire Books, 1982) p. 221.
2. Farley Mowat, *West-Viking* (Toronto: McClelland and Stewart, 1963), p. 20.
3. Paul R. Lofthouse, 'Industrial Liaison'. In: R. J. Congon (ed.) *Introduction to Appropriate Technology* (Emmaus, PA: Rodale Press, 1977), p. 156.
4. Murray Bookchin, *Post-Scarcity Anarchism* (Berkeley: Ramparts Press, 1971), p. 104.
5. Ibid., p. 134.
6. Arnold Pacey, *The Culture of Technology* (Oxford: Blackwell, 1983), Ch. 6.
7. Langdon Winner, *Autonomous Technology* (Cambridge, MA: MIT Press, 1977).
8. Nicholas Jequier, *Appropriate Technology: Problems and Promises* (Paris: Organization of Economic Cooperation and Development, 1976).
9. Murray Bookchin, *Ecology of Freedom*, p. 265.
10. bid., p. 244.
11. Ibid., p. 241.

A Literature of Alternatives

Robert Nicholls

Let's leave the field of protest literature, whose task is to correct lies: that Laos or the zones of El Salvador are not being bombed, when the fact is that they are. Let's leave this field to enter that of literature that inspires, such as the works of Ivan Illich, E. F. Schumacher, Murray Bookchin, Leopold Kohr. This prophetic voice is not one of our modern modes. It belongs to the age of Blake and Whitman, as the gentle moralist voice of Wendell Berry on agriculture is an eighteenth-century mode.

Let's leave the field of protest to the armies of protest and drop our flags, even the one of protesting facts and blocking the State's latest, most catastrophic folly. In other words, as we hear the rumble of the wall collapsing over our heads, we say

'Let it come. . . *in this instant we'll find a way out.*'

In doing this we turn to an alternative literature, that is, a literature of alternatives—insisting as we do that the 'utopian' is a significant and contemporary mode. But there is a difference between utopian *concepts* and utopian *pictures*. To an extent, prophetic literature engages the enemy on his chosen territory. As if it were an argument. As if to persuade were to end the matter. The utopian systematic *concept*, the grand scheme, is a form as unshakably solid as a battleship in the sea-warfare of argument. Because it is abstract, it repels any direct attack. But the utopian *image* is frail, impalpable, and vulnerable. The idea put into flesh is ephemeral.

This is a sticky subject. It is partly a problem of contrasting categor-ies: the conceptual and reasoning versus the entertaining and imaginat-ive. Mark Twain's *Huckleberry Finn* also *thinks*, i.e. thinks concepts through. But in its worst caricature, creative and imaginative fiction can be completely dense. We leave the path, we are lost in the thicket.

The path of books like those of Illich, Schumacher, and Bookchin is to go to higher and higher levels of abstraction; more and more spheres are encompassed and areas explained, using concepts such as domination, planned scarcity, appropriate scale. So that one can almost say there are two vectors going out in opposite directions. One is the high road. And the other goes to the small, the actual set of circumstances, the real thing, the real person.

The prophetic books chart our goals. They are a kind of 'celestial navigation'. At the top, there are these grand and enlightening works. They are our essential guides. At the bottom, there is a real life. At the top are the solutions; what is most meaningful and helpful. As we descend the ladder of conceptualization toward the ground, something is missing and we stumble. The bottom rungs have been left out.

What would be examples of a literature of alternatives? Books of fiction (like *Ecotopia*) that are hopelessly sentimental or trivial must be dismissed (though not their form: character and story in a transformed setting). Paul and Percival Goodman's *Communitas* presents a provocative picture of what life will be like: there are paradigms of three types of societies. But they are little more than models from conceptual premises. We are looking for a specific narrative in the literature of alternatives, the setting of a particular scene. We might think of a story, say, in the year 2010 about social ecologists who have taken over a city, for example, the city of Burlington, Vermont. My own utopian series *Daily Lives in Nghsi Altai* is an illustration of Bookchin's idea of decentralism and a regionally appropriate technology.

The question is: How does the story relate to its political framework? As we would say: 'A nice guy or woman, but what's their politics?', 'A good action, but what were the politics behind it?' We know a good deal of William Morris and the late nineteenth-century socialists. Morris was already a famous poet, and artisan/manufacturer, known for textile patterns, and the Morris chair. For years, he had been a speaker and fundraiser for socialist causes, and was a member in London of the Socialist League. One night, as he describes it, discouraged and depressed after a meeting, he went home and wrote *News From Nowhere:* about what life would be like in England in the years ahead, as if socialism had come.

His relationship to his political associates is complex. One can say that, in some sense, he wrote the book to illustrate the group's socialist ideas. In another sense, he wrote it *against* them, in irritation.

There was the background history up to then, which was fairly typical. Endless doctrinal squabbles. Elitism and sterility in the center, the London metropolis, whereas the main organizing effort was in the countryside, particularly the north of England. There was his own reading of socialism. He was well aquainted with Marx, though less hard-line than Aveling. Perhaps it was a question of temperament. The *picture* that he wanted drawn was different: a harmonizing of the landscape/cityscape; of the intellectual with the artisan and workman.

But these were basic doctrinal issues, articles of belief he would have shared with the rest of the group. They don't explain the sense in which Morris's dream was in *opposition* to it.

Was it simply the tension between the conceptualizing and imagining faculties? There is always this tension: the pressure from the larger reservoir of ideas is channelled, and comes out with extra force. It's hard to put this into words. It is the same impulse the painter has to do a picture and the poet has to do a poem. that is, to make something that is *entirely specific*.

Everyone has had these experiences if they have been actively involved in social movements building alternative institutions. (My own was in the Lower East Side of New York, in 'sweat equity' housing.) The experience—we are all *in* the situation, trying to do something. Begun in high hopes, the experiment is now falling apart, it's about to fail. The cardinal point is one makes these attempts, one does these things with the people who are *there*. Ourselves as we are, not an ideal set. The thing may be conceptually correct. The idea is good, etc. Still, it is failing.

At this point a 'news story' comes out. These stories are by outside people/observers and are written for the general public. Describing how wonderful, how exciting, how radical it all is. (They do not know we are failing). Or the written material might be an evaluation report. Or an application for a grant. The result is farcical.

This is an example of literature (let's call it all 'literature') which is inappropriate, which is at a level of abstraction above the real. We know that there is a situation made up of real events and involving real people. Almost everyone of us has been inside something like this at some time. Enough to know that this is the real thing. But it's a mess, a farce, a mulligan stew, an absolute tangle of life. One needs to get at a distance to make some sense out of it.

We can imagine a literature that might have been less false. Letters home: some of the builders involved in our project were West Indian and Puerto Rican. Interviews on tape: the work meetings could be taped. Diaries. Conversation on the street: gossip, vilification and praise, commentary. An oral history. The situation has produced a storyteller. The point is that this art, because it is a step removed from life, at a level of abstraction and signification above the stew of the real, can give perspective and hope to those of us who are lost in the situation.

I should probably state at this point the thesis of this essay—at this stage of its development social ecology has developed many good ideas, but not enough practice. The main concepts of social ecology, taken in isolation, tend to thin out. For their vitality they need to be connected to *practice*.

But practice is life itself. One can spend one's whole lifetime going forward a single inch in the direction of building an alternate institution! What is needed at this point is a literature, an art of the alternatives, where what we are talking about is shown, described, circulated, given a meaning beyond itself. That is, multiplied (like the world in the Elizabethan eye) in the magic mirror of art.

To approach this, we need to look at the basic terms, usually taken for granted, in a totally new way. We have to ask: What is art in relation to the field of social ecology and to politics? Why is it so neglected? What kind of censorship has been operating? What is the medium itself? Is there an appropriate *art of communication* for this field, as there is an appropriate technology?

But why be solemn? The situation is comic. We spend a week studying some abstruse book on local self-reliance and eight hours in a food co-op serving customers. Then, for entertainment, we go to a movie made by an transnational corporation for an audience of 300 million. We wear shawls and sandals from the Andes and Guatemala, but don't know that our grandparents (if they were farmers) wore pants made out of feed sacks 50 years ago during the Depression—an example of American folk art. Intellectually, we are radicals and self-reliant. Possibly, we do cooperative, autonomous work. But we are mass consumers of images and aesthetic pleasures formed, as for the colonial world, from the outside.

There is a way in which our twentieth-century American reality is a total *gestalt*—one can't call it an artifact, because we are of it, and *in it*. When we think of an 'alternative art', we conventionally think of metropolitan avant-garde experiments, or of a common peoples' art that has disappeared. but we no longer live in villages or the urban neighborhoods of an earlier era.

The situation produces its own storyteller.

It should be clear from the Lower East Side example that I've discussed that we should not be producing 'high' literature made by professionals for the national market. Rather, it should be a literature mired, even be-shitted in its own circumstances. As Rabelais, in analogous circumstances, was also producing 'low' literature.

Let's analyze the elements which distinguish this type from the national market type.

1) It is written for a political community which is taken for granted. The readership is ourselves.

2) We want the writing to be useful. And we accept the stigma that this may be 'bad writing', according to the judgment rendered by some 'professionals'.

We are in the *present*, a relatively short period in history in which the national media have wiped out everything. There was a time not so far back when in North America good verse was composed by miners, voyageurs, and loggers. Now it is collected in learned books as an example of 'folk art', which is now, of course, impossible.

Or to give it a more urban and sophisticated slant: the example of Aristophanes' plays (*The Frogs, The Birds*) written in Athens on the topics of the time, political subjects, and performed by artist-citizens in the hall of congress as entre-acts between legislative sessions. And danced and sung. That is, they were total media.

But now the total media of today have wiped us out.

The contrast remains. There is in almost everyone of us an organic artist. Our pleasures need to be whole. There is the same right proportion between the place and the voice. Athens was a city the size of Buffalo. My own locale in central Vermont is a sophisticated communications network which icnludes several small cities. The impulse of the local artist —using his or her materials—is to speak with eloquence to a circle of immediate hearers.

But this impulse has largely been wiped out.

We have begun to see there are no solutions on the national level; that the competitive market, and capitalist mass-democracy are themselves the problem; that the impetus for initiative has moved from the center to the edges. Bioregionalism is only a word for this, one of several constellations that hold together a set of values: autonomy, ecological balance, appropriate technology and useful work, direct democracy, communalism, etc. The initiative may have begun to build fledgling and alternative institutions. But the overriding and overwhelming fact continues to be the national market, the national bureaucracy that surrounds and represses them. There will be the same law for the lion and the ox, within the same cage.

It is this pressure, inertia, this drag from the past, acknowledged as present reality, that a literature of alternatives tries to throw off. That doesn't mean the need is recognized. The perceived need is for resistance and protest. This is met predominantly by non-fiction, i.e. by criticism, newsletters, and the 'movement literature'. The vitality of this is that it goes hand in hand with action. The precise function of this non-fiction is to resist the encroachment of the market system, the national political culture, etc., to hold it off in order to allow a new thing to happen. But there must *be* something happening. Otherwise there is no replacement for the old. There are many 'movement' small publishers—a good thing. Sometimes, one sees stories and poems. but, in general, economics limits what is published to what is action-oriented and to protest. There is energy for nothing more.

It is because of the very difficulty, the chancy qualities of all these experiments, the density and rawness of fact that I've called 'the stew of the real', that we need all our arts. And, particularly, the art that is not all the time arguing and reasoning and protesting, but, rather, offering the possibility of pleasure, presenting hope in a sensuous medium. The function of an appropriate literature is to be hopeful.

If one looks for a direct connection between imaginative literature and action, one would have to go back to the 1840s. Etienne Cabet's book *Voyage to Icaria* was read by 100,000 French citizens, some of whom went to America to the Midwest to become utopians. In other words, there must be some *political* hope in order for there to be a *literary* hope. One can almost plot a declining curve of hope in literature from the American and French revolutions in the 1780s, through Cabet, Fourier and Owen, through Morris' dream, through to the radical writers of the 1920s and 1930s—Dos Passos, Norris, Dreiser, for whom at least in the background of their thought was the possibility that capitalism could be replaced by another system. After this, the light fades.

The idea of the artist being at the service of politics is totally against the American grain. The tradition of the American writer has been as an independent entrepreneur and professional, detached from the social scene. Yet there are many, myself included, who could help create an alternative literature within the context of a regional political net- work—if there were readers.

A literature of alternatives would include the grand conceptual cri- tique that I've called 'celestial navigation'. And a wide range of non- fiction that is not error-correcting and protesting, but rather is devoted to showing alternatives in finer detail. These could be contemporary accounts of pre-figurative and emergent institutions that have started. Or accounts/descriptions across space—the Mondragon cooperative today in Spain, or the Arc in France. And across time—as early New England town meetings, the nineteenth-century communes, American Indian tribal societies. In other words, what is required for this alterna- tive non-fiction is comparisons, balances, contrasts, juxtapositions, gulfs, resonances; that is, something that gives us distance from the broth of the real and makes some sense out of it.

The fact is, what we are seeking to create today are counter-insti- tutions set up as in a dual society. One foot in this world; one foot in the other one (in the spirit world). Therefore, what we need is a literature which is both multi-spacial and multi-temporal.

We already have the first two of the three modes I have mentioned: the conceptual (if we didn't there wouldn't be a field of Social Ecology), and the detailed factual. The third member of the triad, the third genre, is neglected, almost non-existent. The mode of entertainment and drama has been appropriated by other media. Yet, the possibility of the imaginative mode is to open the utopian vision to the common reader.

An error in approaching utopian (and anti-utopian) fiction has been the tendency to ask such questions as these. Did Morris show socialism correctly? Was Orwell wrong in certain respects? But imaginative utopian fiction need not concern itself with what is 'correct' (though it must not be *incorrect*). Such judgment belongs to the critics. Nor does one expect of this mode exposition/delineation of facts, accuracy, information and scope, truth. These belong to the second genre, not to imaginative fiction.

There will always be a tension between the three modes. It is the prophets from whom the storyteller gets his or her themes. It is the journalists from whom the storyteller gets facts. But these three will never really be friends, they will always distrust each other. The image maker—since he or she is making an image *in the flesh*—will always be conceptually inaccurate, and will always leave something out.

The locus of this genre—not focused upon by the other two—will be *the person*. Of course, the person within the community. It starts with the self, the self woven into a hopeful fiction. An imaginative literature of alternatives is simply about the person in transformed circumstances. It is impossible for this not to be a story. Narrative is our human mode.

Current American fiction is about persons in the 'real situation'. We know this is hopeless and leads nowhere. For this reason, I've called current American fiction 'collaborative'. It is not wedged from its frame by the lever of political alternatives. But the mode of fiction remains. It is the story/narrative. The eternal secret of its success—that wherein it gives the reader pleasure—is that, in reading, one recognizes one's own self moving through the circumstances of the story.

But our story is the transformed circumstances. It is the milieu of the story that is different. The ground is the same, the stew, the tangle of life in which the person is enmeshed, always lovingly, always absurdly. The essential artistry is the same. The shock and pleasure of recognition: 'Yes, that is me. That's how it would be!' The self, the individual, the person who is actual, is the same for all fiction. that person is in some kind of world, familiar enough in the story to be true and recognizable.

That circle is not transformed by utopian dreaming—or *merely* by utopian dreaming. There is always the critique of reason and its themes. The critique of reason, and the impulse of imagining, leads out from the circle of the real, beyond our own space and time. So, of course, the circle becomes a magic circle.

It is as if the individual (drawn, of course, in the round) . . . as he or she is . . . moves through the story, pulled by invisible threads, the ties of fiction, to all that is new and old. That is, to whatever we need for our project, that is appropriate to it.

Of course, it is not the politics of real life, but it is a signification of that. It is a fictional signification. At least it is a kind of flag or emblem held before the hard facts. Or a coat of many colors against the activist's grey. Enmeshed in the hard facts, there will always be time to dream.

Thus the bottom rung of the ladder is restored.

The Saga of the First Ocean Pickup: An Adventure in Applied Social Ecology

Nancy Jack Todd and John Todd

Toward late morning on an overcast Saturday in November of 1982, a crowd of people, well bundled against the light sea breeze, began to assemble on the beach at Vineyard Haven on Martha's Vineyard. The people were as colorfully clad and excited as the day was flatly gray. The focus of their attention was a boat, a newly completed sailing trimaran, that sat perched on the sand, white-painted and angular, with, temporarily, the air of a stranded sea bird. She was not meant to remain beached for long, however, for the upcoming noon was to be the hour of her launching, and her launching was the reason for the continually swelling crowd. The boat about to make its debut was the *Edith Muma*, the first Ocean Pickup, designed by Richard Newick for Ocean Arks International. The history that led up to this moment of launching had been a labyrinthine one, involving, over the years, the founding of two institutes, a number of distant journeys, a stern injunction from Margaret Mead, some detective work, and ongoing financial vicissitudes.

Although the Ocean Pickup is the brainchild of Ocean Arks International, it is also, less directly, an outgrowth of the New Alchemy Institute. With our great friend, the author and biologist Bill McClarney, we founded New Alchemy in 1969 to investigate ecologically sustainable strategies for supporting human populations. We established an institute on Cape Cod and directed our research into the areas of the basic human needs for food, energy, and shelter. The tenet that we adopted for our fledgling institute was nonetheless heartfelt, for all that it might have sounded grandiose to unaccustomed ears. Our letterhead read: 'The New Alchemy Institute: To restore the lands, protect the seas, and inform the Earth's stewards.' By 1976, our various experiments had yielded sufficient data for us to be convinced that viable and realistic alternatives to the industrial paradigm were indeed possible. By about the same time, the Institute was beginning to be sufficiently well known and accepted for many of us to be invited to travel widely to discuss the results and implications of our work. We had realized from the beginning a necessity for what was almost a conspiratorial aspect to what we were doing, living as we do surrounded by a materialistic, consumer-oriented society. We hold the conviction that, no matter how innovative and appropriate an idea seemed at its inception, that, before attempting to implement it, we try to imagine how it will eventually affect the poorest third of humanity. The longer we worked in the field, the more it had become self-evident that true ecological design cannot be divorced from social justice. Biological equity in the form of fair access to, and distribution of, basic resources is inseparably interwoven with the conceptualizing and practice of ecological design. It was through our travels, particularly in the Third World, that we had a chance to observe yet another horn of the dilemma that industrialization and an era of cheap fossil fuels had inflicted on less developed areas. Visiting artisanal fisheries in the Indian Ocean, in the South Pacific, and in the Caribbean, we found that rising fuel costs, supply disruptions, and the unavailability of spare engine parts and gear parts, not to mention the disappearance, through rapid deforestation, of traditional boat-building woods, have idled many offshore fleets. We learned that in many places traditional crafts had been abandoned and modern fishing boats adopted in the period between the end of the Second World War and the early 1970s, a time of worldwide economic expansion, which was also characterized by low interest, easy credit, and expanding world markets. With the present global recession and accompanying diminution of foreign credit and foreign exchange resources, the expanded fisheries became vulnerable to the vagaries of international fuel and finance sources over which they had virtually no control. The need to rethink the basis of transport for coastal peoples was becoming increasingly obvious.

The impressions that we had been gathering from our own traveling were reinforced by reports from other parts of the world from a number of our colleagues. Not the least of these was the late Margaret Mead, who gave us a number of instructions on the direction in which she thought the work begun at New Alchemy should go. She was particularly drawn to the idea of sail-powered shipping, which, as the tall ships have proved, have a power of imagery that is difficult to explain. The heart is moved, and perhaps the soul as well, by their elegance and the incipient sense of adventure that stirs at the sight of swift-moving sails on the horizon. More than anything else, they seem to symbolize the possibilities of rising above, rather than being trapped by, the exigencies of the post-petroleum era.

We knew the naval architect Dick Newick by reputation as the designer of the fastest racing yachts in the world. His trimaran racers hold many transoceanic records, and, in 1980, *Moxie*, his 55 foot trimaran, sailed singlehandedly by Phil Weld, who was then 65, won the TransAtlantic OSTAR Race. John learned that Dick Newick had also pioneered a number of new nautical technologies and construction methods. That he might by sympathetic to our kind of thinking was indicated by the fact that he had also designed *SIB*, a light-weight but sturdy sailing fishing craft named after E. F. Schumacher's *Small is Beautiful*.

Fortunately, Dick Newick is almost a neighbor. He lives on Martha's Vineyard, just a short haul across Buzzard's Bay from us. He liked the ideas from the start. After several meetings, he came up with the design for the Pickup. Dick understood that, to have an appreciable impact, the proposed vessel could not in any way seem like second-hand technology. It would have to be as fast or faster than a motor-powered boat, and just as advanced. Auspiciously, over the last decade, there have been a number of related technological developments which, taken together, represent a major breakthrough that could make possible the rebuilding of artisanal fishing fleets.

For a fleet of Ocean Pickups, the economic prospects for a coastal fishery broaden enormously. Fishing and coastal people would find themselves in possession of a fleet largely self-reliant in terms of fuel and equipment. They would have re-established control of most of the building resources, the technology, and the actual construction of their boats, as, ideally, the boats will be built locally of indigenous woods, relying minimally on imported items like the epoxy. The construction methods should ensure that the boats will be long-lived and require very little in the way of maintenance. The boats would easily be replaced when necessary.

Hidden in our agenda of bringing back working sailing craft for functional transport and transportation is an attempt at land restoration as well, just as during our early work we concentrated on the land, knowing that one day we would turn to the sea. Embodied in the plan for using scrub trees as a building material is the hope that the impulse to plant fast-growing trees, which would be ready for use within a foreseeable time-frame, say 5–7 years, is more compelling than planting trees that take generations to grow. For most people, the pressing demands of the moment make this an almost gratuitous act. In such circumstances, for stewardship to have any meaning, the results have to be perceived as achievable within a realizable period of time. Planting even weed or scrub trees in a world of deserts on the march is a workable first step. A more quixotic hope is that perhaps a few of the remaining giants of the forest may be spared in preference to smaller trees with shorter generation spans.

There was more hope than skepticism apparent in the faces of well-wishers on the Vineyard Haven beach as noon approached on that gray November day. The crowd grew larger, shifting feet moving and regrouping. Greetings and conversation rose and were carried on the cool, light wind. We had invited The Very Reverend James Parks Morton of the Cathedral Church of St John the Divine in New York City, a dear friend and staunch supporter of ecological restoration through his work at the Cathedral, to bless the boat before it was launched. Noon was the time we had chosen because we wished to begin with the United Nation's Prayer for Peace, a prayer intended to be said at noon every day around the world, so that it is continuously circling the Earth. This helped to set the context for the launching of a boat which, like the bioshelter, is intended to help create an infrastructure of non-exploitive technologies to foster a peaceful world.

It was very quiet for a moment as we listened to Dean Morton, many of us half praying, half willing that the Ocean Pickup fulfil its intended promise and help to move us a little closer to peace with the living world and among ourselves. Then the *Edith Muma* was carried across the sand and rose in the water. The crew climbed aboard and set the sails, and she flew off across the harbor.

Subsequent to the launching, the *Edith Muma* underwent a season of testing for both sailing and fishing ability in the cold winter waters of Cape Cod. Having lived up to the expectations of sailors and fishermen alike, she set sail for a 3500 mile voyage to Guyana in South America, where she was tested by Guyanese fishermen for suitability as a replacement for the motor-drive, drift-gill net vessels they could no longer afford to put to sea. The fishermen were delighted with her performance, as were many of the staff of the Department of Fisheries. Elsewhere in the Government there was less enthusiasm, perhaps because a return to sail without fuel restrictions would make it harder to control travel, trade, and smuggling, and the Government bureaucracy showed signs of equivocating indefinitely. Meanwhile, we had received the following letter from the manager of a fishermen's cooperative in Costa Rica, La Cooperativa de Prescadores del Litoral Atlantico.

Dear Sir:

We are very much interested in doing sea trial of your one-ton pick up vessel.

Our association is composed of 208 inshore artisanal fishermen (from the coast of Atlantic Limon, Costa Rica) with a lot of commercial problems.

We think this boat will be of great help to resolve some of our critical conditions, such as high costs of fuel and replacement parts for use of our out board. Owing to these facts, our activity became non-profitable.

We sincerely hope that you will give us the opportunity of testing one these boats.

Our response to the appeal was to set sail once again, this time 2000 miles across the Spanish Main to the village of Puerto Limon, where the fishing co-op is based. As of this writing, the Pickup has been fishing out of Puerto Viejo since March 1984, adapting to local fishermen and conditions and fishing techniques. As the skills of everyone have improved, the Ocean Arks' people getting to know more about fishing in that area and the fishermen adjusting to the boat, performance has gotten better all round. The pickup is unusually stable and has enough deck space for half-a-dozen fishermen to bring their gear on board so they operate it cooperatively as a fishing station. The boat also has the advantage of being able to get to areas beyond the range of an outboard-powered dugout canoe. At dawn, it sails with gill-net fishermen to the mackerel grounds where they set their nets, to return at dusk. During the day, other men from the village use it for handling snapper or diving for lobster. Not long ago, the *Edith Muma* brought back a catch of fish and lobsters to Puerto Viejo that made for the best Christmas in quite sometime.

We are just beginning the next phase of the project, which will include building, locally in the village, newer, smaller versions of the original Pickup. These will be the half-ton catamarans or two-hulled boats, designed by Dick Newick around the specifications of the fishermen who have sailed on the *Edith Muma*. At the rate the *Edith Muma* was bringing in fish and lobsters before Christmas, a half-ton Pickup could pay for itself in a month or less. The idea is to establish a local training and boat-building facility which would employ villagers and use regional forest products to make the boats. Once we start the building program, we also plan to start planting fast-growing trees on eroded hillsides to produce boat woods and, at the same time, begin land restoration in the area. On the sea side of things, we want to test and tend the kinds of equipment being used in the local fishery and to explore currently untapped marine resources.

It is hoped that with time the Ocean Pickup and its fleet of smaller Pickups will enhance and make more independent the economy of the area around Puerto Viejo by acting as a catalyst to a diversified fishery, aquaculture, and agriculture, as well as to local manufacturing. It is, of course, almost impossible to be sure in advance whether any project, however well-intentioned, will achieve the original goals. Inevitably, there will be unforseen side-effects. We continue to learn more and more, *in situ*, about the potential pitfalls, as well as benefits, inherent in ecologically based projects. With the Pickup, as with our work since the early days, part of the ongoing process is to evolve and articulate a theory and a replicable methodology which will prove adapted to diverse natural and social ecologies. The obvious long-term hope is a stable and diverse natural ecology which nurtures and is nurtured by the members of an equitable society. That, quite literally, is the direction in which Ocean Arks has set its sails.

Rights and Reality

Karl Hess

Social Ecology has performed the distinct service of demanding that human action be considered as a factor in the study of natural systems. Legislative acts are seen as transforming the landscape as much, for instance, as a volcanic eruption. Of human actions, none seems more powerful a tool for impacting the natural world than the attribution of rights. Rights are declared in order to empower the endless perturbation of ecosystems. Rights are declared to define ecosystems and to allocate them. Rights are declared to conserve and rights are declared to despoil. The concept of rights is a sword with two edges.

The biblically stated right of human beings to command nature collides impatiently with the scientific method's slow experimental efforts to understand nature. The environmentalist notion of social rights to an uncluttered atmosphere collides directly with the economist's notion of the right to use raw materials in the most efficient way possible while everyone's right to whatever they have in mind collides directly with the politician's mission to define those rights and allocate force to eliminate some and reinforce others. Any concept of rights, in my view, is an invitation to trouble and, perhaps, disaster.

The observable situation is that there are no rights. Every single thing that is called right is and always has been nothing more than a statement of a particular opinion or preference. Consider for a moment what would happen if a right were to be pronounced by people in the middle of a field. Let us say that they pronounce the currently popular 'right for every human being to have enough food to sustain life'. Having pronounced it, let us suppose that they sit down and wait for the right to be translated into action. The people would simply starve. The mere proclamation of the right would not produce food.

Now, what about the right that people have to strike out on their own and seek food rather waiting for it? To be sure, that could be called a right. Unless, of course, uncaring, uncultured, and violent people surround the field and will not permit the people egress. But

THEY have no right to keep the people from seeking food! Sure. Tell that to violent brutes—or to the college-graduate members of an élite police force assigned to contain a certain population in an infertile area.

So long as any discussion of the natural world is one that seeks to state or discern rights, then the discussion should be labelled for what it is—a search for power. Rights are power, the power of someone or some group over someone else. Even considering rights as descended directly from Heaven, with God's signature hot upon them, the very next consideration will be to provide the temporal power to bop upon the head anyone who will not respect (i.e. obey) the right.

The belief that there are rights which seem to be enforced without head-bopping is an illusion. Name one. Neither Christ upon his cross nor Mohammed upon his rock made any provision for what could be called a Sacred Defense Initiative in which some supernatural force would zap anyone not respecting a religiously proclaimed right. After religiously proclaimed rights, of course, it must be obvious that all other rights are human contrivances.

There are those who, admitting that rights are never real, nonetheless feel that they are a powerful rhetorical tool to make discussions of conduct more transcendental than a crude discussion of power. A strong argument is made that there is at least a natural right, professed by most people, asserting that one's personal boundaries should not be violated aggressively and without permission. Most people probably would agree to that—if not as a part of a developed theory, at least as a personal belief.

Even admitting that this is a benign and generally demonstrable statement, I cannot see that it is a wise one. Let in the merest mention of rights, even restricting that mention to the single most agreeable right, and the door is flung open for an ever-escalating war of rights against rights. Introduce rights into any discussion and the chances seem overwhelming that instead of clarity and an endowment of sacred importance, you will get confrontation, bared fangs, bared interests. Rather than discussing possibly mutual interests in non-violent and reciprocal conduct, those who introduce rights into the conversation are actually introducing one or more combative lines which one crosses at the risk of open combat, one person's right facing off, armed to the teeth, against someone else's right.

The right to life, a currently popular right, offers an example. As one bitter commentary puts it, the anti-abortionists believe that life begins with conception and ends with birth. The right of the fetus, in other words, is simply selected out as a particular cause for concern.

Right to life is not stated as an absolute and all-inclusive right, although the very wording certainly suggests such a universal concern. The right-to-life movement does not, to pursue this point, include a correlated statement that all humans have a right to life. To say such a thing, it must be obvious, would be to undercut the power of the very State upon which the anti-abortionists now depend for the eradication of what they see as a particular evil. What they seek, explicitly, is power—the power to punish any who would take the life of a fetus. That is not a right to life for the fetus, which may under circumstances be killed secretly and illicitly. It is a right of punishment for the victors in a legislative putsch.

If the State had no right to kill, then it could not even be a State. Lacking the ability, in the long run, to kill, how would a State impress itself upon other States, or protect itself against them, or even remain sovereign over citizens? The absolute essence of State power, from its ability to collect taxes to its ability to fend off invasion, depends without any equivocation upon its ability (its 'right') to assign its agents to kill someone. The greatest 'good' that it does (say, solace the sick with services paid by taxes) is based upon the State's power to punish and, if need be, kill anyone who resists. But how can that be true in instances when the state merely wants to arrest someone who does not 'have the right' to violate State law? Surely that's not a lethal intent. Nonsense! Unless the right to arrest is coupled with the right to kill, then arrest would be a game roughly like Rugby football, full of bruises and contusions but with precious few appearances in court.

People always have been and always will be killed for trifling reasons, so long as any institution claims the right to protect itself and codify that right into either the legislative act of a democracy or the ukase of a tyranny. But, whether the reason is trifling or profound, the fact remains: the right to life is nowhere on this planet, in any agreed or widespread way, paramount to the might of political power. There simply is not, in short, any right to life. Those who say that there is are, literally, saying only that they feel strongly that people, or some people, should live. No matter how grandly they clothe their statement of rights, it boils down to their own opinion (or ideology), and to become generally effective will do so by raw, brute power; the power to kill. The alternative, in which people voluntarily agree to do something or abide by something is not a right at all, but an agreement.

As given as I am to utopian dreaming, even I cannot imagine a group of people living together on the basis of rights alone. They may agree to certain things and, as a libertarian, I acclaim all voluntary agreements, but they cannot be unmindful that the agreement is just that, and does not constitute any sort of bond beyond that. It can be broken by the will of a human being, just as it was formed by the will of human beings. Powerful and often binding cultures can grow around such agreements, to be sure, but it will be continuity of agreement and not rights which keep them going. And when there is a breach of the agreements, the next decision of interest will be whether the other people involved will want to punish the person in disagreement, to expel the person, or simply ignore the offense. No matter the decision, the lie will be put to the idea that the group was living together on the basis of rights. They were living together on the basis of agreements, the very best thing that human beings can come up with as a guarantor of peace and fair dealing.

Why humans should be ashamed to call their extraordinary capacity to agree with one another just that and only that is beyond me. To agree seems wonderfully human. To talk of rights floating above our heads must invoke the superhuman, the supernatural, the theological. Only by proclaiming rights as divine, it seems to me, can they be elevated beyond the statues of agreements.

In every instance where the capacity to agree has been codified into some right or another, I have seen or sensed mischief. The glorious Bill of Rights of the U.S. Constitution would be altogether glorious if seen as simply a guideline for agreement, a statement of what it is reasonable people might want to assure each other about when settling down to live together.

Alas, it is nothing of the sort. It is, instead, a mere detail in a writ which, as its most overpowering effect, grants absolute powers to the State and even provides that no-one may withdraw from that power no matter how grievously offended they might be. Pardon, the Constitution doesn't actually come right out and say that. What it does is to give a certain group the 'right' to interpret its every word. And, quite sensibly from an institutional point of view, one of those interpretations makes it criminal to secede from the thrall of the Constitution without being granted specific and official membership in some other Nation-State.

How then does the social ecologist go about impressing the good sense of scientific discovery, or intuitive pleas about natural systems upon people who may be inclined to ignore all such knowledge, in much the way a person suspecting a carcinoma might reject any examinations for fear that the data might be depressing? How to impress on anyone that reality, the natural order of things, is even important at all, when so many live in a world populated by slippery, spooky rights which can leap and tumble over mere observation at the prodding of any passion, greed, or interest?

I hope that social ecologists will find ways to do it without proclaiming rights. If rights are all that social ecologists can proclaim, then they will just be making another bit of noise in an already crowded atmosphere in which everyone's rights are jostling everyone else's.

Perhaps, therefore, social ecologists must resign themselves to living on the basis of their own discoveries (being exemplary), sharing their information directly with people whom they know (being good neighbors), sharing it also with people whom they do not know (being publicists and educators), and working toward social organizations in which people must confront directly their own responsibility for making decisions regarding the natural world of which they are a part.

So long as people derive rights from institutions of power, there will be little enthusiasm for the merely objective knowledge of living systems and consequences attendant upon exercising human will in them. The natural system will continue to be seen as subordinate to the rights of the institution.

Where environmentalists may see bad laws as the tools with which their personal concept of proper rights are denied, or good laws as a way to establish those proper rights, the social ecologist should see law itself as a problem. Law is merely specific interest made enforceable. Law proceeds from institutions and contending interests. It can no more be balanced and without bias than the observations of science can be free of the effect of the observer. Living systems, on the other hand, are information that is material. Humans are a part of these systems and endowed with the particular sort of consciousness that makes them able to be concerned about the consequences of their actions.

In social ecology, we are faced, therefore, with an unenviable but inevitable responsibility. We must make as clear as we can that the natural world in which we live presents us with no model for any declaration of rights. It presents us, instead, with certainty that every action has consequences—it does not have any rightness or wrongness, it just has consequences. It is we, and not Nature, who deal in taxonomies of right and wrong. But what a grave responsibility this is!

And yet, should we do more than study and reveal consequences, should we ever become deeply involved in pressing Nature, and our fellow humans, into the mold of our own privilege or preference, we would have stepped from the study of ecology to the practice of law, force, and power.

What humans do is part of, and not apart from, Nature. What they do often seems hideous and, indeed, some feel the entire race to be beyond redemption or even utility. Should that be a sound observation then, of course, the race will end. The rest of the natural world will proceed without it. To be sure, there is a sad possibility here. If, indeed, humans have become a pestilence, then there seems little doubt that they will make their ultimate proof of it in the form of a nuclear or biological war. Should that happen, it would simply end the human cycle. Some life would remain, probably. And even if none did, the barren planet could be re-seeded with life from elsewhere. Or failing even that, the Earth would just join other dead rocks whirling in a universe of such mysterious dimensions that even the dead rocks may be a part of the multi-galactic ecology.

My own feeling is far more optimistic. Perhaps we are as inimical to most life as the most plaguing virus. But we have a not altogether bad record for self-correction. For correction, there needs to be information that is whole and encompassing. We must understand consequences, not as isolated and single items, but as a part of the whole, so that eventually we can begin to see the entirety of life itself. This is the information sought by the social ecologist. And it, not any theory of rights, holds bright promise for our future.

If we become bound in any way to rights, we may once again constrict our study and help restrict all study to matters compartmentally contained within the laws and powers of institutions of force. The ecological view has helped break through those compartments into the good and common sense of whole and related systems. Those whole and related systems, including the zones of our human residency, do not have rights. They simply are.

Discontent with such simple observations have, in the past, led us to mold gods out of thin air and heavy dread, to erect great political structures on concepts of right or wrong, to plunge into wars, to fall into great errors of false pride, to consider ourselves as separate from and not a part of the natural order, to proclaim dominion over even that which we do not understand or cannot see.

The ecological view does not restrain the human mind. That probably could not be done by any view or power short of extinction. Some human mind seems always poised on the edge of mystery, poking and probing for a way past dimness or darkness. We really must live with that. Efforts to stifle human curiosity seem to me inhuman. But reckless refusal to understand the consequences of curiosity is sheer folly. We humans will likely ask every question. We need urgently to understand the changes created in our world by every answer. The ecological view does, all rights and ideology aside, simply bid us to try, to the extent that we may, to try to know what the hell we are doing when we do it.

This is not our right. It is just a thing we can do.

In San Salvador

Grace Paley

I

Come   look   they said
here are the photograph albums
these are our children

We are called   The Mothers   of the Disappeared
we are also the mothers of those who were seen once more
and then photographed   sometimes parts of them
could not be found

a breast   an eye   an arm is missing
sometimes a whole stomach
that is why we are called   The Mothers
of the Disappeared   although we have these large
heavy photograph albums full of beautiful
torn faces

II

Then one woman spoke   About my son
she said   I want to tell you   This
is what happened

        I heard a cry   Mother
mother   keep the door closed   a scream
the high voice of my son   his scream
jumped into my belly   his voice
boiled there and boiled until hot water
ran down my thigh

        The following week I waited
by the fire making tortilla   I heard   What?
the voice of my second son   Mother   quickly
turn your back to the door   turn your back
to the window

        And one day of the third week
my third son called me   oh mother   please
hurry up   hold out your apron   they are
stealing my eyes

        And then in the fourth week   my
fourth son   No

        No   it was morning   he stood
in the doorway   he was taken right
there   before my eyes the parts of
the body of my son were tormented   are
you listening?   do you understand
this story?   there was only one
child   one boy   like Mary   I had
only one son

PART THREE
A NEW VISION OF THE SELF

Human Nature, Freedom, and Spirit
Joel Kovel

The self-regulating character of natural process is an axiom for social ecology. The order, harmony and symmetry of the natural world stand in sharp contrast to the disequilibrium and chaos of human society, manifest as ruthless exploitation of the ecosphere and social domination, with its inevitable train of 'isms—militarism, racism, sexism, and so forth. Non-human life, by contrast, exists within an immense matrix of checks and balances. Its ecological lawfulness stems not from any conscious decision on the part of one creature or another, but from the collective inability of all creatures to step out of line. Each living non-human being pursues its survival interest (as individual or species), at times at the expense of other beings, at times in cooperation with them, but never outside the mutually interrelated framework of all beings. Those creatures who behave with reckless abandon are quickly snuffed out, no matter where they may be situated in the chain of being. And the survivors survive with each other. The most predatory relations between particular living creatures are, from the standpoint of the whole of life, manifestations of utter dependency. Thus, all beings contain each other. The colossal blue whale lives within the being of the tiny krill it consumes by the billion, and vice versa. And so on, upwards, downwards, inwards or outwards, to the edge of the universe.

Except for humans, or as we can say here with genderic accuracy, 'Man'. Man is the only creature who has been able, until now, to step out of line and get away with it. As the only being with the gall to consider himself the Lord of Creation, Man is only too capable of not recognizing himself in the beings subject to his dominion. For Man, reckless abandon is the hallmark of his tenure on earth; and if he has not been snuffed out so far, it is due only to the fiendish ingenuity of the technological means he has developed to squeeze the ecosphere out of ever more 'raw materials' and energy, and to perfect the domination of his fellow creatures.

The ecological—and social-ecological—impulses grow out of the crisis induced by human recklessness. Social ecology in particular is a call for people to rethink their domination of nature, and to change this relationship in practice. The principal insight of social ecology is to identify domination, and the resulting chaos, as a function of estrangement from nature. And its principal practice is that of a reconciliation with nature—a reclamation of our natural tendencies, whether through direct transactions with the material world (food production, nutrition, etc.) or within social relationships (feminism, building community, etc.)

But these laudable projects are predicated on something which is assumed rather than demonstrated, namely, that we have, within our own being, such 'natural tendencies' as should be reclaimed. They are, in other words, statements grounded in a notion of 'human nature'. And this raises a problem, particularly for a movement on the Left, such as Social Ecology. For the Left has something of a taboo towards ideas concerning human nature. The Right, on the other hand, seizes avidly upon the theme. To practice a reconciliation with nature, we have to appeal to human nature; but in so doing we draw on something that has been by and large appropriated by conservative discourse.

It is not hard to see why. For 'nature' connotes what is merely animal, unchanging and prior to human effort. Nothing is better suited than an appeal to nature to deny the possibility of historical change, much less amelioration. If black slaves, 'by nature' are simple creatures, and close to the land, then why bother to free them? This kind of argument was regularly made in defense of slavery (and now of apartheid); and a similar line of reasoning has classically been adopted to prove, for example, that women, being closer to nature, are suited by divine plan for reproduction rather than the demands of 'civilization'. It is hard to find a pernicious tendency that has not been justified by an appeal to human nature. By contrast, people interested in progressive social change take the tack that we are not locked, 'by nature', into any pattern of behavior. This line of reasoning tends to maintain a more or less absolute division between the human and natural world. Animals and other 'lower' creatures have fixed instinctual natures; whereas human nature, if it exists at all, is defined by plasticity and the capacity to transcend instinct. In the classical nature-nurture debate, the Left, with good reason, comes down solidly on the side of the latter term.

There is another aspect to the meaning of human nature, which gives the progressive cause even more grief. This is the exceedingly widespread notion that human beings 'by nature' wicked, sinful, egoistic, and foolish creatures. It is remarkable how many progressive people share in this conviction, which is typically associated with the conservative political philosophy of Thomas Hobbes, but was also articulated by Shakespeare and many of the greatest observers of the human scene, Freud included. Unlike the fallacy alluded to above, this skeptical judgment on human nature does not rely on any pseudoscientific claims about some oppressed group. It is rather a claim about the general essence of human being, something which holds true for all people in so far as they are human. This is a valid use of the term, nature. We say without difficulty, for example, that it is in the nature of dogs to relate primarily to the person of their master, and cats to the master's dwelling. Moreover, it is much more difficult to dismiss this kind of view about human nature, for however ideologically contaminated it may be (as, for example, in the case of Freud), it also has the wieght of truth we associate with high tragic art. Often skepticism about human nature has a peevish, dog-in-the-manger quality to it; but to dismiss it out of hand means turning away from what we generally recognize to be among the greatest products of the human mind. It is not, after all, a very persuasive argument to dismiss the view of human nature as expressed, say, in *King Lear* or *The Brothers Karamazov* as an ideological distortion imposed by the patriarchal family. One might well say that Shakespeare and Dostoevsky are representing the awful truth of the patriarchal family, and that their art, like all great art, has a subversive and critical function because of its utter truthfulness. We might want, because of our experience of this truth, to be rid of patriarchy, as in my opinion we should. But it is impossible to avoid the impression that what they are representing has a deeply 'nature-al' character. We may not be in a position yet to describe very well what this means, but it is hard to avoid an impression that tragedy indicates properties of the self which in some way 'come before' institutional formations, such as patriarchy and capitalism, and are drawn into these as well as other kinds of domination. In any case, I think it fair to say that the claims of a skeptical view of human nature are exactly those of tragedy. If tragedy has any truthfulness for us, if, that is, we think that the representation of human beings as creatures capable of tragic flaws is a deeply true statement, then we are not entitled to make any simple identity between emancipation and human nature.

And this leaves the social ecology movement in something of a quandary. For social ecology is nothing if not emancipatory in intent; and its principal thesis, as noted above, is the reconciliation with nature, which must include our tragic capacity. On what rational basis can we claim that putting ourselves in touch with our 'natural' feelings and impulses will fulfil the project of social ecology? Given the real behavior of people—the copious evidence of egoism, power-hunger, hostility and plain cantankerousness, to mention only a few of the better-known vices—what entitles us to believe that it is not better, in the long run, to actually suppress rather than express our inner nature? Perhaps the truth about human nature is that it indeed breaks with the rest of nature—that we are a sport, a genetic freak who has lost the internal capacity to stay in line with the universe.

I am not going to put these doubts to rest. I am not sure I can do so in any case, but certainly not within these brief confines. I can only offer here some ruminations as might enable us to frame some useful questions with which to address human nature.

I think we should begin by recognizing that, whatever the cause, we remain defined as creatures with a problematic relation to nature. In other words, there is something *essential* about human beings which sits uneasily with the rest of nature, and cannot be collapsed into the kind of mutual interrelatedness that marks the remainder of living creatures. It is no verbal trick to claim that 'human nature' consists of actively establishing some distinction, or separateness, between ourselves and the remainder of the universe. The simple fact that we regard our nature, and the relation with nature, as a problem bears witness to this overriding truth about human beings.

Now there is a great deal to be said about this conjuncture, and I can do no more than suggest a few of the themes which arise from it before passing on to the main portion of my argument. In the first place, the terms 'some distinction' and 'separateness' are very abstract categories, encompassing within their conceptual boundaries a veritable bestiary of implication. We might say, roughly, that the possibilities range between a kind of distinction called 'splitting', and another called 'differentiation'. It will be helpful to bear in mind that when two entities *split* one from another they separate completely, neither being mirrored in one another nor maintaining any connection thereafter. On the other hand, when they *differentiate* from each other, they remain associated, connected, and, indeed, mirrored, so that each could recognize itself in the other. The point of this conceptual byplay is obviously to give us room within the basic framework of human nature for outcomes that we consider bad and those we consider good, and to do so within an ecological perspective. Splitting, in this sense, reflects what we don't want—even if we have to recognize its reality and power over human life; it is the basic property of domination, whether of class, sex, race, or more generally, of nature itself. The dominator, in other words, must dissociate from, and not recognize himself or herself in the dominated. Differentiation, on the other hand, represents what we strive for: it is that outcome of human nature in the direction of ecological interrelatedness and the essential unity of all beings. It is important to keep in mind, however, that neither of these ends of the spectrum represents an absolute (except in death). No splitting ever denies the essential interdependence of all creatures (the master needs his slave, the capitalist his proletarian, the ascetic his body); and no degree of differentiation is ever so finely drawn as to obliterate the essential differentness between human beings and other forms of life—and the tragic implications this holds.

It should also be pointed out that although classical Marxism and social ecology are not on the best of terms, the view of human nature expressed here is Marxist as well as social-ecological. To be more exact, it is a view compatible with a reading of Marxism, although by no means the only compatible view—nor necessarily the predominant view among actual Marxists, including Marx, who is open to much challenge on this point. Nevertheless, there is an approach to historical materialism that is, in my opinion, consistent with a differentiated approach toward nature. We cannot address this theme adequately here, except to say that it builds upon Marx's claim, in his *1844 Manuscripts*, and again in *Capital*, that we are part of nature as well as the transformer of nature. Indeed, there is probably no more fundamental or concise statement of Marx's ontology than this. The labor process is the conscious transformation of nature by means of which we create objects in the world, and, in so doing, create ourselves as transformed beings. Marx's key notion of alienation expresses more or less exactly the idea of splitting as applied to labor and the class struggle. And the revolutionary goal of a classless society is in all fundamental respects the overcoming of splitting and the rise of a truly differentiated, i.e. fully human, being.

But neither Marxism nor classical anarchism has ever bothered much with the actual 'nature' of such a fully realized, differentiated human being. Preoccupied with the external, object world, they fail to investigate the subjective conditions of emancipation and domination. Whether social ecology can go further depends upon the degree it can appropriate what has been left up until now to frank mysticism or bourgeois disciplines such as psychoanalysis: the domain of the self. The track record of radicals in this respect has not been encouraging so far. In the face of all evidence to the contrary, they have continued to assume that rearranging the world will in itself bring about the free realization of human beings. To use the terms we are developing here, in conventional radical practice, subjectivity is split away from the external object world instead of differentiated from it. And this, as they used to say in the 1960s, is part of the problem instead of the solution.

Towards an Ecology of the Self

But can there be an 'ecology' of the self? The term certainly sounds
virtuous. It would make a good slogan, neat and appealing enough to
deflect critical enquiry. Once we take a closer look, however, the fit
is not so neat. In fact, we have to ask whether there is a fundamental
contradiction between the *logos* of the self and ecological fittedness.

Subjectivity, or inwardness, appears to be a property—potential, at
any rate—of living matter. We know it more commonly by the name
of consciousness. Its presence seems to depend on the complexification
of life to the point where nervous tissue appears. We should be open
to the possibility that all life possesses some degree of consciousness,
as is suggested, for example, by studies of plants. Indeed, given a
processual view of physical reality, such as was developed by Whitehead,[1] we should even be open to the presence of some kind of rudimentary consciousness in all matter. Consciousness is not simply passive recognition, it necessarily depends also on an organism's activity
in the world, which is to say, its ecological interrelatedness. In this
respect, all beings are differentiated from each other through their
ecological activity; and their consciousness is the mark of their differentiation. One cannot become conscious of a thing if one is identical
to that thing. Some separateness must occur, some distanciation, if
consciousness is to take place—and this requires a being's activity in
the world, and its alteration of other beings as a result of that activity.
Because being is not passive but gained through an organism's activity,
consciousness is of what one is not. Consciousness registers the alteration made in reality as a result of the activity through which being
has been asserted. This is in line with the Hegelian insight that consciousness arises through negating other beings. Consciousness is of
lack; it registers non-being within being.

Differentiation is therefore not simply a property of humanity, but
characterizes all life. What does it mean, then, for a being to become
human? Only this: that a twofold motion of *hyper*differentiation occurs.
This double transformation consists of the emergence of a particular
gradation within subjectivity, the *self*, and in the same moment, indeed,
as the condition for the emergence of the self, the *projection* of the self
into the world and the alteration of the world to form *objects*. This
latter process we recognize as Marx's labor process; but we now see
(as Marx suggested but never pursued) that the object is subjectified
from the moment of its creation. The world is not simply altered to
make way for an organism; it is not simply negated, in other words.
It is transformed as well to contain the being, now the self, of its
human inhabitant. Indeed, this self-transformed world is nothing other

than 'nature' itself. For infrahuman species, nature as such does not exist: they are already in nature. For us, nature exists because we have lost it. But it never exists 'out there', a passively contemplated object: for us, outside of nature, nature is constructed; it is, and must always be, *Other*. I do not here mean that the Otherness of nature has to be absolute, as it has been constructed by the modern West. In other words, nature can be differentiated as well as split, an ideal that corresponds to the practice of numerous primitive groups. However, even in this ideal case, nature remains Other, as well as constructed. Thus, it makes sense to talk of an alienated relation to nature, and to insist, as social ecologists, that people can achieve this, or at least approximate it very closely. However, lack of alienation means lack of estrangement, and not identity. Nature can be Other, therefore, and still be *recognized*, the way we can love another human being, recognize one's self in him/her, and yet not collapse our beings together (as would happen, for example, in the case of psychosis).

In any case, as soon as humans became such, they insisted upon defining themselves as distinct from nature, even as they recognized themselves in nature. Consider, for example, burial rites, the signs of which tell archeologists that human groups have appeared. To bury its dead with a certain degree of ritual tells us that a creature refuses to accept the facticity of death, with its ultimate dedifferentiation. Only a 'self', a subjectivity with inwardness and self-consciousness, would bother to rearrange and adorn a corpse of its own kind. So it is with the rest of primitive society. The gulf between paleolithic poples, or any aboriginal group, and modern, Cartesianized, atomized 'Man' is enormous. Yet it is not even on the same scale as that between any of these groups and any other living creature, so far as the relation to nature goes.

The same relationship can be drawn from the other end. The self does not arise prior to the transformation of the world, but in the transformation of the world. As the object is made, so is the human subject. As the object is subjectified, so is the subject objectified. The self comes into being only as its being is projected into the world. But this can only mean that human being is divided from the very inception of human subjectivity. We are not merely consciousness, but self-conscious. A reflection has entered subjectivity, and, with it, the world is transformed in human terms.

We know this from common introspection. For the self, the most quintessentially human of developments in the universe, is never (except, perhaps, as the endpoint of extreme mystical practice) homogeneous. Consciousness, the indication of a being's differentiation, is itself differentiated (this is the hyperdifferentiation referred to above) into a center, the 'I', and a periphery containing the object world. Both the I-center and the object-periphery are capable of crucially different variations according to social conditions. But they do not collapse into one another. Setting aside the possibility of mystical experience, to which we will briefly return below, the 'I' remains distinct from its representations even though it has created them and invested them with its own being. This reflects the fact that for human being to come into existence, the self projects itself into objects as it is created. And these objects, however subjectified, belong to the material universe; they are physically other than the self's body. The boundaries of the self always exceed the material limits of its substratum. This is so whether we are talking of the elementary social relation to other body-selves, or of the projection of the self into the natural universe as such. We may express this situation phenomenologically by saying that within the self the object-periphery contains a degree (depending on many conditions, including, foremost, social arrangements) of *Otherness*. Nature, as we have noted, is the universal Other—and God may be described as the absolute Other. But there are many particular Others as well, depending upon history. We cannot of course take them up here, but it is remarkable to what extent history itself is a record of Otherness.

Because the self contains the topology of the I and the Other, any facile identification between the human and natural worlds is cast into a deep shade. The very notion of self means, irrespective of any patho-logical distortions forced upon it by capitalism, patriarchy, or whatever historical condition, a degree of radical separateness from the universe. 'Self' entails an internally coherent point of distinction: an 'I' that posits itself outside the flux of universal being. Whether the self exists 'in-itself' or 'for-itself', it is still itself, standing apart from the universe, non-identical to any other being. There is, in other words, a certain primary alienation to human being, an aloneness outside the living web of interconnectedness which forms the ground of ecology.

I am not lamenting this fact, though it surely underlies the tragic qualities of human existence—and this is at least as true for primitives, who have a highly developed sense of tragic and existential givens, as it is for us.[2] There is no point at all in lamenting the facts, since the 'I' who may bother to lament is a being who owes the capacity to lament to his or her being human. And we may just as well be proud as ashamed of this humanness (though there is no point in this either), since everything we value is a product of our aloneness, or, to be more exact, of our efforts to overcome it. The making of objects in the world—to return to Marx's notion of labor—is never reducible to utilitarian principles. When labor is not alienated—consider the play of a healthy child, or aesthetic production—it is responsive to the need of overcoming the self's aloneness. And because no objective transformation can overcome an ontological condition, labor has to continually rework the object world—this being another way of saying that we are a creative species. Language itself is a product of the self's hyperdifferentiation, for if consciousness were undivided there would be no need to exceed the level of the sign. And if the Other could be named, there would be no poetry. Finally, without the self's ontological isolation, desire would never arise. Human sexuality would be reduced to procreation, and love, as problematical as it may be, would not exist.

Obviously, we cannot pursue these matters here. But perhaps it can be seen how ill they fit into ecological clothes. For each human quality, whether valued like language or cursed like domination, occurs because of a refusal to accept the given—a stepping out of line, we might say. If we were not skewed from the universe, nothing we deem desirable, indeed, the very existence of desire and value itself, would ever come to be. Taken all in all, it seems that the primary ecological relation of the self is that of negation. This does not mean that the self does not also include nature. It does, for the simple reason that we are flesh. But it *defines itself*, i.e. comes into being as a self, through an act of refusal; and nature becomes that which is refused, even as it is reincorporated. How else are we to understand—to take but one, albeit very important, fact—the necessity for preparing, i.e. transforming, food, and eating it in a certain 'anti-natural' way? All the 'natural living' in the world will not eradicate this essential human tendency.

Because of this basic negativity, the relationship between the self and nature cannot be comprehended through any simply extrapolation of an ecological model grounded in unity in diversity. We are too cantakerous a creature for that. It must be stressed, however, that this by no means dooms social ecology to irrelevance: the fundamental, life-threatening imbalance with nature remains in any case, and defines the ecological project. Put another way, being skewed from the universe is one thing, but being berserk is another, and it is the job of social ecology to deal with the distinction. Here Murray Bookchin's principle of not assimilating social ecology to environmentalism or any other biologistically aligned model comes home stronger than ever. If the relation of the self to ecology is negative, then the term, 'social ecology', comprises a dialectical practice defined by the play of opposites and a certain irreducible existential tension. For this very reason, freedom becomes its primary category. And so we have to define the self and its relation to nature in such a way that the category of freedom can be developed.

Ego and Spirit

We have seen that the general notion of human being is expressed in the form of the self. But it is not yet clear as to how the critical qualities of splitting and differentiation can be deployed within varying configurations of selfhood. A moment's reflection tells us, however, that the answer to this problem should be close at hand. As theoretical and abstruse as some of the issues may be, their ultimate point of reference is in lived human life, and must be expressible in ordinary language.

Or rather, at least one pole, that of differentiation, should be express-ible in ordinary language. The other pole, that of splitting, requires an expression standing apart from everyday life, for the obvious reason that its point of reference is in the élite rather than the masses. And for this purpose we have a handy term, recently appropriated by psychoanalysis, but of an ancient lineage and in the public domain— the 'Ego'.

As the Greek term for 'I', Ego refers to self-experience; and as the Freudian term for the effectual, reality-oriented portion of the 'mental apparatus', Ego becomes a good way of describing the self-experience of domination, and the mental organ of splitting. Of course, this is not how the Freudians and the mental health establishment regard the term. For them, Ego has a value-free connotation as a coherent ensem-ble of functional mental relationships. It is what gets us to work on time, represses the unrealistic and threatening mental contents of the 'Id', and in general handles what the eminent ego-psychologist Heinz Hartmann termed[3] (in a deliberate appropriation of biological dis-course) the 'adaptation to reality'. In the most widely adopted psycho-analytic perspective, Ego is refined into an organ of the psyche, as though it were a mental mapping of the central nervous system which is presumed to be its 'seat'. In the harmonious domain of the Ego, the Self is considered one of the Ego's subfunctions, along with reality-testing, motility, repression, and so forth.

This is not the place to take up the poverty of psychoanalytic theory. But a glance at what has been said so far will tell us that once the notion of the Ego has been stripped of its scientistic gloss, it emerges as a pretty fair specimen of what we mean by the form of self-experi-ence called splitting. And we can also see why this should be identified with domination.

If we regard Ego not as an organ in the natural world but a lived form of historical experience (that is, if we reverse the reification of psychoanalysis and place Ego within Self instead of the other way around), we see that egoic being is self-experience in which the rational-istic, all-knowing 'I' crowds out every other phenomenon. In an egoic topology of the self, ontological space is occluded by the I-center. There is no recognition therefore of self in other, and the sharpest of boundaries is drawn between Ego and Id. Three interconnected kinds of practical consequence, each of great importance, result.

1 The object-world is regarded as immediately without value, and is treated in a dehumanized way. If the egoic self is white (which turns out historically to have been the case), it regards any non-white human being as less than human, i.e. in a racist way; if the egoic self is male (which turns out historically to have been the case), it regards any female being as less than human, i.e. in a sexist way; if the egoic self is bourgeois (which turns out historically to have been the case), it regards any proletarian as less than human, i.e. freely engages in capitalist relations. Generally speaking, the egoic position is one that regards all of nature as without value: as inert matter, 'stuff', raw materials. The Ego is therefore the commodifier as such, the pure culturer of exchange-value, the technocrat.

2 The Ego inhabits a purified zone of rationalization. This is masculine, and the forms of Otherness created in the egoic mode are also configured by maleness. In fact, the egoic mode is that species of self-experience whose dynamic of desire is, precisely, the Oedipus complex. The Freudian hypostatization of the Oedipus complex to the status of a universal demands that the Ego be hypostatized too; each concept demands the other. Together, Ego and Oedipus define the subjective relations of domination.

3 Because of the radical distinction between the Ego and its Oedipal desire, a heightened sense of Otherness ensues, continually repelled by bourgeois rationalization, and just as continually returning. Egoic experience gravitates toward paranoia, and is so precisely because of the splitting and domination conjugated into it. The psychoanalytic division between Ego and Id is puffed up techonocratically into a paradigm of rational function. The concrete effects, however, are the repression of the body and the inevitable return of the repressed. Ecologically, nature turns into wilderness which must be 'tamed', i.e. paved, converted into Disneyworlds, or simple raw materials. Thus, the splitting of the Subject results in the dedifferentiation of the Object. From another angle, the sacred is lost, madness appears as radical alienation, and the stage is set for the spectacular persecutions which have graced the twentieth century, age of the Holocaust, anticommunist crusades, and nuclear terror.[4]

Egoic experience reflects one pole of the possibilities afforded to the self, that of non-recognition and splitting with nature. This is manifest subjectively as the split between Ego and Id; organismically as the (Cartesian) split between the all-active, knowing dematerialized Mind and the brutally material body; and historically in the domination of nature. Ego is thus the specific antagonist of any emancipatory project. It is what an ecologically sensitive practice must overcome.

But what possibilities for the Self exist on the other side? What is the emancipatory potential within self-experience? Here, in contrast to the notion of the Ego, we must break with established 'psy' discourse[5] and find our bearings in primitive and elemental existential givens. The reason is self-evident: psy discourse, being technocratic, is established to exclude emancipatory possibilities. By its own 'nature', it is the work of the Ego, and serves to contain the Self within Egoic bounds, as we have seen in the case of psychoanalysis. Thus the term, 'self-actualization', which expresses one way psy discourse tries to encompass emancipation, immediately reveals its egoic limitation. The self, actualized, remains self—more supple and tuned-up, perhaps, but still within itself, still bound away from its own projections in the universe (what Blake would have called its emanations).

On the other hand, we find an immediate recognition of what we are trying to say in the oldest, commonest, and least scientific of terms concerning human existence. For what is the clumsy expression, 'differentiated self-experience', if not another term for the *spirit*? And what is such a kind of Self, if not the *soul*? And is it not a sign of our estrangement to have so much difficulty in recognizing these terms, and integrating them into our practice?

Perhaps, in part, because we mistake them so. Spirit and soul are usually regarded as immaterial, belonging to sublime and transcendent realms and not of the mundane world. This reading, however, is itself confined within the domain of the Cartesian Ego, where consciousness and matter are severed from each other. From the perspective of a being trapped within himself, the world is devoid of being. Any access of vital force refluxes back into the self, pushing it 'higher', into the spirit realm, where it can then be rejected by the Ego as irrational, infantile, syncretic, and savage.

In reality, however, we talk of spirit in order to represent the closest attainment possible, within the confines of the human situation, to an unmediated relation with nature. Spirit occupies the differentiated pole of self-experience: the self recognizing itself in nature, Ego in Id, male in female (and vice versa), psyche in soma.[6] Spirit is directly sensuous; the word itself comes from a direct drawing in of the breath, and the relation to breathing is preserved in all true senses of the term. Although mystical practice pertains to the spirit, spirit is not in itself mysterious or obscure; it becomes obscure only through the agency of the Ego. Rather spirit is a state of direct, vivid experience, felt throughout the widest reaches of being. Indeed, because of the ontological tension between the self and nature, spirit can take the form of a violent eruption with respect to the pre-existent state of being. More, this involves an overcoming of the mind-body split. In a recent important contribution (which explores the ramification of the theme through Merleau-Ponty, Heidegger, Kierkegaard, Buddhism and Presocratic Greek thought, among others), David Levin notes that a great variety of world traditions respect the identity epitomized in the Greek word, *psyche*, which can interchangeably mean 'breath', 'soul', 'spirit', and 'Self'.[7] We could add to this the insights of Reich into the centrality of respiration, as well as those of virtually any 'holistic'—i.e. differentiated — medical tradition. Indeed, wherever the Ego is undone or deconstructed, or wherever we can point to a mode of being prior to the egoic, the unity of spirit and breath is disclosed. This may be mediated by changing oxygen tension in the brainstem; but the phenomenon cannot be reduced to physiology. Spirit is, in the first place, the point at which consciousness and nature come together. Or, since spirit should not be described in dimensional terms, we could say it is the occasion of experiencing the self as united with the natural world.

But spirit is much more than this. 'To inspire' means to draw in the breath, but also, and more frequently (in the words of the *American Heritage Dictionary*), 'to animate the mind or emotions of; to stimulate to an indicated feeling or action; to elicit or create; and to affect, guide, arouse, or communicate with by divine influence.' In sum, spirit represents the subjective condition for actions of great magnitude to be done; and the problem of spirit is also the problem of radical will.

It is amazing how little exploration has taken place of this dimension, which one would think decisive for the future of any social transformation. Made invisible by dematerialization, or reduced to some vicissitude or Oedipal libido by psychoanalysis, the notion of spirit as animating force survives only as a colloquialism. And yet the 'spirit', or lack thereof, of historical agents is rightly invoked as a decisive determinant wherever politics takes place. It is obvious that material circumstances can lead only to social transformation if they are either translated into or combine with spiritual arousal. But it is far from obvious just what the connection is between these phenomena, nor can this be grasped until spirit is understood as a real material force of its own. Indeed, given the redifferentiation with nature implied in the relations of spirit we must insist that spirit be regarded as a material category, no less than that matter be regarded as itself infused with a degree of spirit.

These concepts are historically decisive, and frame what can be called (at the risk of standing against the tradition which bears this name) a historical materialism of the spirit.

What does it actually mean for a torpid mass to take control of their destiny? Under what conditions does a people become, and stay, 'inspired'; and how does this state of being lift them out of their own selves and give them what appears to be superhuman strength, courage, and intelligence? How do we understand the fact that industrial production in the early capitalist period was compatible with a militant, often 'inspired' proletariat, whereas today's workforce has all but disappeared as a conscious political agent? What is the role of the Theology of Liberation in contemporary politics? And how can ecological politics mobilize the spirit?

As what? As the living, indwelling force of emancipation. If the Ego encompasses domination and Oedipal desire, the spirit contains within its own relations a desire turned against the Ego and toward emancipation. The prevailing psy rationalization places Self within Ego and relegates spirit to the Id, or non-rational zone of the psyche. Under these conditions, emancipation can have no rationality. But if spirit is a form of being, as people have always regarded it to be, then it is the negative of the Ego, and the emancipatory negative of the Ego's domination. It places emancipation within the possible relations of being. This was the insight of Gandhi, of Jesus, of the *Tao Te Ching*.[8] It may be the oldest insight in the world, and it is, I would submit, the basis in 'natural law' for the ontological legitimacy of revolution.

And it is not that simple. Or rather, 'natural law' and the insights of prophets are one thing, the 'fallen' human condition, another. Spirit is the possible, perhaps the necessary, ontological ground of emancipation, but it is not yet emancipation, or even something good in and of itself. In the actual world of human beings, the psyche has become so deformed by domination as to be capable of negating the spirit and turning it to evil. Domination, sedimented inward, turns our original nature to 'second nature'. The Ego is a reaction to this cauldron of repressed desire, and turns a polite and reasonable face to the world. Whatever overcomes the Ego and moves toward spirit also removes the inhibitions placed by egoic repression upon the destructivity of second nature. Spirit can become commingled, therefore, with desire of a highly malignant kind. It can animate, in short, what is worst within human beings no less than what is best. No appreciation of spirit should forget, for example, that fascism has an undoubted spiritual appeal, that Hitler valorized the mystical union of the Germanic peoples, through their 'blood', with nature, that Ronald Reagan appeals quite successfully to the 'American spirit' (the spirit of small-town life but also of 'Rambo'), that hundreds of thousands of sophisticated bourgeois people have thrown themselves after the spiritual guru,

Bhagwan Shree Rajneesh, and that the great mass of religious experience has tended, in the real world of Church and State, to impose an ethos of suffering, blighting of intelligence, and passive submission to domination.

Such is the real world. Nature turns inwardly into 'second nature' because of the radical separateness which makes us human. Nature is always Other, always shadowed by loss. Our subjectivity contains the representation of nature, not nature itself; and this very representation is shaped by a desire which always remains ambivalent. Spiritual being, the 'highest' we can attain, activates that desire in all its love and hate, its humility and grandiosity. Hence, the tragic nature of the human condition, which an ontology, that of social ecology no less than any other, must represent if it is not to become banal, a fairy-tale of instant reunification. The great mystics may have been able to approximate unification with nature, but not without passage through 'the dark night of the soul', and not, it must be added, without an eventual return to the mundane, fallen world, which is rejoined in all its concreteness and unfreedom.

It follows that the mark of a genuine spiritual quest (which need not, it seems to me, necessarily be along mystical lines) — as against the perverted specimens alluded to above — is, to use the phrase of liberation theology, an option for the poor and oppressed. If spirit is to be freed from second nature, then the domination embedded in second nature needs to be overcome. And this cannot be begun except through concrete practice. Indeed, one of the few certainties of the human predicament is that personal fulfilment cannot take place without general emancipation. This may mean that it cannot take place at all, which would be another tragic fact about our species. Such is idle speculation, however. As a practical matter, what we mean is that for a spiritual practice to be authentic, it must be on the side of emancipation, and actively so. The tragic character of human experience means at bottom that we are thrown into being and given the chance to be free. And since no one can be free until everyone is free, the realization of our 'nature', and the redifferentiation with nature implied in the relation of spirit, draws us back once again to society and its transfmoration.

REFERENCES

1. A. N. Whitehead, *Process and Reality* (New York: Harper and Row, 1960).
2. Stanley Diamond, *In Search of the Primitive* (New Brunswick: Transaction Books, 1974).
3. *See* Heinz Hartmann, *Essays in Ego Psychology* (New York: International Universities Press, 1964).

4. Joel Kovel, *Against the State of Nuclear Terror* (Boston: South End Press, 1984).

5. Psy discourse refers to the language of the technologies of mind and behavior, i.e. the mental health industries and the whole massive apparatus established to fit subjectivity into late capitalist society. The term was coined by Robert and Françoise Castel and Anne Lovell in their excellent book, *The Psychiatric Society*, (New York: Columbia University Press, 1982).

6. We should observe, although we cannot take up, the marked ambivalence of psychoanalysis here. However, its theory and ideology may tend to enshrine the Ego, the original impulse of psychoanalysis as a praxis remains the dismantling of the Ego, its redifferentiation with Id. Of course, given the association of the Ego with domination, this ambivalence is entirely understandable.

7. David Michael Levin, 'Logos and Psyche: A Hermeneutics of Breathing', *Research in Phenomenology*, 14, 121–147, 1984.

8. John Clark, 'On Taoism and Politics', *Journal of Chinese Philosophy*, Vol. 10, 1983, pp. 65–88.

Toward a Radical Eco-feminism

Chiah Heller

It is one year after the Chernobyl melt-down. As I contemplate the movement of radioactive particles still percolating into the water table and entering into the bodies of those far and near, I cannot help but wonder how we reached this appalling condition. It has become clear to me that we are living out the chilling implications of one of man's most horrible fantasies. We have arrived at a point where confidence in the infallibility of human reason is so great that we build deadly technologies which have the capacity to end all life on the planet unless they are held in check by human reason and control. We are witnesses of a world which embodies man's original fantasy of controlling the 'forces' of nature. In the nuclear age, man lives out his fantasy of control by controlling the very possibility of the planet's extinction.

Feminism, with its analysis of hierarchy and misogyny, has contributed greatly to our understanding of the origins of the present social and ecological crisis. From the earlier liberal phases through to the radical, and cultural phases, feminists have offered distincitive analyses and solutions to the 'problem' of women's exclusion from the building of patricentric culture. Presently, the need for a new wave of feminism has become apparent to women interested in developing a truly ecological theory and praxis for a feminist program. Such a theory would use critique as a tool to propel the body of feminist thought into a new phase which will finally resolve the underlying dualisms between culture and nature which linger within much of feminist theory. By addressing the question of freedom and necessity in nature, I intend to draw out the implicit nature philosophies within liberal and cultural feminisms, making explicit their positions on the relationship between culture and nature. Exploring the implications of an implicit, 'necessitarian' view of nature will open up the possibility of developing a radically new way of looking at nature as a whole. This project is essential for theorists interested in creating a movement that wishes to espouse a truly liberatory view of *human* nature. It is in the interest of liberating female human nature that I now turn to the question of freedom and necessity in feminist theory, making an appeal to feminists to critically examine the nature philosophies inherent in their own theories, and to consider the value of adopting a radical, ecological perspective.

Western man's attempt to place this 'realm of necessity' called nature under strict human control is embodied in Western religion, science, and philosophy. Each discipline holds that nature is a world separate from man, that it is a 'realm of necessity' which man must control, order, understand, and finally transcend. As Murray Bookchin has shown in his essay, 'Freedom and Necessity in Nature', the Victorian concept of a strictly necessitarian nature emerged out of a profound dualism between nature and culture. This underlying dualism has historically spawned a constellation of other dualistic splits such as spirit/matter, male/female, and subject/object.[1] All of these dualisms are reinforced by the belief that there exists a necessitarian nature which is separate from culture.

Dualism as a mode of ordering the world has lethal implications. It is a cognitive mode in which human beings reduce the complexity of their cognitions to such a degree that the intricate, mediated complexity of the natural world becomes reduced to just so many sets of polarized and antagonistic pairs of opposite phenomena. Dualism implies a 'divide and conquer' mentality in which, after dividing the many interconnected, mediated phenomena of the world into pairs of polarized opposites, one then assigns values to each component of the pair. In so doing, one may then justify the domination of the 'more desirable' of the pair over the 'less desirable'. In this way, dualism sets the stage for hierarchy and domination. For example, if we divide up the world of black, white, and all the infinite shades of grey in between into a simple world of black and white, and if we then assign the value of 'bad' to black and 'good' to white, then the domination of black by white becomes 'justifiable'.

However, dualism *per se* is not the only cognitive mode which has lethal social and theoretical implications. As Bookchin has pointed out, reductionism is perhaps an even larger concern for eco-feminist theorists today. Deep ecology, which is currently influencing many eco-theorists, has given sway to the tendency to reduce the complexity of the natural and social worlds to simplistic, monistic categories. This reductionist tendency acts as a lubricant for the smooth functioning of the systems theory some of them have so wholeheartedly embraced.

Dualism and reductionism, in fact, are usually deeply entangled with each other. A crude dualism tends to foster its counterpart in an equally crude monism, one that simplifies all of reality into a single, often homogeneous, agency, force, substance, or energy source. Hegel caustically called this "a night in which all cows are black."[. . .]Reductionism emerges from ways of thinking than are no less mechanisitic, instrumental, and analytical that the hypothetico-deductive mentality that has assumed such supremacy over the past two centuries of Western thought.[2]

For eco-feminism, an understanding of the origins of domination and hierarchy is essential. It is because a dualistic, reductionistic, and exclusively necessitarian view of nature has been used by Western man to legitimate the domination of women and nature that I will now turn to the question of freedom and necessity in nature. In order to reveal the illegitimacy of this domination, we must first expose and dispel the myth of natural law which so depends on dualistic and reductionistic modes of thinking for its own articulation. To dispel the myth of natural law, we must 'radicalize' our view of nature, to use Bookchin's expression, by thinking ecologically. A 'necessitarian' view of nature sees nature as mute, passive and bound exclusively by necessary, inextricable physical laws. A radical view of nature, in contrast, regards nature as active, participatory, and continually engaged in an ongoing process of development out of which emerges ever increasing levels of complexity and diversity. Further, a radical view of nature goes beyond the nature/culture dualism by regarding nature and culture not as separate from each other, but as existing on a developmental continuum in which culture is the realization of the potentiality for subjectivity latent within nature. When regarded this way, we may radicalize our view of culture as well. We may see the possibility within culture for actualizing dimensions of freedom and subjectivity historically latent within non-human nature. By recognizing nature as a realm of potential freedom, we will radicalize our notion of the relationship between culture and nature. Ultimately, this will deepen our understanding of the relationship between women and nature and will open the way to explore the ground for developing an objective eco-feminist ethics.

Previous and current feminist theoretical tendencies have not yet radicalized their concepts of nature. Although most feminists would deny that they subscribe to a necessitarian, indeed hierarchical view of nature, a dualistic quietism still haunts much of feminist theory. This quietism is often not even deliberate; rather, it is caused by the failure of most current social theorists to recognize and articulate the implicit nature philosophies which inform their social philosophies. Eco-feminism must challenge this quietism by drawing out and critically examining these implicit nature philosophies which are often the vestigal inheritance of the misogynist and nature-hating 'academy' which has emerged out of this hierarchical society. By extending Bookchin's extremely innovative concept of nature as a realm of potential freedom to a feminist critique, we will open up the possibility for a 'radical eco-feminism'. Such a critique will dissolve the narrow necessitarian view of nature in feminist theory by proposing a theory and a politics which are committed to a radical, liberatory view of the natural world, a world not completely bound by the fetters of natural law.

It is impossible to explore the question of freedom and necessity in feminist theory without first analyzing the distinctive shifts in feminist thinking on gender and natural law occurring in past and current feminist theory. Early liberal feminists maintained that women's oppression stems from the very belief that gender is determined by natural law. Many of today's 'cultural feminists', however, uphold the belief that gender is determined by natural law and maintain that women's oppression stems from the patricentric negation of female values derived from natural law.

While exploring the differences between liberal and cultural feminisms, one must remember that these two theoretical tendencies are in no way monolithic, theoretical schools of feminist theory.[3] While I recognize the crudeness and the limitations of these labels which cannot adequately reflect the diversity and integrity of feminist theoretical work, I find them useful in my attempt to identify two distinct attitudes in feminist theory regarding the relationship between gender and natural law. When critiquing such theorists, I am not interested in nihilistically throwing away any liberal or cultural feminist 'babies' with their bathwater. Rather, my intention is to improve the quality of the bathwater so that the baby may profit from the bath that much more.

Although both liberal and cultural feminist theoretical tendencies offer very different analyses of women's relationship to patricentric culture, they both share the dualistic view that culture stands in opposition to a harshly necessitarian nature. For the liberal feminist, culture is the vehicle by which humankind may transcend both our internal and our external natures. Culture is the domain of freedom, an enterprise which delivers us from the realm of a necessitarian nature bound by natural law.

Feminist Simone de Beauvoir represents the forebear of this tendency which I will call liberal feminism. In her book *The Second Sex*, de Beauvoir presents a model of a world in which woman will gain freedom and equality with men when she has learned to transcend the world of natural law. For de Beauvoir, women's anatomy, social position and psychology spring from our identification with a necessitarian nature beyond which we may develop. Women's identification with nature reflects an underdeveloped state of 'immanence' which women will overcome when we transcend the laws of the natural world by participating in the building of culture.

For de Beauvoir, the 'masculine world' is the world of male culture and it is precisely this culture which represents the realm of freedom. According to her theory, a feminist program should spell out the means by which women may gain access to this realm of masculine freedom, be it through birth control, abortion, or employment. Anything which obstructs women's entry to the male world of productivity should be eliminated. 'In order to be a complete individual, on an equality with men, women must have access to the masculine world.'[4]

De Beauvoir not only adheres to the traditional, Western nature/culture dualism, she also fails to criticize the culture which she encourages women to enter. She fails to question the structure of this 'masculine world'; a failing in cultural criticism that flares up repeatedly in the theory of many liberal feminists. Liberal feminism is a tendency to take an uncritical look at the patricentric, anti-ecological pie. The proponents of NOW claim that we are all equal and thus we all deserve an equal serving of the societal pie, never questioning whether the pie is edible. An ERA advocate might justify becoming an executive in a hierarchical corporation by explaining simply that, "Anything the boys can do, girls can do . . . ".

Like many liberal and socialist feminists who followed her, de Beauvoir felt that women's freedom will necessarily arise when we gain equal participation in the world of economic productivity.

> It is through gainful employment that woman has traversed most of the distances that separate her from the male; and nothing else can guarantee her liberty in practice. Once she ceases to be a parasite, the system based on her dependence crumbles. . . . When woman is productive, active, she regains her transcendence. . . . [5]

Finally, by implicitly maintaining the dualistic view that nature and culture are conflicting opposites, the liberal feminist also maintains the dualistic view that men and women are polarized opposites. Again, de Beauvoir sees man as the original creator of culture, and women as historically bound by her immanence. To make matters worse, the liberal feminist holds that the conflict between men and women will simply dissolve once women have transcended the realm of necessity.

As I will demonstrate later, profound dualisms rarely 'dissolve'. They are highly resistant and durable thought structures which feminist theory must continually challenge with ecological ways of looking at the world. It is clear that adherents to the tenets of NOW fail to work their way critically beyond gender dualism. Instead of creating an ecological theory of gender which emphasizes diversity and choice, liberal feminists gloss over the historical dualism between the sexes, adopting what I will call 'cheap unity' or a state of bland androgyny. In this state, men and women are 'one' in that they are functionally equal and exchangeable in the economic sphere.

Having achieved the state of 'cheap unity', the liberal feminist now views any difference between the sexes which might impede women's access to functional 'oneness' with men to be deadly. In fact, liberal feminists view women's historical identification with nature as 'red tape' through which women must cut in order to gain access to the sphere of masculine productivity. The liberal feminist cuts this red tape and steps into a state of functional 'oneness' so that in the corporate workplace *both* sexes may look like their briefcases. Here, feminist theory remains within the dualistic, reductionist tradition. By sacrificing the diversity and distinctiveness which exists within and between the sexes for a generic androgyny, liberal feminism fails to transcend dualism.

Cultural feminism, the other general feminist theory that I will explore, also fails to advance beyond its underlying dualisms. Like liberal feminism, cultural feminism also reinforces the dualistic belief that culture is in opposition to a necessitarian nature. Articulated perhaps most audibly by theorists Mary Daly, Andrea Dworkin and Sally Gearhart, cultural feminism holds that the present culture stands in opposition to a necessitarian *female* nature. Instead of regarding culture as the realm of freedom as does the liberal feminist, the cultural feminist maintains that the present culture negates a nature which abides by female natural laws.

The cultural feminist, in effect, believes that women may create a new, improved culture based on female natural law. The implicit nature philosophy within cultural feminism suggests that there exist certain inextricable female principles which women can know and incorporate in the creation of a radical women's culture. Women's 'innate' ability to cooperate, our increased ecological sensibility, and our peace-loving nature are simply a few of the female principles by which female nature abides. Interestingly, women who do not behave in accordance with these female principles are regarded as victims of patriarchal conditioning. No such distinction, it is worth noting, is made between patriarchally conditioned masculinity and biologically determined maleness. Men are viewed as branded by 'innate' male principles, such as competitiveness, aggression, war-like sensibility, and an overdeveloped rationality. This male nature is seen in essentialist terms as existing independently and prior to partriarchal conditioning.[6]

The cultural feminist separates herself from the male culture which is seen as governed by male principles, and commits herself to creating a culture which expresses her innate, true nature. For the cultural feminist, freedom is no longer a transcendence of the laws of nature as in the case for the liberal feminist. Instead, freedom becomes a recognition of necessity, an acceptance and even a reverence for natural law. Here, women must recognize the necessity of female natural law in order to gain their freedom.

Mary Daly, in her fascinating work, *Gyn/Ecology*, proclaims:

> The spring into free space, which is woman-identified consciousness involves a veritable mental/behavioral mutation. The phallocratic categories of good and evil no longer apply when women honor women.[7]

According to Daly, if woman takes this leap into 'free space' by aligning her consciousness with female nature, then the values of patricentric culture will necessarily dissolve. Later in the text, Daly suggests that woman's 'original source' is inherently different from that of man. She suggests that by realigning consciousness to fit female nature, woman will 'release the inherent dynamic in the mother–daughter relationship towards friendship which is strangled in the male mastered system.'[8] The language that Daly chooses reflects her bias towards a metaphysical and rigidly necessitarian view of nature. Words like 'mutation', 'original source' and 'inherent dynamic' all resound with a belief in a scientific and inextricable natural law.

In her novel, *Our Blood*, Andrea Dworkin further delineates female and male natures as strictly necessitarian. She describes male sexual sensibility as that which is 'aggressive, competitive, objectifying, quantity oriented.'[9] The concluding paragraph of the book declares that 'only when manhood is dead—and it will perish when a ravaged femininity no longer sustains it—only then will we know what it is to be free.'[10] According to Dworkin, 'ravaged femininity' or the repressed female principle will necessarily advance into a 'realm of freedom'. Again, freedom consists in the realization of female natural law.

Sally Gearhart presents her vision of cultural feminism in a utopian novel, *The Wanderground*. Gearhart lays out a lesbian separatist world of 'hillwomen' who have decided to create their own community away from the evils of the city men. In this world, even the men who have also embraced the female principle, called 'gentles', are still to be avoided. In the following passage, one hillwoman discusses a gentle's understanding of the necessary separation of the sexes.

> Even beneath his cultivated hard exterior she could feel his understanding of the essential fundamental knowledge: women and men

cannot yet, may not ever, love one another without violence: they
are no longer of the same species.[11]

Again, for Gearhart there is something necessarily violent within male
nature from which women must separate. Women and men, as separate
species, may not coexist within the same culture; when men are left
to themselves, male nature necessarily creates a violent culture, and
female nature necessarily creates a utopia.

This dualistic view of gender gives rise to even more theoretical
difficulties. The cultural feminist can 'resolve' differences between the
two 'species' through segregation. Yet how does the cultural feminist
'resolve' differences *within* the female species? Mary Daly's solution for
gender differences is 'Mister-Ectomy'[12] (a complete separation from
the 'mister') yet Daly says very little about how to address the very
diverse body of women once we have achieved the 'post-Mister-
Ectomy' era. Like many other cultural feminists, Daly glosses over a
problematic and potentially liberating analysis of diversity among
women of different races, personal traits, talents, and proclivities. Like
many liberal feminists, the cultural feminist purchases 'cheap unity' to
achieve oneness within the women's community. This 'cheap unity'
represents the dualistic fall-out which lingers when dualism itself is not
transcended.

Specifically, the cultural feminist purchases a female 'oneness' à la
Wanderground. This 'Wanderground oneness' is a state of affairs where
women suddenly transcend all cultural and racial differences to form
an all-female whole. The cultural feminist tendency toward 'cheap
unity' is equally as lethal as the bland androgyny espoused by the
liberal feminist; both positions purchase 'unity' at any price. Once
again, differences, which should be articulated and celebrated, are
glossed over, and 'unity' acts as a smokescreen for an underlying
monistic reductionism. Unfortunately, 'Wanderground oneness'
cannot accommodate the very real factionalization within the women's
community; tensions between women of different sexual orientations,
race, and political persuasion continue to fester, preventing the unity
which might be achieved if these feminists adopted a libertarian view
of nature which incorporates diversity.

The need for a radical eco-feminist view of nature based on social
ecology becomes increasingly clear when we look at the way in which
both liberal and cultural feminism address the 'woman and nature'
analogy. Both liberal and cultural feminism accept the traditional belief
as a necessary given that women are 'more' connected to nature than
men, differing only in their opinions as to whether to sever or revere
this 'special' connection. To repeat: the idea that women are closer to
nature than men stems from the dualisms between men and women,

nature and culture. Again, men maintain a monopoly on culture while women maintain a monopoly on nature.

The woman and nature analogy is reinforced by the Western, dualistic myth of 'transcendence'. As explained earlier, this myth holds that mankind may transcend the realm of nature by entering the realm of culture. In so doing, man severs his connection to nature, leaving woman behind with her 'monopoly' on the natural world. According to the myth of transcendence, nature is a world that is completely set apart from and opposed to man, an alien substance to which certain subjects are more or less connected. Whereas white men, who are presumably 'closer' to this transcendental world of culture, have fewer connections to nature, peoples of the Third World who live in less proximity to white Western culture are supposed to be more connected to nature. Finally, women make up the general catagory of subjects who are 'most' connected to nature: in fact, as the myth contends, women do not even participate in the building of culture.

The belief that certain subjects are more 'connected' to nature than others is basically dualistic and patently reflects a lack of an ecological sensibility. The study of a social ecology shows us that all beings within an ecocommunity* are interconnected. The possibility of life is grounded in the fact that all living, and pre-organic life forms exist in an interdependent relationship out of which emerges ever new, differentiated, and complex life forms. The Western idea that connectedness is quantifiable reflects an inability to fully grasp the concept of interconnectedness. When we recognize that we live in a world where all subjects are always interconnected, the question of being 'more' or 'less' connected reveals itself as absurd. What is ultimately at issue is the ways in which *all* life forms are interconnected.

The myth of 'quantifiable connectedness' and the myth of 'transcendence' constitute two different sides of the same dualistic coin. The logic of this dualism runs as follows:

1. There exist two separate, indeed, utterly antagonistic worlds.
2. Certain subjects may separate themselves from one of these worlds.
3. Thus, there are some subjects who will be more 'inherently connected' to one of these worlds than other subjects.

It is precisely this kind of dualistic, almost genetic way of thinking

---

*I use the word 'ecocommunity' instead of 'ecosystem' deliberately. As Bookchin has pointed out, 'ecosystem' tends to connote a systems theory version of nature, 'Community' more accurately emphasizes the organic, indeed dialectical, nature of animal-plant interrelationships and preserves the symbiotic character of natural evolution.

which has nourished the present ecological crisis. The problem is that we simply do not think ecologically.

Past and current feminist theory has lacked the necessary ecological, critical analysis of the woman/nature question. In keeping with most social theorists who regard any kind of individual, cultural, or racial difference as problematic, feminist theorists have also regarded woman's 'difference' as a 'problem to solve'. It is bad enough that feminists even attempt to 'solve' such a 'problem'. What makes matters worse, however, is that the solutions which these women deduce are often dualistic or reductionistic. A radical eco-feminist critique of the woman/nature question must articulate a way to break through this dualistic impasse. Once we go beyond dualism or reductionism, we will see that the distinctive relationship between woman and nature is not a problem to be solved. Rather, we will recognize it as a dynamic relationship to be understood developmentally, while critically examining both the liberatory and oppressive implications of woman's difference for feminist theory and praxis.

If we apply the ecological principles of unity in diversity to our understanding of woman's difference, we may broaden our concept of difference altogether. We must understand woman's identity not only in terms of what makes woman different from man, but also we must look at what makes woman different from *non-human nature*. Once we have addressed the latter question, we will begin to understand the potentialities and proclivities that woman also shares with man as part of the human species.

First, let's apply the principle of unity in nature to woman's difference by exploring the unifying principles within human nature. Such principles constitute a common natural history shared by both men and women; this history is characterized by the emergence of several distinctive possibilities which distinguish human from non-human nature. Foremost, woman, as the female expression of human nature, shares with man the capacity to build a 'second nature'. This second nature includes the distinctly human potential to create cultural institutions, a written language, and the capacities for rational thought, intellectual mentation, and self-conscious reflection. The first answer to the 'woman question' must be that woman represents a distinctive expression of second nature: a nature which is the realization of the potential for self-consciousness in 'first nature' (non-human nature). When feminists focus exclusively on woman's difference from man, we cheat ourselves from our evolutionary inheritance, our very birthright to a distinctive role in natural history. We focus so exclusively on that which makes a transcendental, 'female nature' distinctive that we forget to appreciate that which makes female *human nature* distinctive. The history of much of feminist theory has been a series of 'transvaluations of values', to use Nietzsche's term, in which the oppressed merely decide to value the antithesis of the oppressor's values instead of critically examining and integrating what is essentially valuable. Simply because Western, patricentric society overvalues rationality does not imply that women must reject the very quality which distinguishes humans from the rest of nature. Recognizing our unity, or commonality, with the male portion of human nature, allows us to recognize and celebrate that which has been denied to us for centuries: our historically unprecedented potentiality for critical self-conscious reflection which is so necessary for developing an objective, eco-feminist ethics.

Once we have explored the principle of unity within woman's difference, we open up the possibility of creating a 'fuller' feminism, one which recognizes the widest scope of woman's potential for fulfilling her role as the expression of female second nature. Now we may apply the principle of diversity in nature, by looking *within* second nature as a whole to understand the qualities of female second nature which render it, 'diverse', or distinctive from male second nature. We may now understand woman's difference from male second nature not in terms of an enhanced connection to nature, but in terms of a dynamic and developmental relationship to nature. Woman emerges both individually and historically out of first nature in such a way that allows woman to develop an enhanced, often implicit awareness of our interconnected relationship to the natural world. For many different biological and social reasons, male second nature did not historically fulfil its potential for developing this primary awareness of intersubjectivity. Instead, mankind has largely become increasingly dualistic and reductionistic in its thinking and in its way of relating to the world.

It is crucial at this point to emphasize the importance of the word 'tendency' which I so carefully choose to describe the association of enhanced ecological awareness with women. The connection between woman and this awareness is in no way indicative of natural law. I am deliberately describing an inclination, an evolutionary choice which many women have made on an unconscious level. I am pointing to what countless anthropologists and psychologists have described as female empathy. According to Nancy Chodorow, many women exhibit this enhanced relational capacity, this enhanced empathy for other living things. This capacity is correlated both to woman's potential for motherhood and to woman's identification with her own mother.[13] In both instances, woman either experiences an empathetic bond with her young, or she identifies with others in whom she observes this empathy.

Although biological proclivities have been overemphasized by advocates of biological determinism, an understanding of the cultural implications of such proclivities may give us much information about diversity within the human species. Anthropologist Sherwood Washburn points to the prolonged maturation period of the human infant as a factor in shaping the empathetic relationship between the human mother and her young.

> The human mother-child relationship is as unique among the primates as is the use of tools. In all apes and monkeys the baby clings to the mother; to be able to do so, the baby must be born with its central nervous system in an advanced state of development. But the brain of the fetus must be small enough so that the birth may take place. . . . This obstetrical dilemma was solved by delivery of the fetus at a much earlier state of development. But this was only possible because the mother could hold the helpless infant. . . . Bipedalism, tool use, and selection for large brains thus slowed human development and invoked far greater maternal responsibility.[14]

Because the human infant is unable to 'cling' to the mother for survival, the human mother must 'cling' to her young. Historically, an infant's survival has depended on the ability of the social unit to provide the mother with a supportive net of cooperative social relationships. It is perhaps out of this proclivity in the mother to care for her underdeveloped infant, and out of the necessity for a cooperative social unit, that a female ethics of care has emerged.

It is essential to note that the prolonged 'clinging period' of the human mother to her young does not necessitate an ethics of care, nor does it entail an enhanced awareness of intersubjectivity. Motherhood, as a biological event, does not necessarily entail any of these empathetic traits. A true application of the principle of diversity to women's difference requires us to see that each individual woman represents a unique and ongoing development out of her own biological and cultural origins. Certainly, there are empathetic women who choose not to have children, men who are empathetic, and many mothers who do not express their potential for empathetic bonding. Further, many women have accepted the myth of transcendence: notably women in the liberal feminist tradition. Thanks to the NOW movement, more and more women have been struck by corporate-induced cases of empathetic bankruptcy.

Diversity within the human species, or woman's difference, is a crucial issue for eco-feminism. As women recognize and develop our distinctive awareness of the interconnectedness of all things, we begin to see nature as a realm of potential, indeed developing, freedom. We see that in nature all living beings participate together in making unconscious and, even in a rudimentary sense, conscious choices in their own evolution. Nature, when revealed to be a variegated, inter-connected web, becomes active, creative, and participatory. Women will begin to show that natural evolution is a surprisingly free process, not completely subdued by a natural law which has been used to justify our very own oppression. Informed by a *social* ecology, women may develop an ecological standpoint which will radicalize our view of evolution; revealing that evolution is in great part a self-determined process in which all subjects participate together, expressing the infinite latent potentialities for development in the natural world.

When we look at the dimensions of unity and diversity within the woman/nature relationship, we begin to recognize woman's distinctive role as the expression of both second nature and *female* second nature. Now we may begin to appreciate woman's unique opportunity to become the historical subject of an era which so direly needs an objective, social ethics as well as an ecological, empathetic ethics of care. Woman may be the subject who creates the theory and the movement which finally renders nature critically self-conscious. We will realize this possibility when we develop an ecological, empathetic consciousness which is mediated and fulfilled by woman's distinctively human capacity for objective, rational thought.

As eco-feminists become conscious of the connections between historical thought structures and historical actions, we will increase the complexity of our thought structures and will act in a manner which reflects a consciousness of the interconnectedness of life. Thinking ecologically allows us to interact in the world in such a way as to enhance the ecocommunity. A radical eco-feminist revolution begins by moving from dual-logic to eco-logic.

To go beyond dualism, feminists must enhance the complexity of our own thought structures. We need to realize that historically, we as a species have not as yet fulfilled our potential to enhance the interconnectedness of the natural world. To a degree that I hate to admit, patricentric society has reduced our awareness of ecological complexity to rigid, dualistic, and reductionistic thought structures. The effects of such a society can be seen in much of feminist theory which, as I have shown, has unknowingly absorbed such reductionist tendencies.

Our perceptions and cognitions define the shape of our interactions with the world. As eco-feminists, we cannot think reductively and dualistically. Radical eco-feminism entails a revolution in the way we think about nature. We are revolting against a brand of thinking which has simplified our top soil, forests, and air and has simplified our community structures. Hierarchy, patriarchy, the centralization of power, and capitalism are all consequences of having lived out the myth of transcendence. As radical eco-feminists, we know that we can no longer enjoy the luxury of thinking simplistically. When feminists reduce 'woman' to a purely culturally or biologically constructed being, we help to perpetuate the perennial, socially constructed struggle between culture and nature. When liberal feminists focus exclusively on the equality of woman's rational capacities, and cultural feminists focus exclusively on the superiority of woman's empathetic capacities, feminist theory and practice is deprived of the wholeness which we will achieve when we begin to see culture and nature as existing on a developmental continuum, with the former posessing the potential to fulfil the latter. We must go beyond this struggle by integrating the liberal feminist's love for the human capacity for equality, rationality, and excellence, with the cultural feminist's love for woman's distinctive empathetic capacities. As well, we must never forget to include the cultural feminist's deliciously ferocious critique of patricentric society; such an omission would take out of feminism the essential bite which the radical phase of feminism delivered.

Radical eco-feminism incorporates and develops beyond the two previous feminisms by seeing culture not as separate from nature but as a development out of nature. Culture becomes the 'realm of freedom' not because it triumphs over nature, but because it actualizes *potentialities* that are latent within nature. Human beings are born of and live in the natural world. We are, as Griffin says, "Nature seeing nature..nature with a concept of nature . . . ".[15] Our evolution is inextricably interconnected to the evolution of all other subjects in the world.

Thinking through and beyond dualism means realizing that nothing is separate from the 'natural world'. The pencil that I write with, a star a million light years away, a plastic bag—all are interconnected with each other in the natural world regardless of the aesthetic, cultural, or economic values we choose to assign to them. It is essential to realize, however, that just because something is 'natural' or 'interconnected' does not mean it is necessarily life-enhancing. The AIDS virus is a 'natural' event, as is the famine in Ethiopia. Although some Deep Ecologists might disagree, I posit that such natural events do not enhance the complexity and diversity of the natural world. In fact, such 'natural' events reflect the actions of a society which is much more committed to social domination and economic profit than to ecological life-enhancement. Thinking ecologically entails rejecting a 'biological egalitarianism' which would grant the AIDS virus rights equal to those of human life.

As we develop an objective ecological ethics, we will begin to appraise the value of natural events in terms of their ability to enhance the diversity and complexity of the ecocommunity. Such an ethics would make explicit the value of finding a cure for AIDS and of giving aid to the peoples of Ethiopia whose culture has been rendered unsustainable by imperialistic efforts.

Similarly, cultural constructs themselves, as part of a natural continuum, should be explored for their potentiality to increase or decrease complexity in the ecocommunity. For example, it is clear that patricentric cultures which are hierarchical do not enhance the complexity of social life in the same way as an eco-libertarian culture based on social ecology. Patricentric cultures centralize power and decrease the number of active participants in the political structure to a few, élitist figures and bureaucratic agencies. In contrast, eco-libertarian cultural forms may enhance the complexity of political structures by encouraging active participation of all individuals and more rounded communities. There is an actual recycling of power in an eco-libertarian political group: consensus itself requires that each individual take full responsibility for the decision of the group, ensuring a greater distribution of decision-making power and democracy.

As self-conscious women who have lived to seek out the implications of dualistic thought structures, we have come to a point where we may now choose to create a culture which will be life-affirming. Again, radical eco-feminism proposes a non-dualistic, non-reductionistic, indeed dialectical view of nature. When we think dialectically, we see that those phenomena which might appear to be 'opposites' through the eyes of dualism are truly complementary subjects out of which may arise new, even more complex subjects. It is the developmental relationship between different subjects which fosters evolution and complexity. When we think dialectically, with an ecological sensibility, we see that difference does not necessitate conflict. Difference represents an opportunity for creative integration. Dialectical relationships constitute a continual process of becoming which is completely open-ended. This open-endedness is freedom.

As we begin to radicalize our view of nature, we may also generate a radical eco-feminist culture, politics, and a new feminist spiritual sensibility which embodies the complexity and diversity of the natural world. First, we must explore the possibility of building a woman-identified culture and politics which does not need to appeal to natural law for validation. If there is no 'female nature' carved in stone, then we must find a new ground for a woman-identified culture. In fact, we might rethink what feminine nature *is*? I propose that a woman-identified culture celebrate not a feminine nature determined by natural law but a feminine nature constituted of the distinctive experiences of each individual woman in the collectivity. The feminine principle represents a tendency toward a distinctive feminine experience, which is grounded on objective self-directiveness, not on a 'lawful' determinism.

We must articulate the infinite and different evolutionary choices which each woman makes within the context of her own biological and cultural set. We may celebrate the larger tendencies within women's collective history, a celebration which will strengthen our sense of a collective identity and unity. However, we must be ready at all times to look beneath these larger 'feminine' tendencies discussed earlier to see that the very complex and diverse web of woman's shared experience is composed of individual women. Each woman chooses, responds, and evolves in her own distinctive way.

A radical eco-feminist culture draws on the distinctive, larger tendencies within woman's shared history, holding sacred those feminine values which have been misinterpreted as being exclusively biologically determined. Women's tendencies toward cooperation, nurturance, and interdependence are all qualities which we may choose to emulate and incorporate into a woman-identified culture. For example, we may study and celebrate the 'herstory' of woman's art, literature, and music. Cultural feminists have done much to reclaim and revive our unwritten cultural past. Thanks to women like Mary Daly and Susan Griffin, women now have an enriched awareness of woman's past and of the bravery of our 'uppity' foremothers. Because of the women's music movement, we have reclaimed an awareness and appreciation for woman's ability to work together to create music celebrating woman's shared experience.

But we also need to create a larger woman's community; a cross-cultural, even global, community of women. While celebrating the rich diversity of our lives throughout the world, we cannot affort to let our distinctiveness alienate us from each other. As Ynestra King suggests, we must create face-to-face dialogue between women of different nations.[16] We need to learn more about the diversity of our experience as well as our shared experience. The planet is growing smaller: because the universal effects of nuclear technology affect us all, we must use this new awareness to develop an acute sensitivity to how all of our political actions and decisions impact women in different lands. Women must bond together to gain strength and support to fight for the life of the planet we all share as a species.

In order to be free to create a woman-identified culture, women need to fight against the culturally induced fear of bonding which has separated women historically. Women may look to lesbianism as a model for women bonding, and we must constantly fight against the homophobia which tries to prevent this bonding.[17] Each woman must be prepared, if only symbolically, to call herself a 'lesbian', regardless of her sexual preference. In World War Two, the King of Denmark rode through the streets wearing a Jewish star on a band around his arm. By doing this, the king declared that all people must be willing to call themselves Jews in order for all people to reclaim their freedom. In this same way, we must 'de-spook' lesbianism, as Mary Daly might so cleverly say. All women must make it clear that women no longer need fear societal retribution for loving women. Until all women feel pride in wearing a pink triangle around their arms, no women will be free to love women without inhibition.

Lastly, eco-feminists must continue in the struggle to reclaim ownership of our own bodies. As expressions of nature, our bodies too represent the realm of freedom and choice. Women are reclaiming the right to be midwives, healers, and mothers when and if we choose. We are fighting for the right to choose safe and free abortions, and for the right to have access to affordable birth control. In this way, we will increase the spectrum of choices for our own lives.

As we open up human nature as the 'realm of potential freedom' and choice, we can begin to develop an eco-feminist ethics on which to ground a political culture. In short, we must be committed to 'reweaving' the web of our political structures. As Murray Bookchin so brilliantly declares, an ecological ethics in one based on a broad web of participation.

> A politics of participation is a politics that fosters self-empowerment rather than state empowerment. Such a politics must become a truly people politics, organic in the sense that political participation is literally protoplasmic and peopled by assemblies, face-to-face discussion that is reinforced by the veracity of body language as well as the reasoning process of discourse. The political ethics that follows from this ground is meant to create a moral community, not simply an "efficient" one; an ecological community, not simply a contractual one; a social praxis that enhances diversity, not only a political culture that invites the widest public participation.[18]

A moral politics springs from an ecological ethics. We must create an objective ground for determining the ethical value of our political actions so that 'life-affirmingness' becomes a yardstick by which we can measure the ethical content of our political actions.

When we think ecologically, we realize that we must continually challenge homophobia; for we see that homophobia limits the spectrum of human choice and diversity. When challenged by an ecological ethics, we realize that homophobia is life-negating, and thus ethically unsound. In the same way, we see that we must fight against racism, because it represents a desire to degrade the racial diversity of the human species; racism, as a form of reductionsim, is also life-negating. It is essential to fight against nuclear technology because of the destructive effects that radiation has on the ecocommunity. Cancer, eventual genetic mutations, and the production of plutonium used by a few men in centralized governments to maintain their dominant positions in the global hierarchy all reflect a deadly reductionist menace.

We must weigh each political concern carefully to make sure that our goal is to increase ecological-political diversity and participation. As we radicalize our view of nature, we radicalize our view of culture; soon the concept of natural law in its reductionist form will become anachronistic, and we will replace the political structures legitimated by a hierarchical view of nature with a politics derived from a participatory view of nature. To facilitate this shedding away of the old view of nature, we may build a society which is 'reproductive' rather than simply 'productive'. We need to create alternatives to the production-consumption syndrome which drags us closer to ecocide. In our present culture, the processes of both production and consumption function to simplify the ecocommunity. An ecological culture is a reproductive culture where consumption becomes as nutritive as production. The process of consumption must enter into the ecological domain as a mode of enhancing the fecundity of the ecocommunity. As we radicalize our view of consumption, we will develop a sense of ecological responsibility in which all our actions are measured by their ability to increase the fertility of our cultural soil. Just as sexual reproduction can increase the diversity and stability of a gene pool, a philosophy of creative consumption can increase the diversity and stability of our social and ecological relations.

In order to transform our society into an ecological one, we must take direct action. As radical eco-feminists, our politics should be microcosmic expressions of the kind of eco-libertarian society we want to live in. Our direct action must express social ecology's principles of unity in diversity, and the principle of the interconnectedness of life. Our actions should embody the creative, the imaginative and the wrathful, as well as the rational. When I think of direct action, I am reminded of the actions performed by women in both the Seneca and Greenham Common peace encampments. Women weaving colorful pieces of their lives through the barbed wire fences, women helping each other to climb over these walls, women stringing balls of yarn through the trees, police cars, and guns—spinning webs of color that represent our interconnectedness with each other. Eco-action expresses the caprices of a free nature, by showing that we will no longer submit to governmental rule which is legitimated by a hierarchical conception of natural law. I would want our actions to show that we are prepared to go beyond an anachronistic politics by creating a more courageous, *ecological* politics.

Moving beyond anachronistic cognitive and cultural forms opens up the possibility of exploring a new spirituality. As we recognize the dimension of freedom in nature, we might begin to imagine what a spiritual sensibility might be like which does not appeal to a dualistic, hierarchical authority for validation. We might begin to wonder if it is possible to think of an objective, rational ground for spirituality without maintaining the dualistic split between creator and created? What does it mean to think of a nature which is self-creating, a nature which is self-directive? Evolution itself shows us that there is in nature a directiveness toward increasing levels of complexity and diversity within an ecocommunity, that there is a dimension of objective reason in the open-ended horizon toward which nature strives.

And yet, we should never confuse this self-directiveness with transcendental determinism. We cannot look at a leaf and say, 'It could never have been but this way.' Rather, we should look at a leaf and reflect upon the interconnected beings in nature which participated in expressing the potentiality which this leaf represents. There is a rudimentary measure of 'reasonableness' in nature. Nature is 'rational' in its directiveness, yet nature is open-ended. It is this open horizon which may constitute the ground for a new, ecological spirituality.

An ecological spirituality represents a celebration of the interconnectedness of all life and also the distinctiveness of each life form. Respecting species' distinctiveness entails that we do not put ourselves above or below nature; we do not glorify ourselves as transcendental beings over nature, nor do we glorify nature with false humility as something 'above us' or 'wiser' than us. An authentic ecological spirituality goes beyond a spirituality informed by a 'deep' ecology by celebrating the qualities which distinguish human nature from non-human nature as well as celebrating that which makes women different from men. An ecological spirituality informed by social ecology transcends a hierarchical view of nature, revealing the absurdity of professing a greater reverence for non-human life.

Because human nature has far from actualized its full potential for creating and sustaining a truly ecological relationship to both human and non-human nature, it is easy to comprehend why an anti-humanist stance would appear to be a rational stance to adopt. However, we must always look beneath the reality of human behavior to reveal the latent potentiality within human nature to actually enhance and fulfil the natural world. An ecological spirituality expresses an ability to celebrate and articulate the potentiality distinctive to the particularity of each life form.

Spirituality is an awareness and sensitivity that we bring with us to all aspects of our lives. As we derive from nature the ecological principles of interdependence, complementarity, and spontaneity, we may apply these principles to our personal relationships, our political structures, and into our communities. We can begin to create rituals and ceremonies which do not appeal to the 'super-natural'; rather, we can celebrate the arrival of a new relationship with the natural world—a relationship which we can experience with our senses and feel with our bodies. Once we recognize ourselves as deriving from nature, expressing the potential in nature for self-consciousness, we will no longer need to worship nature as something separate from ourselves. Once we have moved beyond dualism, the split between spirit and matter dissolves: we are left only with the sweet awareness that we are, after all, made from this earth.

Ritual itself can help us to demonstrate our new, ecological awareness. Through ritual, we shift our perception so that we become conscious of the liberatory potentialities in nature that are currently not part of our everyday lives. Ritual also helps us to experience and develop our sense of interconnectedness, allows us to make explicit the commitment in our relationships to nature and to each other. Women may create rituals which celebrate our historical and biological relationship to the cycles of the moon; we may derive from nature metaphors and images with which women can identify universally.

Once we see that there really are no rigid 'natural laws' that completely govern us, nature opens itself up before us as a world of patterns, symmetries, and complementary forms, all webbed together, developing in a direction which we can never completely map out, much less 'command'. Evolution itself, which we embody, is something which we may spiritually celebrate within ourselves. We should celebrate the potentiality, the unexpected, and the spontaneous expressed by *human* nature, just as we deal respectfully with human capacities for reason and self-directiveness.

Spirit is not confined to a gender or race, nor does it abide by feminine or masculine principles. Rather, spirit represents the flow of potentiality which exists naturally within the very texture of life. When we assign gender, color or status to our gods and goddesses, we commit idolatry. Symbols represent a transcendental world which is separate from nature. As Murray Bookchin observes, ' "reverence" for nature, the mythologizing of the natural world over the human—all degrade nature by denying the natural world its universality as that which exists everywhere, free of all dualities like "spirit" and "god". . . . A "revered" nature is a separated nature in the bad sense of the term." '[19]

Spiritualism, scientism, and a hypostatization of technology have all been used by man to finally control society as well as nature. Hierarchy, domination, and social oppression have continually appealed to these age-old 'fetters' for legitimation. As women who are now witnessing the implications of the historical errors of a dual-logic, we may enter a time when our personal, political and spiritual lives will appeal to eco-logic for validation; a logic which inheres in the very cells which compose us. Natural law, once meant to ease Western man's sense of discomfort when confronted by the complexity of the natural world, threatens to snap back at us if it is seen as the ubiquitous mode of explaining all phenomena. It threatens to fetter freedom and ultimately our freedom to act. I insist that a radical eco-feminism must revolutionize our view of nature and must arouse us to action. Women must generate a new eco-praxis grounded in social ecology if the natural world, as well as the social, is to survive.

REFERENCES

1. Murray Bookchin, 'What Is Social Ecology', *The Modern Crisis* (Philadelphia: New Society Publishers 1986), p.55.
2. Murray Bookchin, 'Thinking Ecologically', *Our Generation* Vol.18, No.2, p.10.
3. Alice Echols, 'The New Feminism of Yin and Yang', *Powers of Desire* (New York: Monthly Review Press, 1983), p.441.
4. Simone de Beauvoir, *The Second Sex* (New York: Vintage Books, 1952), p.761.
5. Ibid., p.755.
6. Alice Echols, 'The Taming of the Id', *Pleasure and Danger* (Boston: Routledge & Kegan Paul, 1984), p.53.
7. Mary Daly, *Gyn/Ecology* (Boston: Beacon Press, 1978), p.12.
8. Ibid., p. 39.
9. Andrea Dworkin, *Our Blood* (New York: Pedigree Books, 1976), p.12.
10. Ibid., p. 111.
11. Sally Gearhart, *The Wanderground* (Boston Mass: Alyson Pubns., 1984).
12. Mary Daly, op. cit., p. 239.
13. Nancy Chodorow, *The Reproduction of Mothering* (London, England: University of California Press, 1978); Carol Gilligan, *In a Different Voice* (Harvard University Press, Cambridge, 1982).
14. Sherwood Washburn 'Tools and Human Evolution', *Scientific American*, 1960.
15. Susan Griffin, *Made From This Earth* (Cambridge: Harper and Row, 1982).
16. Ynestra King, 'Making the World Live: Feminism and the Domination of Nature'. See Ynestra King's essays on eco-feminist praxis, including 'The Ecology of Feminism and the Feminism of Ecology' in *Harbinger* (Fall 1983), pp. 16–22.
17. Ibid.

18. Murray Bookchin, 'Freedom and Necessity in Nature', *Alternatives* (November 1986), p. 36.
19. Ibid., p. 33.

Nature and Freedom: Thoughts for the 1980s

Patricia Jagentowicz Mills

The most insightful political interventions of the 1960s were directed to the problems and possibilities of a post-Industrial society. The social critiques done by the Frankfurt School (best known in North America through the work of Herbert Marcuse) and the social ecology movement (developed primarily by Murray Bookchin) are two influential strains of radical social thought which contributed to and maintain the innovative politics of the 1960s. For both these intellectual perspectives, the major conflict is seen as that between Industrial society and nature, rather than class divisions within Industrial society: the focus becomes 'domination' rather than 'exploitation'.

Both perspectives point to that which is left out and denied by the domination of nature and in this sense are theoretically central to Women's Liberation, Black and Third World Liberation, sexual liberation, Native struggles, and the peace and ecology movements: all these movements are centrally formed by the repressive power of Industrial society on what is perceived and formed by it as the external Other. As the domination of nature grounds the process of objectification in contemporary society, it entails social and psychic consequences which result in ecological crises, the domination of woman by man, racism, and repressive political forms in both capitalist and socialist societies. The liberation movements of the 1980s, which are rooted in the 1960s, must therefore retain and deepen the critique of the domination of nature in order to attain a theoretical unification necessary for the clarification of political struggles.

This short essay will sketch the development of the concept of the 'domination of nature' through the work of Hegel, Marx, and the Frankfurt School. On this basis, I will criticize what I term the 'abstract pro-Nature' stance current in contemporary political discussions through an analysis of the work of Isaac Balbus in *Marxism and Domi-*

nation. In particular, this critique will suggest that important elements of both feminism and black liberation are ignored by such a stance. By way of conclusion, I discuss the relation of consciousness and nature with reference to the work of Murray Bookchin.

Hegel

The Hegelian problem of the relation between identity and difference is at the heart of the modern project to create a free and equal society. That is, within all the liberation struggles of the 1980s there is now a search for a form of intersubjective recognition (a relation between self and Other) which allows for concrete differences but does not on that account render the relation unequal by dominating the Other. However, a comprehensive approach to Hegel's philosophy reveals the way in which his attempt to include dialectically all oppositional 'moments' presents us with an abstract negation in which nature itself, as immediate and contingent, cannot be fully comprehended in the logical Idea. Adorno has shown that the notion of reconciliation in Hegel's philosophy presents us with a false identity of subject and object in which the sovereign power of thought is an expression *of* the domination of nature. For Adorno (and the liberation movements of the 1980s), 'the matters of true philosophical interest at this point in history are those in which Hegel . . . expressed his disinterest. They are the nonconceptual, the individual, the particular. . . . What Hegel called "lazy Existenz".'[1]

The much-discussed master–slave dialectic is only one brief moment in the Hegelian schema of the movement of Spirit toward universal self-knowledge. For Hegel it is neither work (as objectification) nor the dialectic of dependent-independent consciousness that is most significant. Rather, it is self-consciousness finding itself in an Other, equal self which is required for the reconciliation that leads to universal self-consciousness. While Hegel attempted to ground intersubjectivity in the theory of recognition, his system requires that woman be confined to the family and denied self-consciousness. Woman is said to have a unique relation to nature, in that she never knows the conscious risk of death and therefore never passes through negativity via a contradiction between herself and first nature. For Hegel, woman, like first nature, remains Other and his system reproduces the domination of nature and the domination of woman *as* nature. Thus, while Hegel states the problem of the relation of identity and difference, in the light of contemporary political movements we must consider the problems of the *false* identity of subject and object, the domination of nature, and the domination of woman within Hegel's system.[2]

Marx

Marx's focus on objectification, as the defining human activity through which liberation is to be realized, makes him a proponent of the domination of nature-especially in terms of the technological solution he offers to the problem of social domination. There is a tension between the approach of the early and late Marx to the problem of the domination of nature. Schmidt correctly argues that Marx initially held to a dialectical conception of the relation between nature and human society which revealed 'the mutual interpenetration of nature and society within the natural whole.'[3] Thus, Marx's early understanding of communism focuses on labor as a process which 'humanizes' nature as it 'naturalizes' humanity. In the *1844 Manuscripts*, the schism between nature and human society, which is the 'riddle of history', is to be healed in communism in such a way that nature is to be 'resurrected'. The process of objectification, as a transformation of nature, performed 'in freedom' and 'according to the laws of beauty' does not dominate nature but aids nature to realize itself. In the context of this dialectical understanding, Marx focuses on the heterosexual love relation as the paradigmatic form of intersubjectivity: the love relation between woman and man is the realization of the ideal relation between self and Other. When a woman and a man come together conscious of their sexual need as a need for the Other, a need for another human being, then they are confirmed as both natural and social beings.

The later Marx moves away from his early concern with the intersubjective heterosexual love relationship, in terms of the recognition of the Other, to a concern with the intersubjective relation between workers. These forms differ in that the relation between workers in production is mediated by a process of objectification whereas the earlier man-woman relation is a direct relation. (Even if the Other is seen *as* an object in the direct man-woman relation, it is not a relation mediated by a process of object-creating.) What is required, then, for a critical analysis of Marx is a rethinking of the relation between the early and late Marx in terms of the development of his analysis of intersubjectivity.

Marcuse

It is precisely in the context of the issue of the relation between the early and late Marx that the work of Herbert Marcuse becomes important. Marcuse's self-imposed project is to rescue the critique of the domination of nature in the early Marx as the foundation for all of Marx's later formulations. This project is explicitly carried out in the essay,

'The Foundations of Historical Materialism'. In *Eros and Civilization*, Marcuse attempts to unite Marx's theory with the liberatory potential embedded in Freud's theory of the instincts. He interprets the basic Freudian conflict between the pleasure principle (first nature) and the reality principle (second nature) as a socio-historic conflict. Contemporary society enforces a surplus repression beyond that required by the current stage of civilization. He calls this the performance principle, which is 'a Reality Principle based on the efficiency and prowess in the fulfillment of competitive economic and acquisitive functions.'[4] This historical form of the reality principle defeats the pleasure principle and thereby maintains society as a system of social and self-domination. However, the objectives of the defeated pleasure principle are retained in the unconscious. What civilization represses in the interest of economic performance is retained in the individual's unconscious psyche as a desire for gratification. The project of human liberation is therefore to establish a society beyond the rule of the performance principle where libidinal satisfaction, not domination, is the foundation of human relations.[5]

In the attempt to specify those aspects of instinctual life which are the basis of a *new* reality principle, Marcuse resuscitates nature as an independent moment within a dialectical theory that points to the possibility of a reconciliation of 'man and nature'. This reconciliation, 'the humanization of nature and the naturalization of man', was a central question in Marx's early work (although Marx is never cited in *Eros and Civilization*). Marcuse reformulates or 'extrapolates' the relation between Eros, Thanatos, and the Nirvana principle to reveal the relation between alienated labor and the surplus repression of the instincts. What is most significant in this discussion is the theory of the role of maternal eros. For Marcuse, the dialectical regression beyond surplus repression would be the return of the desire for liberation tied to the memory of infantile gratification rooted in the initial relation to the mother. The mother represents a utopian moment as she represents the pleasure principle against the father as the representative of the reality principle.

Later, in *Counterrevolution and Revolt* and 'Marxism and feminism', Marcuse overrules his theory of woman as mother providing a utopian vision to the son. What is now seen as central to the project of liberation is 'the ascent of Eros over aggression in men *and* women'[6] which is tied to the 'feminine principle' as the definite negation of the male performance principle. Here, again, Marcuse situates the problem of the intersubjective recognition of difference within an analysis of the early Marx. For Marcuse, the free society is to be one in which an androgynous fusion of historically separated differences will occur, but a 'natural' difference will remain. In other words, Marcuse, extrapolating from the early Marx, holds that a new social order could *recognize* different qualities such that the traditional masculine/feminine dichotomy would break down, but society would remain divided by a fundamental natural/sexual difference (male/female) which could never be entirely overcome by social and historical transformations.

Horkheimer and Adorno

The question of the domination of nature is the central question of the social critique most powerfully articulated by the first generation of the Frankfurt School (Marcuse, Horkheimer, and Adorno). However, where Marcuse is concerned with the reconciliation with nature, Horkheimer and Adorno analyze the destructive tendencies of the revolt of nature and oppose any romantic idealization of nature.[7] There are several important theoretical positions developed here: the rejection of labor as the necessary source of liberation; the concern with a changed relation to nature in terms of the constitution of subjectivity; and a theory of the relative autonomy of the psyche, the family, and cultural and political spheres. In articulating these positions, Horkheimer and Adorno show the necessity for departing from the Hegelian system.

Thus, while they are indebted to Hegel and begin from his analysis in their studies of modern culture and fascism, they make an axial turn because of their sustained critique of the notion of reconciliation in Hegel's philosophy, which creates a closed and uncritical system. They reformulate the terms in which contemporary radical social theory must conceptualize 'nature' by revealing the logic of identity in Hegel's philosophy as part and parcel of the domination of nature.

The Abstract Pro-Nature Stance: A Critique of Balbus

Recently, there has emerged a tendency in neo-Marxist and feminist thought that can be called an abstract pro-Nature position. Correctly perceiving that the domination of nature is the underlying issue in the liberation movements of the 1980s, this position suggests that the domination of nature must be rejected root and branch. The positive reception of Isaac Balbus' *Marxism and Domination: A Neo-Hegelian, Feminist, Psychoanalytic Theory of Sexual, Political and Technological Liberation*[8] attests to the fact that this tendency has become widespread. However, as we will see, such an approach entails a highly selective approach to contemporary politics. In particular, the feminist defense of the right to abortion on demand and the fundamental significance of the black movement are evaded by Balbus' position.

Accepting Hegel's analysis that objectification *equals* alienation, Balbus rejects Marx's analysis of reification, which distinguishes between alienated and non-alienated forms of objectification. According to Balbus, the elimination of the domination of nature is to be achieved, not by overcoming the alienated forms of objectification, but by the creation of a 'post-objectifying mode of symbolization' through the *transcendence* of objectification. The thesis of the transcendence of objectification is at first somewhat mysterious. One begins to wonder if there is to be any object-creation in the liberated world. Eventually, we find out that, yes indeed, we are to become capable of a different relation to nature which allows us to transform nature but *not* for the goal of human survival.[9]

Within this thesis of the transcendence of objectification, Balbus claims that we must move beyond the anthropomorphic stance in which humans see themselves as 'the measure of all things' to 'the more modest, ecologically sound assumption that nature cannot be outwitted and that, in fact, "Nature knows best".'[10] Thus, within the post-Instrumental mode of symbolization:

> Humans relate to nature not only in terms of their own purposes but also in terms of the different purposes inherent in *its* various entities; nature for the postobjectifying consciousness is no longer a pure means to exclusively human ends but becomes an end in itself. Put otherwise, nature regains the intrinsic significance that it lost within the Instrumental mode of symbolization; human interaction with nature once again becomes a meaningful experience.[11]

This position does not seem to me very different from the concept of the reconciliation with nature in the early Marx and Marcuse. However, that is not the most important issue here. Rather, this position, which may be useful for the ecology, peace and anti-nuclear movements, creates profound problems for feminists because 'Nature' in its 'wisdom' creates not only ecological balance but unwanted pregnancies.[12] To say that nature must become 'an end in itself' hardly articulates a principle that can ground the feminist politics of abortion on demand. This position, in which the interpretation of the 'end' or *telos* of nature is left in limbo, lends aid and comfort to the abstract pro-Nature position that is gaining adherents within the peace, ecology, and anti-nuclear movements in the United States. Such a position has led some leftists to don 'the seamless garment' of pro-life politics, which entails an anti-abortion stand.[13] Such a position also presents problems for the gay and lesbian movements. Homosexual relationships are not based on the procreative possibilities of the couple and in this sense may be seen as 'anti-nature'. And, if 'Nature knows best,' then it follows that one is either born a homosexual or a lesbian or these sexual orientations are 'unnatural'. This leaves no room for the analysis of lesbianism as a *political* choice, which was an important development in the women's liberation movement. In addition, the artificial insemination of lesbians, which sometimes involves an attempt to secure a daughter rather than a son, may also be seen as 'dominating nature'.

Against the abstract understanding of nature as benign and omniscient, what is required for a feminist analysis is a comprehensive understanding of nature which includes the aspect of mere nature 'red in tooth and claw'. Such an understanding can be found in the work of Theodor Adorno. For Adorno, the origin of the domination of nature is a contradiction within nature itself: 'The suppression of nature for human ends is a mere natural relationship.'[14] Here, the domination of nature is seen as a consequence *of* nature. It is therefore only the memory of suffering that results from domination which can animate the project of liberation – not 'Nature itself'.[15]

In his effort to theorize and generate new possibilities of critical consciousness, Balbus points to the necessity for a transformation in child-rearing practices. Since the mode of child-rearing is seen to significantly determine our unconscious life, and thereby to establish the limits of our ability to transform society as adults, a non-dominating stance toward nature and others is to be achieved through shared heterosexual parenting. Leaning heavily on the work of Dorothy Dinnerstein, Balbus claims that we must have fathers as well as mothers involved in the care of infants if we are to eliminate the development of an unconscious process in which the need to deny the power of the mother entails the domination of the Other as woman, nature, or political adversary. Once both men and women share the responsibility for child-care, the mother will no longer be seen as all-powerful and with the dissolution of the first powerful (M)Other, the logic of domination will disappear.

Within feminism in general, and within Balbus' analysis in particular, there has been a shift away from the politics of abortion (non-mother-hood) to a concern with reclaiming motherhood. But the liberatory roots of the attempt to reclaim and reconstruct motherhood *began* with women who found themselves suffering from the alienation of enforced motherhood – women who found themselves pregnant when they did not want to be and were forced either to have an unwanted child or to risk death with an illegal abortion. The politics of reproduction cannot forget its origins: it cannot be reduced to a form of shared heterosexual parenting as Balbus suggests, but must remain first and foremost woman's right to choose *not* to reproduce, the right *not* to mother. In addition, such a politics must articulate the right to choose the form of birth (midwife/hospital) and to choose between heterosexual shared parenting and woman-only motherhood.

The reclaiming of motherhood is a contentious issue within feminist theory. Balbus, following Dinnerstein and Chodorow, sees only negative features in human development due to the absence of the father from early child-care: male domination of woman and the domination of nature are seen as reactions to the overwhelming and unbearable power of the mother experienced by the pre-verbal, pre-rational infant. This analysis, however, is quite different from the feminist ones in which female mothering is seen as the basis for the transformation of society. Feminists like Rich, Ruddick, Ryan, and Whitbeck see positive features in mother-raised children and want to use these features to ground a model of the non-dominating relation between self and Other. For them, equality and the non-dominating stance toward nature are not necessarily incompatible with the sexual division of labor. Rich, for example, sees woman-bonding or sisterhood as the solution to the oppressive character of motherhood as an institution. Thus, the central issue is perceived as the social domination of woman rather than the sexual division of labor or the process of gender differentiation. Even those who agree that shared heterosexual parenting is the goal recognize that there are potential dangers. For example, men are not nurturers by training and so may not be able to give the infant the nurturance he/she requires; men are the source of most familial incest; and men may attempt to divest women of their children in situations in which women have little else.[16]

In contradistinction to Balbus' theory, Horkheimer and Adorno develop a theory of the domination of nature in which social oppression rather than child-rearing patterns is shown to be central. In the *Dialectic of Enlightenment*, they reveal the connection between the domination of women and the domination of Jews in which women and Jews are seen *as* nature. They write:

> Women and Jews can be seen not to have ruled for thousands of years . . . and their fear and weakness, the greater affinity to nature which perennial oppression produces in them, is the very element which gives them life. This enrages the strong who must pay for their strength with an intense alienation from nature, and must always suppress their fear.[17]

Here it is social domination which requires that the Other be kept alive and suppressed as nature; and the Other is seen to acquire a relation to nature that keeps alive the hope of liberation. This analysis can be extended to include the domination of blacks in a way that Balbus' analysis cannot.

Any theory of contemporary liberation movements must recognize the foundational role of the black movement in the development of the counterculture and the New Left in the United States. The infusion of black music and black politics into the white psyche was a major force in the radicalization process of the 1960s: from the explicit sexuality of black music to the militant opposition of the Black Panthers, blacks were seen as saying something to whites and whites were listening. What developed was the New Left identification with blacks ('student as nigger') and a support for their struggles (as well as support for Third World struggles). It is simply not good enough to say, as Balbus does, that one did not participate in the black movement. One must recognize the importance of black culture and black politics for *all* the liberation struggles of the 1960s, especially if one's stated project is the search for a unification of these struggles.

What is central here is that Balbus develops an argument concerning the role of child-rearing patterns in the creation of radical activists that eliminates the possibility of understanding black activism. According to Balbus, it was upper-middle class professional families, raising their children according to the child-centered patterns developed and expounded by Dr Spock, that created the white radicals of the 1960s.[18] But Black Panthers rarely came from such families.[19] It was not family dynamics, but the unique configuration of institutionalized racism, which sent an inordinate number of blacks to fight and die in Viet Nam, that created black activism in the 1960s.

For Balbus, the domination of nature is a 'collective neurosis' originating in the process of our separation from the mother within 'mother-monopolized' child-care which leaves us unable to accept our own death. Thus, the problem of death (Norman O. Brown) rather than objectification/alienation (Marx) or sex (Freud) is the central one. He admits that feminism is the weak link in his argument for the unification of the feminist, ecology, and participatory democracy movements. However, he believes that this is because the prolonged pre-Oedipal identification between sons and mothers creates a radical male psyche able to support ecology and participatory democracy, but this psyche retains an unconscious need to dominate women. Against this claim, I believe that the political insufficiencies of this work are rooted in the theoretical eclecticism of an abstract pro-Nature stance, and come to grief when the issues of abortion and black liberation are raised.

Reconciliation with Nature?

Within the Frankfurt School there is a tension between the liberatory (Marcuse) and repressive (Horkheimer and Adorno) aspects of nature. From this perspective, the 'abstract pro-Nature stance' (Balbus) advocates a naïve, direct, and immediate unity of humanity with nature which does not take into account the danger, compulsion, and scarcity of untransformed nature. Any adequate theory of the domination of nature must retain this tension rather than attempt to avoid it. The work of Murray Bookchin, which has been influenced by the Frankfurt School, understands the complexity of this issue. In *The Ecology of Freedom*, he writes:

> . . . an ecological ethics is not patterned on a naive vision of the natural world–either as it exists today or as it might exist in a 'pacified' social future. The wolf has no business lying down with a lamb.[20]

However, Bookchin has a deep disagreement with the Frankfurt School over the source of this tension in nature. Whereas Horkheimer and Adorno maintain an essential distinction between consciousness and nature and see dominating reason as 'still too natural', Bookchin regards nature as already imbued with consciousness. He writes:

> From the biochemical responses of a plant to its environment to the most willful actions of a scientist in the laboratory, a common bond of primal subjectivity inheres in the very organization of "matter" itself. In this sense, the human mind has never been alone, even in the most inorganic of surroundings.[21]

This disagreement between the Frankfurt School and Bookchin touches on the most fundamental issue raised by critiques of the domination of nature. This short essay cannot hope to resolve the issue. Rather, it suggests that in order to come to a comprehensive conclusion concerning this disagreement it is necessary to rethink the sources of these concepts of nature. The Frankfurt School derives the distinction between consciousness and nature from German Idealism through Marxism. Bookchin's work, rooted in an anarchist perspective, argues for the necessity to step outside this tradition. In a speculative vein, it seems to me that Bookchin's conception of nature bears a deep affinity with the origins of American nature philosophy as found in Emerson and Thoreau.

The necessity to think through the concept of the domination of nature comes out of recent political movements and the urgency of their projects. A critical appropriation and extension of this concept prepares the way for the 'mutual aid' of these movements. But the history of the domination of nature is not *merely* the history of an error as the abstract pro-Nature stance supposes. Our political agenda requires a more profound thinking through of the sense in which we may be 'reconciled' with nature.

REFERENCES

1. Theodor W. Adorno, *Negative Dialectics* (New York: Seabury Press, 1973), p. 8 (amended translation).
2. *See* my article on 'Hegel and "The Woman Question": Recognition and Intersubjectivity.' In Lorenne M. G. Clark and Lynda Lange (eds.) *The Sexism of Social and Political Theory: Women and Reproduction from Plato to Nietzsche* (Toronto: University of Toronto Press, 1979), pp. 74–98.
3. Alfred Schmidt, *The Concept of Nature in Marx* (London: New Left Books, 1973), p. 80.
4. Herbert Marcuse, 'Marxism and feminism', *Women's Studies*, 2, 279, 1974.
5. Herbert Marcuse, *Eros and Civilization. A Philosophical Inquiry into Freud* (New York: Vintage Books, 1962), pp. 15–18 and 220.
6. Herbert Marcuse, *Counterrevolution and Revolt* (Boston: Beacon Press, 1972), p. 75.
7. This is not to suggest that the philosophical positions of Horkheimer and Adorno are identical. Despite their collaboration on *Dialectic of Enlightenment*, one has only to compare Horkheimer's *Eclipse of Reason* to Adorno's *Negative Dialectics* for their differences to become apparent. See Susan Buck-Morss, *The Origin of Negative Dialectics*. (New York: The Free Press, 1977), Ch. 4.
8. Isaac D. Balbus, *Marxism and Domination: A Neo-Hegelian, Feminist, Psychoanalytic Theory of Sexual, Political, and Technological Liberation* (Princeton: Princeton University Press, 1982). An earlier version of my critique of Balbus was published as 'Man-Made Motherhood and Other Sleights of Hand', *Phenomenology + Pedagogy*, Vol. 3, No. 3, 1986.
9. Ibid., p. 374.
10. Ibid., p. 365.
11. Ibid., p. 285.
12. In fact, it is not only feminists who are affected by this abstract 'pro-Nature' stance. For example, native groups who live by hunting wolves, seals, or bears now find themselves in conflict with urban-based groups who oppose all killing of animals. And of course, 'Nature' creates famine, flood and disease as well as ecological balance.
13. The conflict between an abstract pro-life politics and a feminist perspective was revealed most clearly in a recent issue of *The Village Voice* (July 16, 1985). See especially Nat Hentoff's article 'How Can the Left Be Against Life?' (p. 18 and 20) and the rebuttal by Ellen Willis 'Putting Women Back into the Abortion Debate' (p. 15, 16 and 24). *See also* the feminist critique by Katha Pollit 'Hentoff, Are You Listening?' in *Mother Jones*

(February/March, 1985). The same debate is raging in the pages of *The Nonviolent Activist*, a publication put out by the War Resisters' League. See the May-June and July-August issues, 1985. According to a report in *off our backs* (August-September, 1985, p. 7) a new anti-abortion group called Feminists for Life has been spawned by this debate.

14. Theodor W. Adorno, *Negative Dialectics*, p. 179.

15. In my book, *Woman, Nature and Psyche* (1987, Yale University Press), I explore this position from a feminist perspective.

16. *See*, for example, Rosalind Pollack Petchesky, 'Reproductive Freedom: "Beyond A Woman's Right to Choose" '. In: Catharine R. Stimpson and Ethel Spector Person (eds) *Women: Sex and Sexuality* (Chicago: University of Chicago Press, 1980); Adrienne Rich, *Of Woman Born: Motherhood as Experience and Institution* (New York: W. W. Norton & Co., Inc., 1976); Sara Ruddick, 'Maternal Thinking'. In: Joyce Trebilcot (ed.) *Mothering: Essays in Feminist Theory* (Totowa, New Jersey: Rowman & Allanheld, 1984); Joanna Ryan, 'Psychoanalysis and Women Loving Women.' In: Sue Cartledge and Joanna Ryan (eds) *Sex and Love: New Thoughts on Old Contradictions* (London: The Women's Press Ltd., 1983); Patsy Schweickart, Review essay entitled 'Feminist Utopias – Going Nowhere?'. In: *The Women's Review of Books*, Vol. 11, No. 10, July, 1985; Caroline Whitbeck, 'Maternal Instinct' and 'Afterword.' In: Joyce Trebilcot (ed.) *Mothering;* Iris Marion Young, 'Is Male Gender Identity the Cause of Male Domination?' In: *Mothering*.

   The new emphasis on the reclaiming of motherhood in the United States often obscures the fact that there are still many unwilling mothers bearing unwanted children and women dying from illegal abortions all over the world.

17. Max Horkheimer and Theodor W. Adorno. *Dialectic of Enlightenment* (New York: Herder & Herder, 1972), p. 112.

18. Balbus has some difficulty trying to explain white female activism. While the sons of the revolution were mothered by child-centered women, the daughters it seems had 'Supermoms': mothers who were not only child-centered but successful career women. These mothers, however, were ambiguous about their success in the public world and tended to maintain the family as the primary source of their identity (pp. 394–95).

19. Nor did the Young Lords, Native Indians, or working-class activists.

20. Murray Bookchin, *The Ecology of Freedom* (Palo Alto: Cheshire Books, 1982), p. 277.

21. Ibid., p. 276.

The Social Ecology of Communication

Stephen Duplantier

There are no maps showing the lay of social and ecological utopias.

Present mapmakers show the abundant Nation-States in pastel colors on political maps of the world. A light-olive Mongolia nestles under a tawny-orange Soviet Union. A sunset-purple Bolivia lies landlocked in South America. The atlases are full of information on coffee-bean production in Brazil and tungsten deposits in Australia. Some newer environmental maps, inspired by remotely sensed satellite imagery, are much more realistic. All these maps have their place. But where are maps of the imagination and atlases of utopias?

We need cartographers who could do for maps what Jorge Luis Borges had done for literature. A mapmaker who could give us thematic maps of mindforms (world distribution of melancholy, the geomorphology of pity, maps of grace and desire, honor and madness, abnegation and contentment) would be someone who could help reduce the present poverty of imagination. A natural history of fanciful creatures and unthreatened nature would be a useful guide for *prolepsis* — leaping ahead to pre-experience the life, society, and environment which is most desirable.

Murray Bookchin is such a cartographer of the imagination: his maps are prose depictions of possibilities and potentialities which wait as impatiently and irascibly as he does for history to catch up. His logic is *ecomorphic* — the 'wayward logic of the organic' — logic which takes the shape of an ecosystem. His writings are as diverse as a rainforest, full of bewildering complexity and intricate mazeways of interconnected energy flows.

Murray Bookchin's lifework is the development of the ideas of social ecology; his style is *ecolectical* (ecologically dialectical, as is the logic of nature). The strategy of his writings is to get the reader to co-evolve with his texts 'critically and querously . . . but with empathy and sensibility' for its arguments against domination and for freedom.[1] Bookchin's rhetoric of social ecology is a 'process-oriented dialectical approach' which stands at odds with analytical approaches. Process dialectic is capable of modeling the primal person who lives and understands the flood of natural phenomena which are co-equal with their lives. The old ways of being human, of understanding and living, can be recovered and partially restored. Our minds are forever different from those of our ancestors, so a literal return to the primitive is not possible. But what can happen, according to Bookchin, is the 'quasi-animistic respiritization of phenomena—inanimate as well as animate— without abandoning the insights provided by science and analytic reasoning.'[2] The ambition of social ecology is a true dialectic which would conjoin the subjectivity of our primal past (itself, no less an *episteme*, a 'science', or way of knowing) with the analytic science of today (just as much a fiction and piece of story-telling as the conscious mythopoeia of the primal person).[3] The blending of these two mythologies by good mapmakers and tale-tellers is the pressing need of today. This book is an attempt to tell some of the new stories.

Bookchin's goal of quasi-animistic respiritization is part of the 're-enchantment of the world' which Berman has been charting.[4] Re-enchantment is necessary because of the disenchantment of the world described by Max Weber. Disenchantment followed from the 'transcendentalization of God', or, in Berman's translation of Schiller's phrase, 'the disgodding of nature'. Respiritization is a re-godding, although Bookchin would avoid the 'quasi-theological trappings' of god-language. Despite this, *The Ecology of Freedom* is self-admittedly messianic.

'Messianism' here means that Bookchin is hopeful about a coherent future which is also radically new. That future so fervently described in the book is, he says, the working out of 'reason'. Bookchin acknowledges his unorthodox use of the word. For him, 'reason exists in nature as the self-organizing attributes of substance; it is the latent subjectivity of the inorganic and organic levels of reality that reveal an inherent striving toward consciousness.'[5] The working out of this immanent world reason seems uncomfortably monotheistic. This kind of reason seems like a replay of the ontogeny of the Western religious ethos. Still, even if Bookchin's ecological philosophy bears some of the shadows of religious history, his methodology is decidedly anti-dogmatic. His work is a *Summa Ecologica*, not in the sense of a complete catalog of every biological relation in ecosystems, but more of a magisterial rendering of what humans need philosphically in order to live ecologically. His *Summa* is not dogmatic like the treatises of the medieval Schoolmen, but open-ended, intuitive, and interactive—the very model of the social ecological principles he is teaching. The participatory and 'unfinished' quality of *The Ecology of Freedom* encourages readers to complete it themselves. His work is an explicit theory and methodology of a libertarian rhetoric, important for its imaginative blend of rigorous analysis and freeplaying respiritization.

In the spirit of what I take Bookchin to be teaching, I will not simply summarize his complex thought. Those formidable ideas are already well presented in his books and articles. Rather, I will follow his advice to engage in imaginative, proleptic, and utopian discourse.

This essay is about two issues which have a bearing on social ecology and communication. The first is *teleproxemics*—the name I have given to the problem of the confusion of near and far caused by modern media of communication. The second is *polytheism*, which is about the question of the one and the many. Preceding these is a discussion of reason, speech, and freedom.

Eco-epistemology—the Dialectic of the Rational

Reason and the rational may be less the willed-for and attained climax of human development than an evolutionary trait of which human beings are the heir.[6] Reason as consciousness, in Bookchin's unorthodox usage, needs to be untangled from the progressivist bias that sees reason as the crowning achievement of humankind. Wartofsky shows that reason is natural – like the opposable thumb and the human voice— definitely not supernatural. Reason developed 'because it functions optimally for human survival.'[7] In view of the catastrophes of the twentieth century, there exist critical questions about the ability of reason to be adequate as a means for total ecospheric survival. In fact, the reasonableness, and even the dangerousness, of reason is worth pondering. Bookchin concludes that humans ' . . . are a curse on natural evolution, not its fulfilment.'[8] This is the dialectic of reason.

On the one hand, passionate defenders of the human would insist that reason is all that is good about human life. Detractors might say that the bad must be taken with the good and not merely repackaged as 'unreason'. Reason's nightmare is when it turns into its opposite.[9] Bookchin's solution of identifying reason with 'consciousness', and especially with the ultimate self-consciousness of humanity, is not an answer to the problem. Reason as consciousness, while it may not be as grand and pretentious as some kind of 'Omega Point', nonetheless implies that a pinnacle is reached in mankind-transcendent. I think it is fair, and not merely fashionably cynical or anti-human, to question human consciousness as an ultimate. Reason as consciousness remains ecolectical: the pressure of natural selection against reason must still be admitted. If reason has evolved non-teleologically, then it can devolve as well.

Reason easily turns into its opposite while keeping the appearance of the rational: it can seem 'reasonable' while becoming repressive and instrumental. A serious question is whether rationality is a danger to the species.[10]

The scholastics had the concept of *recta ratio* (right reason). The antithesis of right reason is an unreasonable reason which seems to have evolved along with the tools, art, bipedalism, large brain, small pelvis, social structures, as well as everything else we know as human nature and culture. The dialectic of right reason and its negation are part of the natural history of human ecology.

Can reason be saved? Are the defects of reason only pseudo-reason, or are they the inescapable shadow of reason? The answers are not clear.

Reason and rhetoric are very closely related. Rhetoric is by definition instrumental. 'The aim of rhetoric . . .' says a recent account, 'is to affect the giving of sound decisions: i.e., good judgements.'[11] There is a brotherhood between rhetoric and practical reason, since the purpose of rhetoric is to influence the making of 'preferred or more defensible decisions.'[12]

'Communication' is a more neutral term than rhetoric. Communication is the branching and extended kinship of discourse and interchange, while rhetoric is the practice of 'persuasive possibility'. If communication is 'unfettered sharing' in thought and feeling, then rhetoric shows the limits of communicative possibility. Rhetoric's reasonableness must be suspect, based on the history of the Western world. Farrell has noted that neither the rhetorical tradition nor the communicative philosophy tradition 'depict accurately the reality of ongoing communicative practice.'[13] This is the realm of the ecology of communication which has been missed by both traditions. Traditional rhetorical theory sees the connections between speech and democracy.[14] Traditional liberal democracy, rhetoric, and communication meet here. C. Wright Mills describes the process:

> The people are presented with problems. They discuss them. They decide on them. They formulate viewpoints. These viewpoints are organized and they compete. One viewpoint 'wins out.' Then the people act on this view, or their representatives are instructed to act it out, and this they promptly do.[15]

This is a fairy tale, according to Mills. The mass media are part of the reason why this kind of naïve democracy is extinct. Mills sees media as destroyers of discussion and interchange of opinion. And what is just as bad, the media are themselves part of the increased means of control and power at the disposal of the élites of power and wealth.[16] But media-as-evil was preceded by media-as-salvation.

The field of communication and media studies in the US started with high promise in the writings of Dewey, Cooley, Park, and Mead. Dewey noted the deeper-than-etymological relationships between *common, community, communion*, and *communication*. 'Men live in a community in virtue of the things they have in common; and communication is the way in which they come to possess things in common.'[17] Dewey's early insight into communication had a practical, though progressivist, slant to it. Dewey thought communication was wonderful enough to be the fulfilment of the promise to restore the face-to-face small town community, with its accompanying values, in a nation which was hell-bent on industrializing and expanding (and in the process, running over small towns and their ways).[18] But the Chicago School—the grandfathers of communication studies in the US—saw in the newer technologies of information exchange (spawned by industrialization) potentialities for the transformation of society. The information made available by the new media would augment and improve public discourse, they thought. In their ideal democracy, if more information is made available, the decisions of the public could be more rational and therefore more democratic. Of course, the dream of a return to a small town face-to-face democracy by a media-made 'great community' was never possible, as Mills pointed out.

Carey calls the 'transmission view' that which is concerned with 'who does what to whom with what effect?'[19] This view is linked to the dominant mode of the West: discovery, exploration, exploitation, and domination. Transmission means sending and receiving, but not necessarily equally or mutually. Transmission means transportation and the conquering of distance; it is inextricably bound with hegemony, colonialism, corporate plunder, profit, and imperialism.

The next period of communication studies in the US after the community-focused Chicago School was the 'effects tradition'. This approach accepted the transmission view and a positivist method. It was practiced from the 1930s on by figures like Lasswell, Lazersfeld, Lewin, and Hovland. The rise of separate departments of communication in universities took place while the effects tradition was dominant. Today, most communication scholars in the US were schooled under this approach.

The monopoly of this tradition has been broken by critical approaches, mostly imported from Europe. The minority view in the US is increasingly critical. Carey has called the effects tradition 'intellectually stagnant and increasingly uninteresting.' It has devolved into a 'mere academicism: the solemn repetition of the indubitable.'[20]

Communication-as-transmission leads to effects studies which are not merely neutral social science. The knowledge and data generated are most usable by government, institutions, and corporations. The benefits generally give the established regimes more power and control. This is the realm of 'administrative' studies which positivistic social science serves so well.

But another style and approach to communication and rhetoric is indifferent, if not opposed, to entrenched power structures. Carey calls this alternative the 'ritual view'. The style of this kind of communication is one of sacred/secular ceremonies which can bring people together in fellowship and commonality. Symbol and ritual-making in the service of better symbolic environments is a kind of utopian communication. Hamelink has looked at the varieties of utopian communication research. The question is whether such research can give us the knowledge to 'understand and change social reality.'[21] The assumption underlying the notion that we need a utopian science of communication is the dystopian nature of present societies and communities. Communication theory should be guided by a vision of a wished-for society. The knowledge produced by communication research should make the present understandable and the future possible. Hamelink sees in the development of an 'emancipatory science of art, of accidental and irrational moments which give birth to new ideas', a tool which can liberate people from the predominant mode of knowledge generation.

This is the promise of art, ritual, and communitarian ecology which goes back to a sacred, archaic world-view.[22] The 'old ways', which make up 99% of human experience, go at least as far back as the Paleolithic era of 50,000–100,000 years ago. The social ecology of communication in such organic societies went as follows, according to Bookchin:

> . . . the blood that flows between the community and nature in the process of being kin is circulated by distinct acts of the community: ceremonials, dances, dramas, songs, decorations and symbols. The dancers who imitate animals in their gestures or birds in their calls are engaged in more than mere mimesis; they form a communal and choral unity with nature, a unity that edges into the intimate intercourse of sexuality, birth and the exchange of blood. By virtue of a community solidarity that such widely bandied terms as stewardship can hardly convey, organic societies 'hear' a nature and 'speak' for a nature that will be slowly muffled and muted by the 'civilizations' that gain ascendency over them. Until then, nature is no silent world or passive environment lacking meaning beyond the dictates of human manipulation. Hence social ecology has its origins in humanity's initial awareness of its own sociality—not merely as a cognitive dimension of epistemology but as an ontological consociation with the natural world.[23]

Bookchin calls this the 'outlook of the organic society'. This picture of organic society is not a blueprint for a modern ecological society, but it is the ontological matrix of a society, not of communicative *rationality*, but of communicative *ecstasy* (to suggest an improvement over Habermas' goal). This type of participatory, ecstatic, sensuous, aesthetic, imaginative, kinesthetic, celebratory society represents a storehouse of social riches and diversity which no merely rational community can ever hope to match. With enough social ecological evolution, a recapturing of the best of past and present organic societies might be possible. Reason's saving grace, even with its auto-nemesis lurking just inside itself, is its ability to transcend itself. When it is reasonable to go beyond reason to a newly remade, neo-organic, socially ecological community, then reason, both as *ratio* and as consciousness, can make the move.

The Ecology of Distance

Communication can be thought of as an attempt to regain and restore what was once whole. The separation by distancing, which is what communication is trying to overcome, can be psychophysical as in the birth trauma (with the subsequent loss of the womb—the center of warmth and security.) It may be a multi-leveled, existential alienation. Or the separation may even be expressed archetypally in the primordial, cosmological story (whether expressed as myth or science) of the Big Bang—the headlong rush of the universe away from its center.

The clue that the original wholeness existed is the 'foreground radiation' of the individuated wholeness of self, which is visible and recoverable. The end of our personal and cosmic story will be the ultimate collapse back to the center of the universe.

The general systemic dialectic of near and far is as much a problem of philosophy as it is of astronomy. Problems of distance are everywhere: the dislocation between word and thing is an abyss into which humans have fallen. Original unity and wholeness, psychic integration, at-one-ment are what is so earnestly sought after. Communication leads to consciousness which most successfully bridges the separation of being far from the center.

The body is the first human medium of communication. People touch, kiss, and make love in silence. When words are added, complications and misunderstandings take place. Bodies in passion are successful without words. Intimate proxemic distances do not require verbalization.[24] In fact, moans, soft sounds of tongues, sharp inhalations, and long exhalations are perfectly adequate as a most wonderful poetry. As the distance apart increases, first whispers, then soft voices are heard (sweet nothings). Giggles and laughs are eloquent. *Post coitum*, the sadness is not due to guilt, but because words are now necessary. Explanations, discussions, excuses, and analysis all become necessary.

Voices rise and words proliferate. At less personal distances, speech gets loud, formal, stilted, and frozen. The stentorian public voice means truncated ideas, little subtlety, shouting, and incoherence. The increase in distance between communicating bodies has a built-in limiting factor. Over enough distance, communication between bodies is impossible and unnecessary. Finally, there is only silence.

Mechanical media, from Sumerian clay tablets to interactive computers and satellite links, do not so much extend the ordinary senses of humans (as McLuhan has put it) as bring the far away up close. The name I have given to this property of modern media is *teleproxemics* — when the far away seems close. Teleproxemics signifies having the appearance of being near while actually being far away. When what sould be at a distance is brought up close, then misperceptions occur. With electronic media, teleproxemic events are a relocation: the perceived phenomenon is presence without substance. Telephones, television, and radio bring the appearance of living and speaking people to the eye and ear of the observer, but these media bring no matter or physical presence. Edmund Carpenter used a line from Don Quixote as the title for his book on media: *Oh What a Blow the Phantom Gave Me.*[25] Teleproxemic reality is a sensual paradox in which phantoms seem real.

The remote sensing of electronic media perception is also a theological problem. Teleproxemic media are like the literal interpretations of angels and transcendent deities — supernatural beings in another realm, not seen, not present in substance but powerful (more or less) in effect.

Teleproxemic realities are anti-earth and anti-ecology because they are not part of local bioregions. The catastrophe seen on television does not require any action because it is dematerialized. The mediabody, the eyes that 'see' phantom electrons on a screen assemble into people and things and the ears that 'hear' the reconstituted voices and music from a speaker, is not one of extended senses but of fractionated senses. Media do not eliminate space, as McLuhan says, but give only the appearance of doing so.

Teleproxemics is the confusion of distance between the near and the far which plays havoc with the idea of community and ecosystem. The current phrase 'think globally, act locally' is usually thought of as a balanced strategy for understanding and action. But thinking globally is possible only in a teleproxemic sense. It can only mean to *conceive* ideas globally, not *perceive* them. Global perception is not generally possible, though the illusion of it is. Teleproxemics creates this illusion in an authorial 'I', an ego conceived as a center through the distorted perception of the distant as near. Teleproxemic perception disrupts the balance and redundancy of the senses and endangers the more accurate perception of local phenomena.

Theologically, in teleproxemic perception, the ground of being is lost. The result is a search for supernatural beings 'out there', when actually the ground is literally where the body is standing.

Ecological perception and consciousness is wholeness and localness in the extreme. 'Sense of place' should not be thought of merely as an idea or as of a vague feeling of loyalty for a specific locale, but as a mode of perception as well as a topophilic commitment to the rocks, waters, and biological diversity of a bioregion.

The early medieval Benedictine vow of stability of place is more difficult to comprehend than the companion vows of poverty, chastity, and obedience. Benedictine monks still vow permanent connection, not with the idea of monasticism, but with their particular monastery. Although a traveling monk would be welcomed at another monastery, there is always a permanent home monastery to which he must return. The commitment to a particular place does not incline the Benedictines to be missionaries (religious/temporal empire-building 'warriors', like the Jesuits).

The pilgrim finds out through the pilgrimage away from home that what is being searched for was never lost. Psychically, culturally, ecologically, the message is, as poet Wendell Berry has put it, 'fragmentation is a disease'.

Teleproxemic perception and media threaten the health and wholeness of individuals and of communities by the dislocation and unbalancing of forces and centers.

Bateson tries to solve the problem of near and far, or 'immanence and transcendence' in his terminology, through what he calls 'cybernetic epistemology'.

The individual mind is immanent but not only in the body. It is immanent also in the pathways and messages outside the body; and there is larger mind of which individual mind is only a sub-system. This larger mind is comparable to God and is perhaps what some people mean by 'God', but it is still immanent in the total interconnected social system and planetary ecology.[26]

Bateson's immanence is extended but not ethereal. He sees mind as inseparable from the structures in which they are immanent. This puts mind/God back where it belongs—in circuit in the system. The distancing involved in traditional ways of thinking about humans and nature causes mistakes to be made. Distrust is natural when someone is not near enough at hand to be a friend, neighbor, acquaintance, or friendly presence. The distant is alien because it is unfamiliar. But Bateson is saying that this is an erroneous way of thinking. Selves are excessively concretized objects which can fall prey to pathological epistemology. The new way of thinking has been understood by poets who saw the false separations between self and experience. The boundaries of the ego may have been incorrectly mapped or may even be fictitious. Distance is the enemy: 'It is the attempt to separate intellect from emotion that is monstrous, and . . . it is equally monstrous—and dangerous—to attempt to separate the external mind from the internal, or to separate mind from body.'[27]

Human reason and consciousness are not all there is to 'nature made self-conscious', but, rather, are only a part of a whole system of self-consciousness. No one species possesses the self-consciousness of the whole; it is shared among the members of the ecosystem. It is erroneous to try to localize the first instance of the emergence of consciousness in humans. Recent work in animal thinking may tend to further reduce human hubris.[28] But Bateson's eco-epistemology is even more radical than admitting that animals share consciousness. Even inanimate beings are part of the dance of mind through the system.[29] Rocks, biogeographical, and hydrological cycles are part of immanent mind. The ecumenism of this view is extraordinary: the only thing not explicit enough in Bateson's theology is the apparent monotheism of his one big 'Mind'. Locality and distance, the problem of the near and the far, is solved by immanence-in-circuit, but the problem of the one and the many (diversity) remains.

An immanent Mind may be godlike, as Bateson suggests. But minds (in the plural) are a richer and more accurate ecological image. Eco-theology requires polytheism. Monotheistic thinking is 'abstract, formal, logical and speculative thinking', a kind of intellectual and rational fascism. A 'one-party dictatorship of the mind which forcibly supresses feelings and intuition expressed in concrete images and symbolized by the telling of stories.'[30]

The death of God is the death of a monotheism which means, as Miller puts it, 'single minded and one dimensional thinking' not only in religion, but likewise in politics, history, society, ethics, and psychology. Miller writes: 'Socially understood, polytheism is eternally in unresolvable conflict with social monotheism, which in its worse form is fascism and in its less destructive forms is imperialism, capitalism, feudalism and monarchy.'[31] Polytheism is not heresy but a social reality and a philosophical condition. Men and women experience polytheism when single logics, grammars and symbol systems cannot describe their experiences. Polytheism is in the air when 'metaphors, stories, anecdotes, puns, dramas and movies, with all their mysterious ambiguity, seem more compelling than the rhetoric of political, religious and philosophical systems.'[32]

Polytheistic sensibility is ecological. A principle of ecology is 'unity in diversity', but these terms are permanently dialectical. The diversity does not disappear because of the unity. The unity is not an overarching super Mind (the one big Divinity). The unity resides in the pantheon. All the gods are necessary to compose a pantheistic ecology—all the species and beings become gods for one another. Bear and Coyote were god-like for many of the peoples of North America. In turn, in animal theology, humans may have been (and maybe still are) gods to Bear and Coyote. Maybe, if we do not think of animals as beasts but as gods, they will do the same for us.

If nature is made self-conscious through humans, it is made more wily and clever through Coyote, and strong and patient through Rock. Damselflies are nature made light and delicate. All the species and beings are necessary to make up the pantheon. 'The things of heaven and earth are such a wide realm that the organs of all beings together only can provide comprehension.'[33]

Deep Communication

These ideas have been offered as part of the utopian dialogue needed for the emergence of social ecology and neo-organic societies. The work and play of building ecological societies can benefit from an awareness of the dangers of teleproxemic perception. Polytheistic thinking can reduce the persistent tendency in many people to think monotonically. The ritual view of communication goes well with the prospects of forging new communities and revitalizing old ones. Bioregional communities need the deep ecological perspective created by rituals. Finally, non-teleproxemic, immanent, polytheistic, socially ecological communication might be multi-sensuous, tactile, more silent, less verbal, more musical, filled with more dancing, leaping, and kinesthetic experiences. As guides to this kind of communication, the shamans of the world's primal cultures are an inspiration. But we do not have to rely solely on antique rituals. Contemporary ritualists like Dolores La Chapelle know how to orchestrate this kind of communication for people in Western society. She is an extraordinary guide to what we can call *deep communication*.[34]

With more of the right kind of earth-bonding rituals in neo-organic, bioregional cultures and a reduction of instrumental communication, there will be less domination and unfreedom in the world. The attainment of the degree of 'muteness' and silence required to balance the excesses of discursive communication will demand some, as yet, uncertain strategies and efforts on our part. But the resulting liberation and freedom coming from non-pathological knowledge, practice, and community will be sufficient reward.

REFERENCES

1. M. Bookchin, *The Ecology of Freedom* (Palo Alto: Cheshire Books 1982), p. 13.
2. Ibid., p. 14.
3. *See* M. Landau, 'Human Evolution as Narrative', *American Scientist* 72: 262–268, 1984.
4. M. Berman, *The Reenchantment of the World* (Ithaca: Cornell University Press, 1982).
5. M. Bookchin, op.cit., p. 11.
6. M. W. Wartofsky, 'Is Science Rational?' In: W. H. Truitt and T. W. G. Solomons (eds) *Science, Technology and Freedom* (Boston: Houghton Mifflin Co., 1974).
7. Ibid., p. 207.
8. M. Bookchin, op.cit., p. 238.
9. A. Gouldner, *The Two Marxisms: Contradiction and Anomalies in the Development of Theory* (New York: Seabury Press, 1980).
10. M. W. Wartofsky, op.cit., p. 202.
11. T. B. Farrell, 'The Tradition of Rhetoric and the Philosophy of Communication,' *Communication* 7: 1983, p. 162.
12. Idem.
13. Ibid., p. 176.
14. L. Thonssen and A. C. Baird, *Speech Criticism* (New York: Ronald Press, 1948).
15. C. W. Mills, *The Power Elite* (New York: Oxford University Press, 1948).
16. Ibid., pp. 314 and 315.
17. John Dewey (1915) quoted in D. Czitrom, *Media and the American Mind — from Morse to McLuhan* (Chapel Hill: University of North Carolina Press, 1982).
18. D. Czitrom, op.cit.
19. J. W. Carey, 'A Cultural Approach to Communication,' *Communication* 2:1–22, 1975.
20. J. W. Carey, 'Overcoming Resistance to Cultural Studies'. A paper presented to the Qualitative Studies Division, The Association for Education in Journalism and Mass Communication. Memphis. 1985.
21. C. J. Hamelink, 'Emancipation of Domestication: Toward a Utopian Science of Communication,' *Journal of Communication* 33:74–79, 1983.
22. G. Snyder, *The Old Ways* (San Francisco: City Lights Books, 1977).
23. M. Bookchin, op.cit., p. 48.
24. E. T. Hall, *The Hidden Dimension* (Garden City: Doubleday and Company, Inc., 1966).
25. E. Carpenter, *Oh, What a Blow the Phantom Gave Me* (New York: Holt, Rinehart and Winston, 1972).
26. G. Bateson, 'Form, Substance and Difference,' in R. Grossinger (ed.),

Ecology and Consciousness (Richmond, CA: North Atlantic Books 1978), p. 40.
27. Ibid., p. 41.
28. D. R. Griffin, *Animal Thinking* (Cambridge: Harvard University Press, 1984).
29. G. Bateson, *Steps to an Ecology of Mind* (New York: Ballantine. 1972).
30. D. L. Miller, *The New Polytheism — Rebirth of the Gods and Goddesses* (Dallas: Spring Publications, 1981), p. 46.
31. Ibid., p. 26.
32. Idem.
33. Symmmachus, quoted in D. L. Miller, p. 93.
34. D. La Chapelle, *Earth Wisdom* (Silverton, CO: Finn Hill Arts, 1978) and *Sacred Land, Sacred Sex — The Rapture of the Deep* (forthcoming).

Hegel's Lament

Jonathan Stevens

There is no blue
in the sky above us
there's too much blood
in the soil below
Destiny
is a pit between us
and your owl
is a deadly crow

There is a hand
that kills in the shaking
a poison kiss
that seems so right
a summer dream
that has no waking
a kind of love
that smothers light

(Chorus;)

And this is not the sacred mountain
the eternal circle
is the barrel of a gun
don't try to sing
along beside me
because the number
is not One.

Your sacred dance
is a walk of numbers
your guru's mass
a halloween ball
your pyramid
is full of cobwebs
no exit sign
on the labyrinth wall

The stars align
as do the zealots
sarificial fire
has been re-lit
Donations
have been collected
so the Prophet falls
into the Holy fit

(repeat chorus)

You call me brother
and bid me drink
from this water
you say is wine
your music soothes
but does not think
that there is hunger
beyond your mind

(repeat chorus; end)

Hegel's Lament

Verse I

There is no blue in the sky a-bove us, there's too much blood in the soil be-low, Destiny is a pit be-tween us, and your owl is a deadly crow / And this is not the sacred

chorus:

mount-ain, the eternal circle is the barrel of a gun, don't try to sing along be-side me, because the number is not one.

Postscript: Ecologizing the Dialectic*
Murray Bookchin

It is eminently *natural* for humanity to create a second nature from its evolution in first nature. By second nature, I refer to humanity's development of a uniquely human culture, a wide variety of institutionalized human communities, an effective human technics, a richly symbolic language, and a carefully managed source of nutriment. Dualism, in all its forms, has opposed these two natures to each other; they are normally seen as antagonists. Monism, in turn, often dissolves one into the other, be this monism Marxist, liberal, fascist, or, more recently, a very extreme form of 'biocentrism' that more closely approximates an inhuman form of 'anti-humanism' than the more equivocal forms of 'biocentrism' that are currently in vogue. These monist ideologies differ primarily in whether they want to dissolve first nature into second or second nature into first.

What the dualist and monist views share is their conception that the two natures are at least parallel to each other. Classically, the counterpart of the 'domination of nature by man' has been the 'domination of man by nature.' Just as Marxism and liberalism see the former as a desideratum that emerges out of the latter, so acolytes of 'natural law' accept the latter as a fact that is all but tainted by human efforts to achieve the former. Some recently arrived voices in the ecology movement have added a new wrinkle to this imagery: they seek a cosmos in which humanity will essentially resign itself to the rather indisputable fact that it is 'part' of nature. This would be a truism if it were not exaggerated into a moral 'democracy' in which humanity's 'right' to

* Murray Bookchin contributed this essay as an expression of his most recent thinking on many of the issues addressed in this collection. A more extensive version has been published as 'Thinking Ecologically: A Dialectical Approach' in *Our Generation* 18: 3–41, and will be included in a forthcoming volume from Black Rose Books. It should be consulted for a more detailed presentation of his ideas on Deep Ecology, bioregionalism, Eastern thought and other topics.

live and fulfil itself is equatable with the 'right' of butterflies, ants, whales, apes, and—yes—pathogenic viruses and germs to live. The logical problems this ballet of ideas produces, particularly when it is played out in the wings of the philosophical stage rather than in the centre, are too complex to examine at this point. Suffice it to say, for the moment, that every one of these images as it now stands is deeply flawed—not only because it is conceptually one-sided or simply wrong, but because of the way it is philosophically structured and worked out.

The real question, I submit, is not whether second nature parallels, opposes, or blandly 'participates' in an 'egalitarian' first nature.[1] Rather, it is how second nature is *derived* from first nature. More specifically, in what ways did the highly graded and many-phased evolution from first nature into second give rise to social institutions, forms of inter-action between people, and, in the best of cases, a mutuality between first and second nature that enriched both natures? The ecological crisis we face today is very much a crisis in the emergence of society out of biology, the contradictions (the rise of hierarchy, domination, patri-archy, classes, and the State) that unfolded with this development, and the liberatory pathways which provide an alternative to this warped history.

The fact that these two natures exist and can never be dualized into 'parallels' or simplistically reduced to each other accounts in great part for my use of the words '*social* ecology'. Additionally, social ecology has the special meaning that the ecological crisis that beleaguers us stems from a social crisis, a crisis which a crude biologism tends to ignore; still further, that the resolution of this social crisis can be achieved only by reorganizing society along ecological lines, imbued with an ecological philosophy and sensibility.

Such a philosophy and sensibility cannot be patched together from the bits and pieces of alien outlooks like mechanism and mysticism or from traditional, indeed 'common-sensical' logic and Eastern theos-ophy. One can respect a consistently Eastern mystical view or a consist-ently Western mechanistic view, however much either one may seem one-sided or erroneous. Neither view, I submit, can fruitfully derive second nature from first nature organically—that is to say, by using a mode of thought that distinguishes the phases of the evolutionary continuum from which second nature emerges and yet preserve first nature as part of the process. Common sense betrays us by its demand for conceptual fixity. Mysticism, in turn, deflects us from developing a rationality that goes substantially beyond poetic metaphors. What is wrong with a good deal of ecological thinking, today, is that it partakes of both modes—the mechanistic and the mystical—in an opportunistic, 'catch as catch can', manner rather than by restructuring its mode of thought in an authentically organic manner.

This much should be clear: the purely deductive logic we use to build bridges, budget our income, plan our everyday lives, and calculate our chances of 'making out' in the world offers no promise of grasping the richly articulated or mediated development that both unites and differentiates second and first nature. Common sense demands only inference, consistency, and the verification provided by ordinary sensory experience. Apart from the inductively acquired particulars that help us arrive (often quite intuitively) at the concrete premises for our inferences, we normally tend to deduce our ideas schematically, as a series of well-ordered and rigidly fixed concepts. Truth in this everyday logical domain is normally little more than consistency. Thus, we are held to be 'logical' only when our conclusions can be framed into fixed categories, supported, to be sure, by those atomized isolates we deliciously call 'brute facts'. We celebrate this achievement as 'clarity' and its results as 'certainty'. To conceive of anything other than a hypothetico-deductive logic is evidence of 'fuzzy-headedness'. Facts, you know, are facts, and truth is truth. Consistency, the syllogistic 'if . . . then' propositions that make up formal logic, together with our image of experiences as a sequence of 'clear-cut' data and the eminently practical results formal logic achieves—all, taken together, verify the judgement that we 'think clearly' and understand the 'real world'.

Yet, there is a highly personal sphere of life in which we think very differently from the habitual rationality we exercise in our practical affairs. We do not deal with children, for example, the way we deal with our business affairs and the pragmatics of our everyday living. We see them as *developing* beings who pass through necessary 'stages' of growth and increasing capabilities. We try not to impose more demands upon them than they can adequately handle (assuming, to be sure, that we are rational and humane people). Nor do we try to afflict them with problems they cannot resolve. We sense that there is a *flow* in their lives that involves the actualization of their potentialities at different levels of their development. It requires no unusual perceptive qualities to recognize the infant that lingers on in the child, the child that lingers on in the adolescent, the adolescent that lingers on in the youth, the youth that lingers on in the adult—in short, the *cumulative* nature of their development in contrast to the common-sensical attitude of substitution, succession, and supplantation. Only a fool believes that the man or woman could—or should—completely replace the boy or girl. Properly understood, a mature person is not an inventory of test results and measurements. He or she is an individual *biography*, the developmental embodiment of wholly or partially realized qualities which environment surely conditions (today, radically so) but whose inherent 'make-up' should ultimately determine his or her development; that is, if society acquires a rational form.

However intuitive it may be, this kind of thinking is structured not around deduction but *eduction*. If deduction can be said to consist of the 'if . . . then' inferential steps we take, with due reverence for consistency, to arrive at unshakeable and clearly defined judgements about 'brute facts', eduction can be said to render the latent possibilities of phenomena fully manifest and articulated. Clearly, then, eduction implies a phased process in which 'if' is not a purely hypothetical premise but rather a *potentiality*.[2] 'Steps' in the logical process are not mere inferences, but, rather, stages of *development*. 'Consistency', far from being an imposed canon of logic based on the classical 'laws' of 'identity', 'contradiction,' and the 'excluded middle', is that immanent process we properly call *self-development*. Finally, 'then' is the full *actualization* of potentiality in its rich, self-incorporative 'stages' of growth, differentiation, maturation, and wholeness. That the 'mature' and the 'whole' are never so complete that they cease to be the potentiality for a still further development represents an ecological change in the dialectical that Hegel, given his strong theological bent, terminated in an 'Absolute' which encompasses the full unfolding of the world in an identity of subject and object.

Which brings us to the problem of what we are obliged to modify in the dialectical philosophy of its two most outstanding voices, Aristotle and Hegel, in order to render it an ecological mode of thought.[3] To do this, we must briefly summarize what an ecological dialectic shares with the Aristotelian and Hegelian, often at the risk of anticipating what I hope to examine more fully at a later point.

Dialectical philosophy moves from the undifferentiated abstract to the highly differentiated concrete while most common-sensical forms of thought move in the very opposite direction. In this respect, dialectic picks up and goes beyond the thread of classical education from the implicit in bare potentiality to its realization in a fully articulated actuality. For much of Greek philosophy, this problematic of development was expressed as the emergence of the Many from the One. In Aristotle, whose work marks the apogee of classical thought, 'a conception of substance, or the real, as the goal toward which develops a potential being that, save as ultimately realized, is neither real nor intelligible, dominates the whole course of . . . speculation,' observes G. R. G. Mure in a very pithy formulation. 'Follow him as he applies it in every sphere which he investigates; watch it grow from this initial abstract formula into a concrete universe of thought; and you may hope to grasp the essential meaning of his philosophy.'[4] The same can be said for Hegel, whose elaboration of this Aristotelian motif is more subjectivized and informed—at times, even cluttered—by a mountain of problematics in philosophy that were added to Western thought since Aristotle's time.

An ecological dialectic would have to deal with the fact that Aristotle and Hegel did not work with an evolutionary theory of nature, hence the natural world was seen more in terms of a *scala naturae*, a ladder of 'being', rather than a flowing continuum. Ecology, in effect, would have to introduce evolution, not only logical derivation and education, into this 'ladder', indeed replace the notion of a 'ladder' or *scala naturae* by a richly mediated continuum. Both thinkers, too, were more profoundly influenced by Plato than their writings would seem to indicate, with the result that in Hegel we usually move more within a realm of concepts than history, however historical Hegel's dialectic invariably proves to be. Which is to say that Hegel is strongly preoccupied with the 'ideal' of nature rather than its existential details, although this fixation, too, is honoured in the breach. The overarching teleology of the two philosophers tends to subordinate the element of contingency, spontaneity, and creativity that marks natural phenomena as we know them today.[5] In an ecological dialectic, by contrast, there is no terminality that could culminate in a 'God' or an 'Absolute', as is clearly the case with Hegel. 'Actuality', which is often used in a very special sense interchangeably with 'reality', is almost the momentary culmination of maturity so that the objectivity of the potential, which I hold to be crucial for developing a truly objective ethics, is subordinated to its actualization. By giving an emphatically historical priority to nature as the ground for intellectuation, an ecological dialectic obliges us to reformulate Hegelian terms like the 'real' and the 'actual'. English translations of certain passages in Hegel often render 'real' and 'actual' as synonyms, such that the Hegelian 'real' is conceived as the *actualization* of the potential, a failing that I believe should be corrected. What is less 'real' than *Hegel's* 'reality', notably the 'brute facts' or the given 'is' of common sense, would more closely correspond to 'the apparent' (*das Erscheinende*). From an ecological viewpoint, this could lead to a very confusing use of terms, hence I have used the word 'real' to simply mean 'what is', not what is necessarily latent in the potential. 'Actuality' remains very much what Hegel meant it to be: the rational realization of the potential as distinguished from the 'real' as the existential.[6] Finally, the creative role that Hegel imparts to strife, often seen as mere 'antithesis', would have to be greatly modified, although not without ignoring the presence of strife in human history. An ecological view of the dialectic would tilt dialectical philosophy toward differentiation rather than conflict and redefine progress to emphasize the role of social elaboration rather than social competition. Additionally, progress would be seen as growing self-consciousness and mutuality rather than the result of 'Spirit's' self-elaboration, with its hidden historical agenda beyond the understanding of the people who make history.

Dialectic, let me emphasize, is not merely 'change', 'motion', or even 'process', all banal applications of these terms to dialectical philosophy to the contrary notwithstanding. Nor can it be subsumed under the mere term 'process philosophy'. Dialectic is *development*, not mere 'change'; it is *derivative*, not mere motion'; it is *mediation*, not mere 'process', and it is *cumulative*, not a mere continuum. That it is also change, motion, process, and a continuum tells us only part of its true content. But denied its immanent self-directiveness; its phases that yield unity in diversity; its entelechal eduction of the potential into the actual, this 'process philosophy', indeed this remarkable notion of *causality*, ceases to be dialectic and becomes a mere husk that our current flock of eco-journalists reduces to 'kinetics', 'dynamics', 'fluctuations' and 'feedback loops', indeed a mechanistic salad of verbiage that dresses up systems theory as a developmental philosophy.

As Hegel warns us in the course of educing the complexity of the dialectical processs: knowledge has 'no other object than to draw out what is inward or implicit and thus *to become objective.*' But if

> that which is implicit comes into existence, it certainly passes into change, yet it *remains one and the same* . . . The plant, for example, does not lose itself in mere *indefinite* change. From the germ much is produced when at first nothing was to be seen; but the whole of what is brought forth, if not developed, is yet hidden and ideally contained within itself, the principle of *this projection into existence* is that the germ cannot remain merely implicit, but is impelled toward development, since it presents the contradiction of being only implicitly and yet not desiring to be so.[7]

Thus dialectic is not *wayward* 'motion', the mere 'kinetics' of change. There is an 'end in view'—not preordained, to state this point from an ecological viewpoint rather than a theological one, but as the actualization of what is implicit in the potential. Every 'if . . . then' proposition is not premised on *any* 'if' that springs into one's head like a gambler's hunch; it is the positing of a potentiality that has its ancestry in the dialectical processes that preceded it.

Reductionism breaks this process down to the most undifferentiated interactions it can formulate. But it does so at the cost of demolishing the integrity of the various phases or 'moments' (to use Hegelian terminology) from which the process is literally constituted. A living being is clearly an ensemble of chemicals. While reductionism can explain its existence as a mere physico-chemical *being*, it cannot comprehend it as a remarkably complex form of *life*. Chemical analysis provides us with no substitute for the multitude of forms, relationships, processes, and environments that the organic creates for itself as it metabolically sustains its own 'selfhood' in differentiation from other 'selves'. Indeed, carried too far into another level of phenomena, reduction leads to dissolution so that the very integrity of a given level, be it social, biological, chemical, or physical, simply disappears into mere 'matter' and 'motion'. A kind of ideological entropy occurs in which thought no longer has the differentia with which to define its subject matter, much less explore it. By a process of trimming down the complex to its 'irreducible' components, the whole which forms the very premises of thought disappears into a meaningless, indeed formless heap of 'matter', thereby erasing the very boundaries that give definition to a phenomenon as a component of a more complex 'whole'.

In the organic world, the metabolic activity of life-forms constitutes the sense of self-identity, however germinal, from which nature begins to acquire its rudimentary subjectivity. This subjectivity (which reductionism necessarily cannot encompass) not only derives from the metabolic process of self-maintenance, a process that defines any life-form as a unique whole; rudimentary subjectivity extends itself beyond self-maintenance to become a *striving* activity, not unlike the development from the vegetative to the animative, that ultimately yields mind, will, and the capacity for freedom. Conceived dialectically, organic evolution, like social development, is, in a very loose way, subjective in that life-forms and the communities they establish strive to be other than what they are, a perception that stands very much at odds with that clearly definable fixidity of conceptions we blissfully call 'clear thinking'. Systems theory enters into this reductionist tableau in a very sinister way. What renders the theory so Kafkaesque is that, by dissolving the subjective element in life so that biological phenomena can be treated as mathematical symbols, evolutionary interaction, subjective development, even process itself, are taken over by '*the* System,' just as the individual, the family, and the community are destructured into 'the System' embodied by the economic corporation and the State. Life ceases to have subjectivity and becomes more of a mechanism in which the striving of life-forms toward ever greater differentiation is replaced by 'feedback loops', and their evolutionary antecedents are replaced by programmed 'information'. A 'systems view of life' is literally life conceived as '*a* System', not only as 'fluctuations' and 'cycles'—mechanistic as these concepts are in themselves.

Leaving aside all the external selective factors which Darwinians invoke to describe evolution, the striving of life toward a greater complexity of selfhood—a striving that yields increasing degrees of subjectivity—constitutes the internal or immanent impulse of evolution toward growing self-awareness. This evolutionary dialectic constitutes the essence of life as a self-maintaining organism that bears the potential for a self-conscious organism. A dialectical orientation, in effect, is not merely a 'logic' or a 'method' that can be bounced around and 'applied' promiscuously to a content. It has no 'handbook' other than reason itself to guide those who seek to develop a dialectical sensibility. Dialectic can no more be applied to problems in engineering than Einstein's general theory of relativity can be applied to plumbing. These problems can best be resolved by traditional forms of logic, common sense, and the pragmatic knowledge acquired by experience. The content which dialectic explicates must be a developmental phenomenon just as systems theory properly explicates the workings of a system with its fluctuations and cycles. The kind of verification that validates or invalidates the soundness of dialectical reasoning, in turn, must be a developmental phenomenon, not relatively static, or, for that matter, 'fluctuating' kinds of phenomena.

Hence, it distorts the very meaning of dialectic to speak of it as a 'method'. Indeed, dialectical philosophy, properly conceived and freed of vulgar Marxian presumptions, is an ongoing protest against the myth of 'methodology': notably, that 'techniques' for thinking out a process can be separated from the process itself. This sensitivity for the concrete, even when Hegel distills it into 'concepts', is what renders dialectic such an existentially vital and palpably organismic philosophy. It was Hegel's genius to reintroduce Plato's supramundane world of forms—an *exemplary*, and hence a *moral* world, I should emphasize, not merely a metaphysical one—into reality and develop Aristotle's notion of entelechy into a concept of 'transcendence' (*aufhebung*) that nuanced processes as mediated 'moments in the self-fulfillment of their potentialities.' Freed of its theological trappings, dialectic *explains* with a power beyond that of any conventional wisdom how the organic flow of first into second nature is a reworking of biological reality into social reality. Each phase or 'moment', pressed by its own internal logic into an antithetical and ultimately a more transcendent form, emerges as a more complex unity in diversity that encompasses its earlier 'moments' even as it goes beyond them. Despite the imagery of strife that permeates the Hegelian version of this process, the ultimate point in the Hegelian *aufhebung* is reconciliation, not the nihilism of pure negation. Moreover, norms—the actualization of the potential 'is' into the ethical 'ought'—are anchored in the objective reality of potentiality itself, not as it always 'is', to be sure, but as it 'should be' such that speculation becomes a valid account of reality in its 'truth'. Hegel, I would argue, *radically expands the very concept of Being in philosophy and in the real world to encompass the potential and its actualization into what it 'should be'*, not only as an existential 'what is'.[8]

Dialectical speculation thus becomes projective in a sharply critical sense, quite unlike 'futurology', which dissolves the future by making it a mere extrapolation of the present. It is in this sense that Hegel can truly call his dialectic 'negative philosophy' in its restless critique of reality. By the same token, speculation also becomes creative by ceaselessly contrasting the free, rational, and moral actuality of 'what could be' that inheres in nature's thrust toward self-reflexivity with the existential reality of 'what is'. That speculation can thereby ask 'why'—not only 'how'—the real has become the irrational, indeed, the inhuman and anti-ecological, derives precisely from the fact that dialectic alone is capable of grounding an ecological ethics in the actualization of the potential, that is, in its objective possibilities for the realization of truth.

This objectivization of possibilities—of potentiality conceived as continuous with its yet unrealized actualization—provides the ground for a genuinely objective ethics as distinguished from an ethical relativism that is subject to the waywardness of the opinion poll. An ecological interpretation of dialectic, in effect, opens the way to an ethics that is rooted in the objectivity of the potential, not in the commandments of a deity or the eternality of a supramundane and transcendental 'reality'. Hence, the 'should be' or 'could be' acquires not only objectivity, but it forms the objective critique of the given reality.

Human intervention into nature is inherently inevitable. It is utterly obfuscatory to argue whether this intervention 'should' occur: humanity's second nature is not simply an external imposition of human society on biology's first nature. Rather, it is the result of first nature's own inherent evolutionary process. What is at issue in humanity's transformation of nature is whether its practice is consistent with an objective ecological ethics—an ethics that has yet to be rationally developed, not one which is haphazardly divined, felt, or intuited.

Minimally, I would argue that such an ecological ethics definitely involves human stewardship of the planet. I say this all the more because a humanity that fails to see that it is the embodiment of nature rendered self-conscious and self-reflexive has separated itself from nature morally as well as intellectually. Second nature in such a situation literally becomes divested of its last ties to first nature; worse, the vacuum which the departure of consciousness leaves is filled by blind market-oriented interests and an egoistic marketplace mentality. In any case, there is no road back from second to first nature, any more than second nature as it is now constituted can rescue the planet from destruction with its 'technological fixes' and political reforms.

Given the massive ecological crisis that confronts us, intellectual confusion in the ecology movement may yield harmful results of immeasurable proportions. To carelessly heap fragments of ideas on each other and call this 'ecophilosophy' is no longer an affordable luxury in the present period of history. In advocating human stewardship of the earth, I do not believe it has to consist of such accommodating measures as James Lovelock's establishment of ecological wilderness zones or attempts to patch up environmental dislocations with half measures. What it can mean—and what it should mean—is a radical integration of second nature with first nature along far-reaching ecological lines, an integration that would yield new ecocommunities, ecotechnologies, and an abiding ecological sensibility that embodies nature's thrust toward self-reflexivity. To write an active human presence out of nature would be as unnatural as a rainforest that lacks monkeys and ants. Dialectic, it should be noted, is no less a critique of one-sidedness and simplicity as it is of existing reality and a mentality adaptive to the status quo. Cast in radical ecological terms, it calls for a denial of *centricity* as such, be it 'anthropocentricity' or 'biocentricity'. A philosophy of organic development is above all a philosophy of wholeness in which evolution reaches a degree of unity in diversity such that nature can act upon itself rationally, defined mainly by coordinates created by nature's potential for freedom and conceptual thought.

To speak concretely: in the intermediate zone between first nature and second that saw the graded passage of biological evolution into social, social evolution began to assume a highly aberrant form. The effort of organic societies like bands and tribes to elaborate their non-hierarchical, egalitarian social forms was arrested. For reasons that involve complex evaluation, social evolution was diverted from the realization and fulfilment of a cooperative society into a direction that yielded hierarchical, class-oriented, and Statist institutions. Whatever could have been rescued from the more cooperative past was still further distorted by the rise of the Nation-State and, ultimately, the rise of a capitalist economy. In our own time, we have seen an even more serious distortion of second nature by the massive penetration of this economy into society as a whole. The market economy, which all cultures resisted to one degree or another from antiquity to recent times, has essentially become a market society. This society is historically unique. It identifies progress with competition rather than cooperation. It views society as a realm for possessing things rather than the elaboration of human relationships. It creates a morality that is based on growth rather than limit and balance. For the first time in human history, society and community have been reduced to little more than a huge shopping mall.

Unless ecology explores this warped development systematically—that is, unless it unearths its internal logic in a reasoned and organismic way—its critical thrust will be entirely lost and its very integrity will be hopelessly impugned. Today, the most serious obstacle to the realization of this critical project is eclecticism and reductionism: a hodge-podge of disconnected, even contradictory, ideas degraded to their lowest common denominator. This kind of approach may appeal to lazy minds that prefer slogans to reasoned studies of society and its impact on the natural world. But with lazy minds come lazy thoughts and a passive-receptive mentality that increasingly renders people vulnerable to authoritarian controls.

We must try to bring the threads of our discussion together and examine the important implications dialectic has for ecological thinking. A 'dialectical view of life' is a very special form of process philosophy. Its emphasis is not on change, but on development. It is eductive rather than deductive, mediated rather than merely processual, and cumulative rather than continuous. Its commitment to objectivity begins with the actuality of the potential, not with the mere facticity of the real, hence its ethics seeks to define the 'what could be' as a realm of *objective* possibilities. That 'possibilities' can be regarded as objective in contravention to simplistic forms of materialism is dialectically justified by the perception that potentiality and its latent possibilities form an existential continuum that constitutes the authentic world of *truth*—the world of the 'what should be', not simply the world of the 'what is' with all its incompleteness and falsehood.

From a dialectical viewpoint, a change in a given level of biotic, communal, or, for that matter, social organization consists not simply of a new, possibly more complex, ensemble of 'feedback loops'. Rather, it consists of qualitatively new attributes, interrelationships, and degrees of subjectivity that express and radically condition the fact that a new potential has emerged, opening a new realm of possibility with its own unique self-directive mode of activity—not a greater or lesser number of 'fluctuations' and 'rhythms'. Moreover, this new potential is itself the result of other actualizations of potentialities that, taken together historically and cumulatively, constitute a developmental continuum—not a bullet 'shot from a pistol' that explodes into Being without a history of its own or a continuum of which it is part.[9]

Dialectical logic is an immanent logic of process—an *ontological* logic—not only a logic of concepts, categories, and symbols. This logic is emergent in the sense that one speaks of the 'logic of events'. Considered in terms of its emphasis on differentiation, this logic is provocatively concrete in its relationship to abstract generalizations, hence Hegel's use of the seemingly paradoxical expression the 'concrete universal.' Dialectic thereby overcomes Plato's dualistic separation of exemplary ideas from a phenomenal world of flawed 'copies', hence its ethical thrust is literally structured, cumulatively as well as sequentially, into the concrete. Emerging from this superb, basically Hegelian, ensemble is a world that is always ethically problematic, an ethics that is always objective, a recognition of selfhood and subjectivity that embodies non-human and human nature, a development from meta-bolic self-maintenance to rational self-direction, which thereby locates the origins of reason *within* nature, not in a supramundane domain that exists *apart* from nature. The social is thus wedded to the natural and human reason is wedded to non-human subjectivity through processes that are richly mediated and graded in a shared continuum of develop-ment. This ecological interpretation of dialectic not only overcomes dualism but through differentiation moves in the very opposite direc-tion away from reductionism.

Ecology cleanses this remarkable heritage of European organismic thought of the hard teleological predeterminations it acquired from Greek theology, the Platonistic denigration of physicality, and the Christian preoccupation with human inwardness as soul and a reverence for God. And it is only ecology that can ventilate the dialectic as an orientation toward the objective world by rendering it co-extensive with natural evolution—a privilege, I may add, that has been possible only with the appearance of evolutionary theory in the last century.

As such, dialectic is not only a way of thinking organically; it can be a source of *meaning* to natural evolution—of ethical meaning, not only rational meaning. To state this view more provocatively: we cannot hope to find humanity's 'place in nature' without knowing how it *emerged* from nature with all its problems and possibilities. Our result yields a creative paradox: second nature in an ecological society would be the actualization of first nature's potentiality to achieve mind and truth. Human intellectuation in an ecological society would thus 'fold back' upon the evolutionary continuum that exists in first nature. In this sense—and in this sense alone—second nature would thus *become* first nature rendered self-reflexive, a thinking nature that knows itself and can guide its own evolution—not an unthinking nature that 'seeks its own balance' through the 'dynamics' of 'fluctuations' and 'feedback', at the cost of needless pain, suffering, and death. Although thought, society, and culture would still retain their integrity, they would also consciously express the abiding tendency within first nature to press itself toward the level of thought and conscious self-direction. (Here, I cannot help but contrast again the eductive approach of dialectic which presses toward the differentiation of phenomena with the deductive approach of systems theory which presses toward the symbolic reduction of phenomena.)

In a very real sense, in fact, an ecological society would be a trans-cendence of both first nature and second nature into the new domain of a *free* nature, a nature that could reach the level of conceptual thought—in short, a nature that would wilfully and thinkingly cope with conflict, contingency, waste, and compulsion. In this new syn-thesis, where first and second nature are melded into a free, rational, and ethical nature, neither first nature nor second would lose its specificity and integrity. Humanity, far from diminishing the integrity of nature, would add the dimension of freedom, reason, and ethics to first nature and raise evolution to a level of self-reflexivity that has always been latent in the very emergence of the natural world.

To deny this transcendence and synthesis of first and second nature into a free nature is to open ecological thinking to all the waywardness of those 'if . . . then' propositions that threaten to overrun and brutalize it. These propositions are triggered off like bullets 'shot from a pistol' (to use Hegel's blunt mataphor). Generally, it makes no difference what the target may be as long as the 'aim' is 'accurate', hence the common-sensical fetishization of consistency rather than truth. Common sense 'brainstorms' rather than thinks, and throws ideas into the air with the prayer that mere probability will provide us with a meaningful pattern.

The results of this desystematization of thinking are often ludicrous when they are not simply cruel, even vicious. *If* all organisms in the biosphere are equally worthy of a right of life and organic fulfilment, as many biocentrists believe, *then* human beings have no right, *given the full logic of this proposition*, to stamp out malarial and yellow-fever mosquitoes. Nor does the logic of this proposition give humanity the right to eliminate the AIDS virus and other organic sources of deadly illness.[10] It hardly helps us to learn that the notion of 'biocentric equality', to re-word the language of Bill Devall and George Sessions, the authors of *Deep Ecology*, is hedged by a qualifier like 'we have no right to destroy other living beings without sufficient reason.'[11] A qualification like 'sufficient reason' is ambiguous enough to divest the entire notion of its logical integrity. Logic, in fact, gives way to a purely relativistic ethics. What may be a 'sufficient reason' for Devall and Sessions—all their well-meant and desirable intentions aside—may be very 'insufficient' to a large array of people whose well-being, indeed whose very survival under the present 'system', conflicts sharply with the authors' views. Given this kind of argumentation, which divests ethics of its social basis and second nature of its derivation from first nature, 'centricity' bifurcates into an opposing body of values called biocentrism that makes humans and viruses equal 'citizens' in a 'biospheric democracy', or, alternatively, makes humans into self-centred sovereigns in what is presumably a 'biospheric tyranny'. That both views are in error is an essential point in this work. In any case, 'deep ecology', taken at its word, leads us into a foggy and dangerous logical realm from which there is usually no redemption but a recourse to Eastern mysticism.[12]

There is no 'biospheric democracy' nor 'tyranny' in nature other than what human second nature imparts to non-human first nature, just as there is no hierarchy, domination, class structure, nor State in the natural world other than projections that the socially conditioned human mind extends into non-human biological relationships.

'Rights', in any meaningful sense of the word, are the product of custom, tradition, institutional development, social relationships, an increasing self-consciousness of historical experience, and *mind*, that is, conceptual thought that painstakingly *formulates* a constellation of rights and duties that makes for an empathetic respect for individuals and collectivities. Leopards recognize no 'rights' among themselves and certainly no 'rights' to life, much less 'fulfilment,' among the animals on which they prey. As mammals, these predators may be more self-aware than, say, frogs, because of their more complex neurological and sensory apparatus. Hence, they may be more subjective, even more rational in a dim way.

But their range of conceptualization from everything we know is so limited, often so immediately focused on their own needs, that to impute ethical judgements involving 'rights' to their behaviour is to be truly anthropocentric, often without even knowing so. When 'biocentrists', 'anti-humanists', and 'deep ecologists' flagellate us with claims that life-forms have 'rights' to life and 'fulfilment' which we, as humans, fail to 'recognize', they unknowingly introduce a hidden humanism—essentially, a feeling of empathy and identification—that we bring to all forms of life. They work from *within* our human feelings, indeed the best that constitutes our humanism, to incarnate 'rights' and the notion of a 'biospheric democracy' that emerges from the human *social* sphere and to ways in which human communities *institutionalize* themselves that require careful social analysis and radical institutional change. A human empathy and sense of identification that yields a profound respect and sensitivity for the non-human world should not be confused with sophisticated ethical 'rights' and 'democracy' that have moral and political meaning—that is, unless we are ready to reduce the meaning of these terms to a point where they lose their authentic social content for human society and human intellectuation. Ironically, if there is to be anything that approximates a 'biospheric democracy' in the non-human world, it will be shaped by human empathy, which *presupposes* the rational and ecological intervention of human beings into the natural world. This will entail the infusion of human values into nature and of human mind into non-human subjectivity.[13]

Biocentrists and anti-humanists can hardly have their cake and eat it. Either humanity is a distinctive moral agent in the biosphere, which can at least bring the prospect of a 'biospheric democracy' into the natural world by practicing an ecological stewardship of nature—or else it is 'One' with the whole world of life and simply dissolves into it. If the latter is true, humanity's exploitation of the planet to suit its own ends is a 'biospheric right' that cannot be denied any more than can the 'rights' enjoyed by a leopard to kill and feast on its kill—only less 'effectively' and 'efficiently' than human beings. To change the whole level of the argument by reverting to mere expediency and to claim that the despoliation of the earth by plundering 'humans' (whoever they may be) will ultimately boomerang on the human species becomes a pragmatic problem of a purely instrumental character. The issue is reduced from a problem in morality to one of engineering new technological 'fixes' and the deployment of mere human cunning. Nature, bereft even of subjectivity, not to speak of its accessibility to one of its own products, mind, thus reverts to a Darwinian jungle that is morally neutral at best or riddled by a duel between human cunning and animal mindlessness at worst.

On the other hand, if human beings are indeed moral agents because natural evolution confers upon them a clear responsibility toward the natural world, their unique attributes cannot be emphasized too strongly. For it is by virtue of this uniqueness, this capacity to think conceptually and feel a deep empathy for the world of life, that makes it possible for humanity in an ecological society to reverse the devastation it has inflicted on the biosphere. Not only does this imply that humanity, once it has come into its own humanity as the actualization of its potentialities, can be a rational expression of nature's creativity and fecundity, but that human intervention into natural processes can be as creative as that of natural evolution itself.

By virtue of this evolutionary and dialectical viewpoint, which derives the human species from nature as the embodiment of nature's own thrust toward self-reflexivity, the entire structure of the argument around competing 'rights' between human and non-human life-forms changes radically into an exploration of the *ways* in which human beings intervene into the biosphere. Whether humanity recognizes that it is a fulfilment of a major tendency in natural evolution or whether it remains blind to its own humanity as a moral and ecological agent in nature becomes a *social* problem that requires a *social* ecology. For 'biocentrists' and 'anti-humanists' to throw the word 'arrogance' around whenever human beings are seen as ethical and mental referents for nature and natural evolution is manipulatory. The 'stigma' feeds on a self-effacing quietism and 'spirituality' that afflicts a sizeable, often highly privileged sector of Euro-American society, notably human types so consumed by a 'Love' of 'Nature' and 'Life' that they can easily ignore the needless but very real suffering and pain that exist in nature and society alike.

REFERENCES

1. Let me make it clear, at the outset, that I believe that nature is neither hierarchical nor egalitarian, terms that are meaningless unless they can be conceptualized at least morally and institutionalized socially—all of which presupposes a human presence in the biosphere, e.g. second nature. What we encounter in first nature is *complementarity*, the mutualistic interaction of life-forms in maintaining a non-human ecological community. My use of this term in *The Ecology of Freedom* has since been picked up with minimal acknowledgement by 'natural law' acolytes and turned into a '*law* of complementarity', a regressive use of the concept if there ever was one.

2. Much as I would like to avoid a technical discussion of Prigoginian systems theory, I feel obliged to note that a system of positive feedback allows for no concept of potentiality. We only know from Prigoginian 'fluctuations' that when a system approaches a 'far from equilibrium' situation (that is, when it is about to swing into disorder) there is no way to determine whether the system will simply fall apart into 'chaos' or assume an immanently predictable form. Given 'far from equilibrium', disorder, or a succeeding orderly system, speculative thought is reduced to mere observation. In the succession of systems, development seems to give way to thermodynamics and phases of growth to 'dissipative structures'. Prigogine's emphasis on the irreversibility of time, appropriate as it may be in exorcising a mechanistic dynamics based on time's reversibility, is not congruent with process and evolution; it is merely a presupposition for these phenomena. Indeed, in Prigoginian systems theory, it is chance and stochastic phenomena that act as 'mediating' phases between one 'dissipative structure' and another; not potentiality and immanence. *See* Ilya Prigogine and Isabelle Stengers, *Order Out of Chaos* (New York: Bantam Books, 1984), pp. 291–310.

3. Let me state very emphatically that I am not speaking about 'dialectical materialism' which, whatever the intentions of Marx and Engels, uses Hegelian terms and concepts to formulate what is little more than a scientistic 'dialectical' mechanism. My purpose is not to flesh out the skeleton of dialectical philosophy with 'materialism', or what is actually a latterday form of nominalist physicality, but, with the limited space afforded by an article, to bring nature into the foreground of dialectical thought in an evolutionary and organismic way.

4. G. R. G. Mure, *Aristotle* (New York: Oxford University Press, 1964), p. 7.

5. Which is not to say that Hegel sees 'teleology' as an inflexible predetermination of the development of the 'real' in its beginnings. Hegel's *Logic* exists on a different level from the existential reality we experience in history and everyday life. Its 'purified' categories are developed with a 'logical necessity' from each other and, in a metaphoric sense, could be seen as a rational level parallel to the existential level from which they are abstracted. This *logos*, as it were, could be taken as an exemplary and thus inherently critical vision of the world in a highly subjectivized form whose 'logic' yields a distinct rational conclusion, just as Plato's domain of forms has been regarded by many Platonists as exemplary in a *normative* sense as distinguished from the flawed world that we experience around us.

6. The confusion is by no means Hegel's, but, rather, that of some of his translators, among whom translators of Frederick Engels are very much to blame. The German word *Wirklich* has a family of meanings which include 'real' as well as 'actual', Hegel is quite scrupulous in distinguishing the 'real' from the 'actual' in his *Science of Logic*, where 'reality', as he puts it in his discussion of 'Determinate Being', seems 'to be an ambiguous word' while 'Actuality is the *unity of Essence and Existence* . . .' (*See* the Johnston and Struthers translation, *Science of Logic* (New York: MacMillan, 1929), Vol. I, p. 124, and Vol II p. 160, respectively.) The rub comes when Hegel's famous maxim, *Was vernünftig ist, das ist wirklich; und was wirklich ist, das ist vernünftig*, is often mistranslated as 'All that is real is rational; and all that is rational is real.' The mischief this maxim has produced in the historical interpretation of Hegel's ideas is matched only by the confusion it has produced in translations of the maxim itself. Engels, ironically, was to clarify its historical meaning wonderfully. (*See* Frederick Engels, 'Ludwig Feurbach and the End of German Philosophy' in Marx and Engels, *Selected Works* (Moscow: Progress Publishers, 1970), Vol III, pp. 337–38.) The correct and philosophically meaningful translation, of course, is 'What is rational is actual and what is actual is rational'. Let me note that I am not engaged in nitpicking here; the odium which Hegelian philosophy acquired as an apologia for the Prussian State rests in no small part on the failure to properly interpret — and translate — this famous maxim in Hegel's *Encyclopedia Logic* and his *Philosophy of Right*.

7. G. W. F. Hegel *Lectures on the History of Philosophy* (New York: Humanities Press, 1955), Vol. I, p. 22 (my emphasis). Let me note in passing that here Hegel is describing the dialectic in unknowing nature. 'In Mind (*Geist*, or Spirit) it is otherwise' he is quick to note: 'it is consciousness and therefore it is free, uniting in itself the beginning and the end — that is to say, intention, striving, and predetermination' (p. 22).

8. Unfortunately, this has not been noticed in most commentaries on Hegel's *œuvre*, much less in philosophy generally, which seems more occupied with establishing what Heidegger means by 'Being' than with investigating other concepts of Being in Western thought.

9. Viewed from this standpoint, there is a sense in which Hegel's 'objective idealism' was more objective than his materialist critics realized. That possibilities, i.e. the actualizations of very existential potentialities, could be regarded as 'objective' is quite as valid as the notion than an oak tree objectively inheres in an acorn. Ethically, this is a highly illuminating approach. It establishes a standard of fulfilment — an objective 'good', as it were — that literally informs the existential with a goal of objective fulfilment, just as we say in everyday life that an individual who does not 'live up' to his or her capabilities is an 'unfulfilled' person and, in a sense, a less than 'real' person.

10. Long after these lines were penned, I was startled to learn that this argument is regarded as an authentic problem among anti-humanist 'ethicist'. No 'logical line can be drawn,' observes Bernard Dixon in a discussion of biocentric ethics in *The New Scientist*, between the conservation of whales, gentians, and flamingoes on the one hand and the extinction of pathogenic microbes like the smallpox virus on the other, which, according to one 'anti-humanist' wag (David Ehrenfeld), is 'an

endangered species'. Hence logical consistency would require that we try to rescue the smallpox virus with the same ethical dedication that we bring to the survival of whales. *See* Bernard Dixon, 'Smallpox—Imminent Extinction, and an Unresolved Problem,' *New Scientist* 69 (1976). For an 'anti-humanist' position that verges on sheer misanthropy, *see* David Ehrenfeld, *The Arrogance of Humanism* (New York: Oxford University Press, 1978).

11. Bill Devall and George Sessions, *Deep Ecology* (Salt Lake City: Peregrine Smith Books, 1985), p. 67.

12. Or else by looking at the human condition with ugly indifference, as witness Foreman's response to starvation and deprivation in the Third World. I have personally encountered a misanthropy, indeed an *inhumanity*, masked as 'biocentrism', 'deep ecology', and population control, that provides a brutal mandate for human suffering and authoritarian State controls. We must face the fact that ecology, on these terms, threatens to become an ideology that can be designated only as cruel, not as caring or cooperative. Attempts to compost a great variety of views under a common rubric like 'deep ecology' or 'bioregionalism' are gravely misleading: there are differences within the ecological movement, such as it is, that are utterly at odds with each other to a point where their divergences are more important than their so-called 'common goal'.

13. The more one examines the literature of 'biocentrists', 'anti-humanists', and 'deep ecologists', the more one senses an undertaste of manipulation. Their appeals to very human feelings like empathy and identification are translated into 'rights' that rest heavily on the historic development of humanism. Humanism involves not simply a claim to humanity's 'superiority' over the non-human world, but, far more significantly, an appeal to human reason, care, and a social ethics of cooperation. Great social movements, uprisings, and ideologies, not to speak of self-sacrificing individuals, were committed to the achievement of these monumental goals—causes and individuals who are simply effaced from much of the literature on 'biocentrism', 'anti-humanism' and 'deep ecology'. Often, their place is taken by a nagging denigration of the human spirit with decorative metaphors lifted from Eastern philosophy and theosophy. Social analysis tends to be minimized and even deflected by a privileged and inward concern with abstractions like 'Humanity', 'Connectedness', 'Oneness', and 'Spirituality'—this in a society that is riven by genuine conflicts between rich and poor, privileged and denied, man and woman, not to speak of 'deep', 'deeper', and the 'deepest' ecologists.

Green Print

Green Print is an independent publisher of books on green and environmental issues, or written from a radical green perspective.

Our list is wide-ranging. We publish books on politics, education, economics, public health, women's issues, cookery, diet, animal welfare, energy, environmental hazards, gardening, spirituality, cooperative games and green travel. We also publish two green diaries.

New titles are being added all the time. We publish in paperback, our books are well designed and competitively priced, and most of them are printed on recycled paper.

To receive a free catalogue of our books, phone us on 071-267 3399, or write to Green Print (RE), 10 Malden Road, London NW5 3HR. And ask your bookseller to show you our latest titles.